What Your Fossils Can Tell You

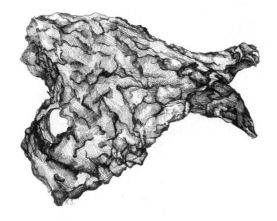

UNIVERSITY PRESS OF FLORIDA

Florida A&M University, Tallahassee
Florida Atlantic University, Boca Raton
Florida Gulf Coast University, Ft. Myers
Florida International University, Miami
Florida State University, Tallahassee
New College of Florida, Sarasota
University of Central Florida, Orlando
University of Florida, Gainesville
University of North Florida, Jacksonville
University of South Florida, Tampa
University of West Florida, Pensacola

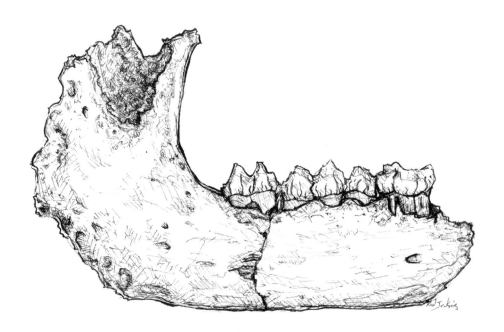

What Your Fossils Can Tell You

Vertebrate Morphology, Pathology, and Cultural Modification

ROBERT W. SINIBALDI

University Press of Florida
Gainesville/Tallahassee/Tampa/Boca Raton
Pensacola/Orlando/Miami/Jacksonville/Ft. Myers/Sarasota

15   14   13   12   11   10   6   5   4   3   2   1

Library of Congress Cataloging-in-Publication Data
Sinibaldi, Robert W.
What your fossils can tell you : vertebrate morphology, pathology, and
cultural modification / Robert W. Sinibaldi.
p. cm.
Includes bibliographical references and index.
ISBN 978-0-8130-3425-6 (alk. paper)
1. Vertebrates, Fossil—Collectors and collecting. 2. Paleontology. I. Title.
QE841.S56 2010
566.075—dc22   2009037082

The University Press of Florida is the scholarly publishing agency for the
State University System of Florida, comprising Florida A&M University,
Florida Atlantic University, Florida Gulf Coast University, Florida Interna-
tional University, Florida State University, New College of Florida, Univer-
sity of Central Florida, University of Florida, University of North Florida,
University of South Florida, and University of West Florida.

University Press of Florida
15 Northwest 15th Street
Gainesville, FL 32611-2079
http://www.upf.com

For Mary, Dominic, and Rosanna
For all who can see beauty in old bones, professional and amateur alike

There is no need to possess the remains, except as a story.

John Allen

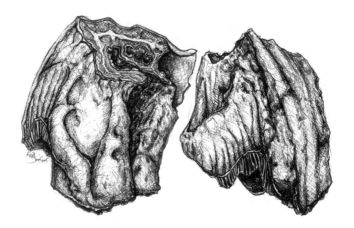

Contents

Figures

Preface

The following story originally appeared in the *Tampa Bay Fossil Chronicles* many years ago. It was a tongue-in-cheek example of how easy it is to go astray in identification of specimens or determination of their meaning. I've resurrected the story here because, after this somewhat embarrassing moment, I committed myself to not making the same type of error again. This entire book, in some respects, represents the culmination of that quest; however, the closer I moved toward completing this project, the farther I seemed to be from finishing. I finally realized I could never know it all, but only become as informed as possible and become more careful when it came to speculating on what I did and didn't know. With only a few minor editing revisions, here is the article "I Didn't Always Know It All" as it first appeared:

As an author of three books and a past president of the Tampa Bay Fossil Club, one of the largest amateur clubs in the nation, I get my fair share of questions. To the amazement of most, I always have an answer. Either I'll answer the question outright or point the person in the right direction. Over the past 12 years I've read over 200 books on paleontology or related subjects. This information has been a great resource to me in answering the endless stream of questions I field at club meetings. As my wife is quick to point out, I'm a know-it-all. Unfortunately it didn't always used to be this way. Unbelievable to some, there was a time when I made "a" mistake. Following is the unabridged story of my "one" mistake identifying a fossil. The story begins back before the days I became a know-it-all.

On March 31, 1994, I finally talked my wife, Mary, into diving with me in the Peace River in Florida. We loaded up the canoe early that morning and headed down river from the sleepy little town of Arcadia. After a while we pulled the canoe over and I suited up in my dive gear. I knew this spot would be productive because I had read a book telling me what to look for on the banks that would indicate a good fossil hunting locality and we had stayed in a Holiday Inn the night before.

Sure enough, as soon as I stuck my face mask in the water I found a section of camel jaw with three teeth in it. Only an emerging know-it-all at the time, I was reasonably sure it was a camel jaw. I would have to confirm it in an identification book and show some senior members of the Tampa Bay Fossil Club that I had just joined. To my wife, though, I had already unequivocally declared that the specimen was a fossilized camel jaw.

Moments later I found a curious piece of bone which I was not totally sure how to identify. It had obviously been "worked" by Paleo-Indians. I knew I had found a genuine Paleo-Indian artifact on my first river dive! The bone was puzzling though, in that it was intentionally smoothed flat on both sides. Surely these clever Indians had processes for doing such incredible workmanship. But what was this bone used for? Why and how would these early Indians do this to a bone?

Excited, I came out of the water to show my wife. "Looks like an old pork chop bone," she said. Knowing-it-all, I calmly corrected her. I pointed out the black color and the fact it was found in association with a camel jaw and other bones that were at least 10,000 years old. "Then those Indians must have shopped at Winn-Dixie." she quipped. Patiently, only the way a loving husband could, I corrected her once again.

The following Saturday night would be a Tampa Bay Fossil Club meeting. I could show off my camel jaw and be vindicated and heralded on my first Paleo-Indian artifact. Upon arrival, two senior members of the club, Mike Nipper and George Overhuls inspected the camel jaw. "Very nice," they said. "Hey guys, how about this worked bone from the river?" I asked. With raised eyebrows, Mike pulled out a lighter while George just smiled. Mike held the lit lighter to the corner of the "fossil" while George explained to me that non-fossilized material would smell like burning hair when exposed to a flame. Well, not only did it smell like burning hair, my wife claimed she could also smell a trace of barbecue sauce.

So even though I've come a long way in my knowledge base since this incident, the most important thing I've learned is that no matter how much you learn you will never know it all. My wife never lets me forget the "paleo-pork chop" from my early days. However, now when this topic surfaces, I inform her of my newly identified specimens that will soon go to the Florida Museum of Natural History for comparative study. These specimens, all of which are new to science, I have confidently identified as a Unicorn jaw, a Cyclops skull, a Sasquatch toe bone, and a Centaur pelvis bone. (See fig. 7.127.)

I hope the following pages will help you get to know a little more about your collection and maybe even spare you the embarrassment of acting like a know-it-all when there is just too much to know. The corrective feedback I received on early versions of this manuscript was humbling to say the least. Each of the almost 500 specimens presented in this book is a case study unto itself. If a picture is worth a thousand words, you have almost a half million bits of information to process in the following pages. I hope you find them informative and useful, and, most of all, I hope they move you to seek even more information beyond that encapsulated in this book.

CHAPTER 1

Introduction

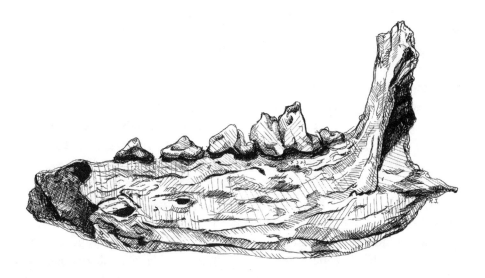

The fossil hunter does not kill, he resurrects.
George Gaylord Simpson

The purpose of this book is to provide fossil enthusiasts with a deeper understanding of the fossils they collect or see at museums. Most amateur and professional paleontologists alike take the first step toward understanding their finds: identifying the specimens in their collections. Often, though, the search for knowledge about a fossil ends after its identification. Some may even take the second step to finding out about their fossils by asking the question, how old is it?[1] At this point, most collectors are satisfied with knowing what their specimen is and how old it is; however, each bone and tooth has its own story to tell if one knows how and where to look for clues about its form, structure, and purpose. In the author's desire to gain more information about specimens, he came to realize that not many books have been published for the avid amateur or beginning professional in this field that go beyond identification or age.

What Your Fossils Can Tell You: Vertebrate Morphology, Pathology, and Cultural Modification is an attempt to fill the gap between determination of identification and age of a specimen and a fuller understanding of the specimen's significance. This book is divided into four sections: Morphology of Bones and Teeth, Natural Alterations of Vertebrate Fossils, Pathologies of Bones and Teeth, and Cultural Modifications of Vertebrate Fossils. The reader need not possess previous knowledge of morphology, pathology, or cultural modification as they relate to fossils; the reader may, though, need to bring to this effort patience and good will to get through some of the sections. As many photographic examples as possible are provided to enable the reader to generalize and apply the concepts presented in this book to a personal collection. Scientific and common terms are paired, whenever possible, to enhance comprehension of the subject matter. Whenever common terms are not available, the scientific term is defined in the text.

The majority of specimens pictured in this manuscript are from Florida collections unless otherwise noted, but the concepts presented should generalize to any collection geographically or temporally worldwide. The fossils are generally from Eocene to Pleistocene in age (54 million to 10,000 years old). Culturally modified bones are generally from 10,000–12,000 years old to approximately 500 years old, or pre-Columbian (before first contact with Europeans). The pictured specimens following the text may not always be museum quality examples, but they are the specimens to which the author had access and are representative of the concepts presented. The morphologies, pathologies, natural alterations, and cultural modifications presented in this text can be generalized to a wide range of species geographically and geologically through time. Each picture is accompanied by a size scale, common and scientific names, and time period. In some instances pathological and culturally modified specimens are pictured next to "normal" specimens if their abnormalities or alterations are not apparent in order to highlight their diagnostic features.

It is the hope of the author that this document can take the reader a few steps deeper into an understanding of fossils. It is also hoped that this deeper understanding will lead the reader to a greater appreciation of fossils in general, as a collector, museum visitor, patron, school presenter, or collaborator with the professional community. It is very difficult to infer behavior and physiology with complete certainty from the fossil remains of extinct animals. The fossils represented here, as in most museums, are all the result of a fatal crisis and generally do not represent typical behaviors (only trace fossils can represent typical behavior).[2]

Finally, the author does not purport to be an expert in any content area covered in this book. He simply wanted to gain a fuller understanding of what his specimens represented. *What Your Fossils Can Tell You* is an outgrowth of that curiosity, hours of research, and collaboration with experts who were willing to share their time, collections, and knowledge of the many subjects covered here.

What Is a Vertebrate Fossil?

A fossil is any evidence of past life embodied in the remains of a plant or animal or in traces of its activities. Most fossils have gone through a chemical change that encased the original organic matter within inorganic matter.[3] Some fossils may have organic materials remaining, such as carbon film, cellulose, lignans, original bone, etc. The fossilization process may involve mineralization, molding, casting, carbonization, distillation, or incrustation. Preservation *in toto* such as amber, mummification, or freeze-drying is also a special case considered a form of fossil.[4]

Vertebrates are animals with backbones from marine (sea) and terrestrial (land) habitats. Marine vertebrates include sharks, rays, whales, dolphins, manatees, sea turtles, and fish, among others. Terrestrial vertebrates include mammals, reptiles, amphibians, and birds. A vertebrate fossil, therefore, is the fossilized remains of a marine or terrestrial animal with a backbone. The majority of vertebrate fossils have gone through some type of mineralization. If the mineralization process is not complete, the specimen is termed a subfossil.[5] Because of lack of availability to the author and the vastness of the subject, dinosaurs and their kin, although vertebrates, are not covered in this book;[6] however, the majority of the principles and concepts in morphology, pathology, and natural alterations of fossils apply equally to dinosaur and earlier materials. Fossils of invertebrates (animals without a backbone, e.g., mollusks, insects) also have a plethora of morphological and pathological issues and many have been culturally modified, but invertebrates, like dinosaurs, go beyond the scope and sequence of this book.

What are Morphology, Pathology, Natural Alterations, and Cultural Modifications?

Each fossil has a unique story to tell, and the language of the specimen is written in the morphological features, pathological features, natural alterations, and cultural modifications of bones and teeth. Once a paleontologist knows how to translate this language, his or her specimens will begin to tell their own unique stories.

Broadly defined, morphology is a branch of biology that studies the external form and structure of animals and plants. A narrow spectrum of the morphology of vertebrate fossils is covered in chapter 2 of this book, where bone topics, including growth plates, tendon and ligament attachment scars, types of joints, and density are presented.[7] Various types of teeth are presented in the third chapter. Teeth can provide a great amount of information about their original owners. Was the animal a carnivore, herbivore, or omnivore? Was the animal young or old? Male or female? Many of these questions can be answered by looking at animals' teeth.

Natural modifications to bones and teeth can happen before, during, or after the process of fossilization. The four categories of natural alterations—biological, geological, hydrological, and atmospheric—are covered in chapter 4. It is important for professionals and amateurs alike to understand these processes and the effects they produce before looking at pathologies or cultural modifications of bones and teeth. Natural alterations may often mimic effects attributed to a pathology or to modifications by humans (cultural modification).

Pathology is the study of the essential nature of diseases, especially the structural and functional changes produced by them. For the purpose of this book, only structural and functional changes to fossil bones and teeth produced by injury, disease, attack, or feeding are covered. Pseudopathologies, markings left on bones and teeth with no evidence of healing, are also discussed in some detail. Fossil bone and tooth pathologies are important studies and are covered in chapters 5 and 6, respectively. This subject produces information on the ways in which prehistoric animals survived or perished after an affliction or attack of some kind.

Within the scope of this book, cultural modification, covered in chapter 7, can be defined as bones, antlers, or teeth that have been worked or modified by Native Americans, ranging from the first Paleo-Indians[8] to those existing right before contact with Europeans, termed pre-Columbian Indians. These modifications can be either intentional (e.g., tools, ornaments) or unintentional (resulting from butchering).[9] Cultural modification, along with natural alteration, falls under the broader topic of taphonomy, the study of postmortem processes that affect death assemblages. Often a taphonomist must decide whether natural, cultural, or a combination of factors was involved in modifying bones, teeth, or antlers from their original state.

Why Study Morphology, Pathology, Natural Alterations, and Cultural Modifications?

Scientists study the morphology, pathology, natural alterations, and cultural modifications of fossils for various reasons. Their studies can lead to discovery of important information in many areas. Evolution, paleoecology, prehistoric diets, diseases in prehistoric populations, and the natural resources used and modified by pre-Columbian Indians are just a few of the subjects scientists include in the study of fossil bones and teeth.[10] Interested amateur paleontologists may want to know more about morphological features, pathological features, and cultural modification of bones and teeth to aid in identification of scientifically relevant specimens for donation to museums or universities. Additionally, this knowledge may help them better understand their own personal collections. Furthermore, a comprehension of the morphology, pathology, and cultural modification of bones and teeth will enable fossil enthusiasts to fully appreciate museum collections. The majority of amateurs, however, want knowledge simply because they love their hobby. These are all valid reasons for wanting to learn more about fossils beyond simply identification and age determination.

Using This Pictorial Guide

Knowing how to interpret the figures, correlate dates with time periods, understand scientific directional terms, and use the endnotes will enable the reader to gain the best understanding of the main text of the book. *What Your Fossils Can Tell You* is designed to be read straight through and therefore has a logical sequence. Judging from past experience with pictorial guides, however, it is likely that many readers will continue to use this book as a reference guide; therefore, each figure is presented in a consistent format using directional terms, scientific time periods, and a brief description of the phenomena discussed in the main text. Once one knows where to find the information about each specimen pictured, one can quickly place the fossil in geological, geographical, biological, and temporal contexts. Scientific terms are defined in the text the first time they appear. If they appear several times in the text, they can be found in the glossary at the back of the book. Based on past experience, the author knows how frustrating it is when a technical term, abbreviation, or acronym is defined only within the text, then crops up several pages or chapters later with no explanation. Without a glossary the reader must attempt to look it up in the index or leaf aimlessly through the text looking for the definition.

Figures

The information for each figure is presented in the same location for every specimen. Figure 1.1 is an example of a photo of a specimen with an explanation of the information shown. Once the reader is familiar with this format, finding information on any specimen should be easy.

Geological Time Scales

The geological time divisions encompassed in this book span approximately the last 65 million years. Time divisions comprise eras (large divisions of time), divided into periods (smaller divisions of time), divided into epochs. Each division of time can be distinguished by its own distinct fauna and flora. The actual

Figure 1.1

Horse
(common name)
Partial Lower Jaw
(body part)

Equus sp.
(scientific name)
Pleistocene
(time period)

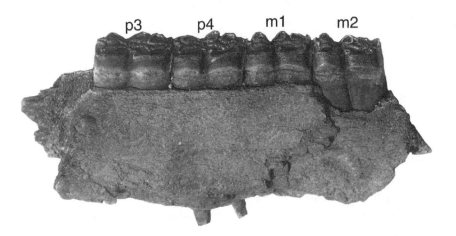

Peace River,
DeSoto County, FL
(location of discovery)

Collection: R. Sinibaldi
(where specimen resided at
time of publication)
Size: (approximate size of specimen
in inches and centimeters)

Figure 1.1. This partial horse lower jaw has 4 teeth: the 3rd and 4th premolars and the 1st and 2nd molars. (Caption includes information relating picture to text that referenced the item.)

time frames were developed on the basis of chemical decomposition rates of radioactive decay of various isotopes of specific elements. The geological time frames presented here are approximate and being continually refined as scientists develop new and more accurate techniques for dating rocks and fossils.

Cenozoic Era—65 million years ago (mya) to present (roughly from the time the dinosaurs became extinct until now).
Tertiary Period—65 mya to 1.9 mya (sometimes referred to as the age of mammals).
 Paleocene Epoch—65 mya to 54 mya
 Eocene Epoch—54 mya to 37.5 mya
 Oligocene Epoch—37.5 mya to 24.5 mya
 Miocene Epoch—24.5 mya to 5 mya
 Pliocene Epoch—5 mya to 1.9 mya

Quaternary Period—1.8 mya to present (includes the ice ages up to present day).

Pleistocene Epoch—1.9 mya to 10,000 years ago

Holocene Epoch—10,000 years ago to present

American Archaeological Time Scales

Archaeological time stages are also subject to constant refinement and may have a variety of names, depending on the literature. A very general archaeological time frame is presented here that is relevant only to North America and occurred at the end of the Pleistocene Epoch or during the Holocene Epoch of the fossil and archaeological records respectively. Archaeological stages in Europe, Asia, and Africa go deep into the Pleistocene Epoch and include more stages to cover the complete spectrum of human development.

Paleo-Indian Period—12,000 years ago to 9,000 years ago[11]

Archaic Period—9,000 years ago to 4,000 years ago

Ceramic Period—4,000 years ago to 500 years ago

Historic Period—From first contact with Europeans to present.

General Directional Terminology

The following general directional terms appear throughout the book and assist scientists and amateurs alike in specifying the direction a view is facing. An anterior view is of the front or head. A posterior view is of the rear or tail of a specimen. A lateral view is of the side (outside) and a medial view is of the middle of the interior side. A proximal view is the side nearest the body, and a distal view is the side of a specimen farthest from the body of an animal. A labial view (sometimes referred to as the buccal view) is of the cheek side of teeth or jaw farthest from the tongue, and a lingual view is of the side closest to the tongue. The occlusal view of teeth is of the chewing surface of premolar and molar teeth, where they make contact with teeth in the opposite jaw (fig. 1.2).

Endnotes

Each chapter contains more information in endnotes, denoted by superscript numbers. The endnotes may contain more explanation of the subject, information on where to find deeper inquiry into the subject, or tangential information that might be of interest to the reader. The purpose of the endnotes is to bring the reader to a fuller understanding of the subject without interrupting the flow of the main text.

Figure 1.2

(a) Camel Toe Bone
(b) Oreodont Skull

(a) *Hemiauchenia macrocephala*
(b) *Merycoidodon culbertsoni*
(a) Pleistocene
(b) Oligocene

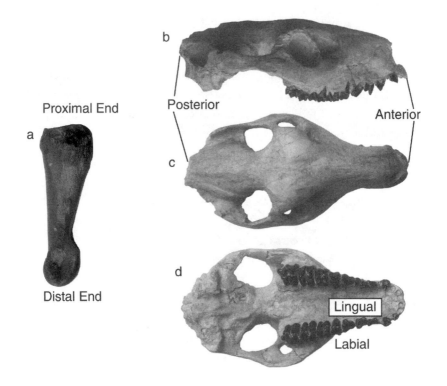

(a) Peace River, FL
(b) Crawford, NE

Collection: R. Sinibaldi
Size: (a) 3.75 in.\9.7 cm
(b) 8.25 in.\21 cm

Figure 1.2. The camel toe bone (a) is shown in an anatomically correct position, with the proximal end closer to the body. The oreodont skull (b) is shown in three views to demonstrate terms for directionality explained in the text; (c) is a dorsal view, and (d) is a ventral view of the skull.

CHAPTER 2

The Morphology of Fossil Bones

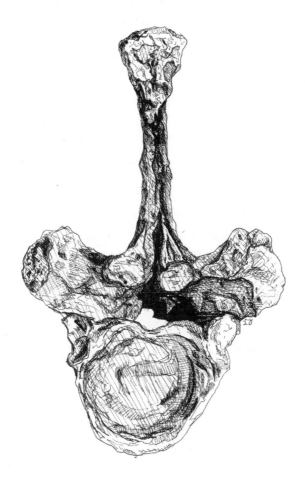

The fossil hunter is always seeking to bring extinct animals back to life.
Henry Fairfield Osborn

Introduction

Bones and teeth are the hardest parts of a vertebrate animal's anatomy while it is living. After death, therefore, bones and teeth usually have the best chance of becoming fossils. Bone morphology is presented in this chapter; tooth morphology is covered in chapter 3. Under ideal circumstances bones can become fossilized in their entirety. Fossilization is often so complete that not only the main elements (ends, shafts) of the bones fossilize, but also sometimes minute details such as tendon and ligament attachment scars, artery impressions, nerve canals, skin attachment scars, and other morphological features.

Morphological features can tell us many things about the animal's behavioral and physical traits when it was alive. Type of diet and locomotion, where it lived, size, strength, speed, and age are all items of information that can be inferred from bone morphology.[1] Even auditory and visual range can be determined to some extent by examining the fossil record. When the information gathered by examining all the morphological features is combined, a fairly accurate picture can be painted of an extinct animal. In fact, this technique is literally the way artists, working closely with scientists, re-create prehistoric animals on canvas, three-dimensionally, or for the movies.[2] Furthermore, studying **extant** (living) closely related counterparts (termed **phylogenetic analogues**) of **extinct** animals is often a way scientists confirm the hypothetical representations they make from the fossil record.[3] Use of a modern phylogenetic analogue diminishes in effectiveness the farther back in time the extinct counterpart lived as speculation about habitat and lifestyle becomes less certain.

Scientists also study morphological features from the fossil record to determine whether a particular characteristic was developed by natural selection through processes such as **adaptation** or **exaptation**. Gould and Vrba (1982) define adaptations as those "characters that are currently enhancing fitness and that were constructed by natural selection to function in that particular role; their selection context has not varied historically. By contrast, exaptations are characters that now perform a current function that is subject to selection, but they initially either were not shaped by selection at all or were shaped by selection for a different role." Concepts such as adaptation and exaptation can be studied only by looking deeply into the morphological features of the ancestral past of a species through its fossil record.[4]

The following documentation of morphological features is by no means exhaustive. Scientists have studied, labeled, and determined the usefulness of virtually every process, "bump," or "knob" (feature) of every bone from most animals, both extant and extinct. The author has chosen those features that are both commonly found and easily described and understood. The morphological features on human bones have been extensively studied, and most processes are **homologous** to those on other mammals; however, there is not much of a human fossil record in North America, as humans were among the latest arrivals to the faunal habitat.[5] Furthermore, possession of human (fossil, Native American, or other) remains in private collections is not ethical, nor in most cases is it legal to possess human remains in the United States. Therefore, with the exception of one Cro-Magnon skull cap from a private German collection, no human fossils have been used in this document.

Before we look at the various types of bones, some common features are characteristic of most bones. Bones generally have three layers: the outer layer or cortex, the middle or spongy layer, and the inner layer filled with marrow. The cortex layer is covered with a membrane called the **periosteum**. Tendons and ligaments actually attach to the periosteum and not directly to the bone. **Tendons** are dense, fibrous connective tissues that attach muscles to bones, whereas **ligaments** are dense connective tissues that attach bones to other bones. The cortex layer of the bone is extremely hard and gives bones their strength. The spongy layer of the bone is where calcium is deposited by the blood for future bone growth. The marrow layer, a fatty red substance, is where red and white blood cells are formed. The **articulating** ends of bones are generally covered with cartilage that keeps them from wearing down. The cartilage can work as both a link and a cushion.

Types of Joints

Since bones of necessity are not very flexible, joints are needed between bones to allow them to move relative to each other. Joints are formed in a way that allows some movements while preventing others. Some joints such as sutures are entirely inflexible later in life, but flexible earlier (see below). Different joints have very different movement demands; therefore, many different types of joints exist, each with a unique solution for efficient form and function.[6] The five main types of joints are **cartilaginous**, **gliding**, **hinge**, **ball and socket**, and **sutures**.[7] Once again, this is not a comprehensive coverage of existing joint types, but a description of the most common.

Cartilaginous Joints

The term *vertebrate* denotes those animals with a backbone composed of numerous vertebrae protecting the nerve cord and supporting the body. The vertebral column in mammals is usually divided into five distinct areas.[8] The first three zones are the **cervical vertebrae** of the neck, the **thoracic vertebrae** of the upper back that articulate with movable ribs for breathing, and the **lumbar vertebrae** of the lower back. The lumbar vertebrae may or may not also have associated ribs. Some reptiles have ribs in their lumbar regions, and other animals have vestigial ribs fused to the transverse processes of the lumbar vertebrae, called **pleurapophyses**. The second area of the vertebral column is the **sacrum**, usually consisting of several fused vertebrae. The last section of the vertebral column consists of **caudal** or tail vertebrae.

Vertebrae protect the spinal column (fig. 2.1) while articulating by means of cartilaginous joints that allow some movements while preventing others. Each articular surface is covered with a thin layer of cartilage, and the bones are

Fig. 2.1

Horse
Thoracic Vertebra

Equus sp.
Early Pleistocene

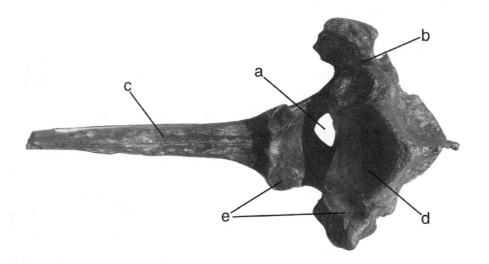

Leisey Shell Pit,
Hillsborough County, FL

Collection: R. Sinibaldi
Size: 6.75 in.\17 cm

Fig. 2.1. The spinal cord travels through the neural arch, the opening at (a), with nerves exiting through openings at (b). Tendons and ligaments attach at (c), with the centrum or main body of the vertebra at (d) gliding against the next vertebra separated by a small disk. At (e) are various facets (surfaces) that also glide or articulate with facets on the next vertebra in the spinal column or the associated ribs for that vertebra.

connected with a plate of **fibrocartilage**.[9] Processes on the vertebrae also provide ligament and tendon attachments. In most mammals, reptiles, and birds, each vertebra contains interlocking processes of bones called **zygapophyses** (fig. 2.2). A front pair of **prezygapophyses** from one vertebra interlock with a back pair of **postzygapophyses** from the next vertebra. This pattern continues down the spine, from the neck to the sacrum (fig. 2.3). These bony processes restrict movement of the back and neck and prevent dislocation of the spine. The interlocking zygapophyses also provide body support against the forces of gravity.

Beyond the sacrum, caudal (tail) vertebrae have diminishing to no zygapophyses to restrict their movement (fig. 2.4). In addition, most caudal vertebrae lack a **neural spike** and **neural canal;** however, exceptions always occur, and proboscideans and alligators are examples of animals with neural spikes and canals in their tail vertebrae. The diminishing zygapophyses in the tails of most

Fig. 2.2

Horse
Cervical Vertebrae

Equus sp.
Late Pleistocene

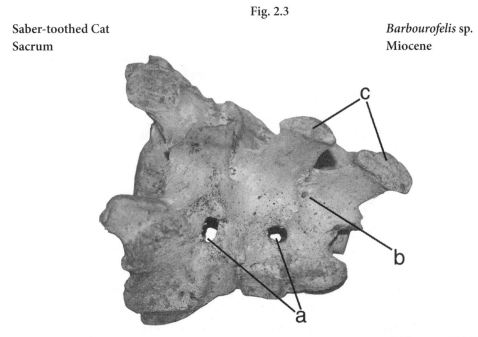

Withlacoochee River,
Marion County, FL

Collection: A. Kerner
Size: 3.5 in.\8.5 cm

Fig. 2.2. The zygapophyses from these two cervical (neck) vertebrae are shown separated, then interlocking, with the lower surface of the postzygapophyses at (a) interlocking with the upper surface of the prezygapophyses at (b) from the next vertebra.

Fig. 2.3

Saber-toothed Cat
Sacrum

Barbourofelis sp.
Miocene

Love Bone Bed,
Alachua County, FL

Collection: FLMNH
Size: 5.25 in.\13 cm

Fig. 2.3. This sacrum clearly shows the foramina or holes (a) where the nerves exit the spinal cord. Smooth surfaces at (b) are where muscles would have run next to the bone but not attached; rough surfaces at (c) are where tendons and ligaments would have attached to the bone.

Fig. 2.4

Glyptodont
Caudal (Tail) Vertebra

Glyptotherium floridanum
Late Pleistocene

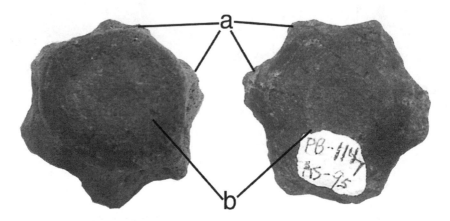

Peace River,
DeSoto County, FL

Collection: R. Sinibaldi
Size: 1.5 in.\4 cm

Fig. 2.4. Note that no zygapophyses occur at (a), and the only articular surfaces on caudal verte-brae occur at the centrum (b). To the left is the anterior view and the right is the posterior view of the same vertebra.

vertebrates make them very flexible. In contrast, the zygapophyses of the verte-brae in the neck region are usually very pronounced (fig. 2.5). They are formed in such a way as to allow maximal movement, up to a point, without allowing dislocation. This configuration protects the spinal cord in this region, where it initially exits the skull and contains the most nerves. Note that some texts group the cartilaginous joints in with the gliding joints (discussed next).

Gliding or Plane Joints

Gliding joints have generally flat or near flat articular surfaces called **facets** that allow the opposing bones to slide or glide across one another. Movement in gliding or plane joints is generally very limited and often depends on the cu-mulative movements of several joints together, such as in the wrists and ankles of most mammals. Some types of gliding joints are the **carpals** and **tarsals** in the ankles, feet, wrists, and paws of many animals. Carpal bones are those in the wrist or forelimbs; tarsal bones are located in the ankles or hind limbs. Many examples of these bones can be found, and every animal has numerous carpals and tarsals. Generally, carpal and tarsal bones are quite dense, fossilize well, and are therefore quite common in the fossil record. A few examples are provided (figs. 2.6–2.8), however, carpal and tarsal bones are very difficult to identify even with a comparative collection at your disposal. As mentioned,

Fig. 2.5

Running Rhino
Cervical Vertebrae

Hyracodon nebraskensis
Oligocene

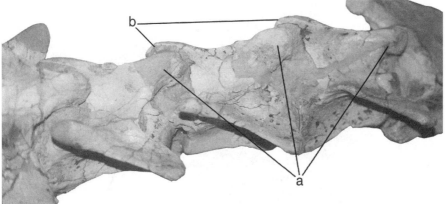

South Dakota

Collection: F. Garcia
Size: 11.5 in.\28 cm

Fig. 2.5. Three cervical (neck) vertebrae demonstrate pronounced zygapophyses at (a). These pronounced zygapophyses allow for maximal movement of the joint while preventing dislocation and injury to the spinal column. They interlock with postzygapophyses (b) from the adjoining vertebrae.

Fig. 2.6

Horse
Carpal Bone

Equus sp.
Pleistocene

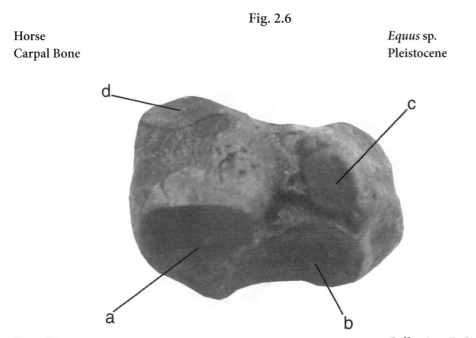

Peace River,
DeSoto County, FL

Collection: R. Sinibaldi
Size: 1.63 in.\4.5 cm

Fig. 2.6. This small carpal bone has four facets (a, b, c, d) on the side pictured for articulating with adjacent bones.

Fig. 2.7

Sloth
Carpal Bone

Undetermined species
Pleistocene

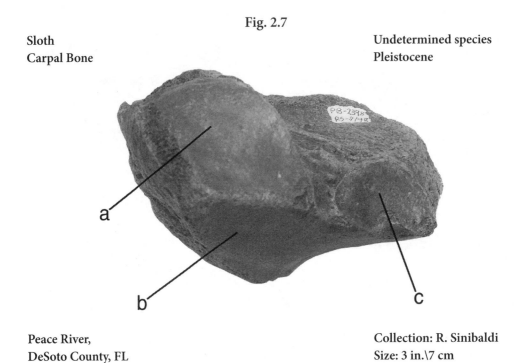

Peace River,
DeSoto County, FL

Collection: R. Sinibaldi
Size: 3 in.\7 cm

Fig. 2.7. This large carpal bone has three distinct facets at (a), (b), and (c).

Fig. 2.8

Carpal Bone

Undetermined species
Pleistocene

Peace River,
DeSoto County, FL

Collection: R. Sinibaldi
Size: 1.5 in.\4 cm

Fig. 2.8. This carpal bone with three facets (a, b, c) remains unidentified. Carpal bones come in so many sizes and shapes that it takes an expert with a comparative collection to identify those that are not common.

most carpal and tarsal bones work in conjunction with several bones in their immediate vicinity. Doing so makes them easily recognizable as they generally have multiple distinct articular facets on each surface of the bone. The overall effect is a joint with many movement capabilities. Along with their movement capabilities, carpal and tarsal bones also work as natural shock absorbers in the limbs of animals.

Hinge Joints

Hinge joints are found generally between toe bones, finger/claw bones, leg bones (at the knee), and jaw bones. Hinge joints provide only one type of motion: rotation around one axis like the hinge on a door (fig. 2.9). In fact, a deep groove on the articular surface of one bone usually corresponds to a projecting ridge on the articular surface of the adjacent bone of a hinge joint (fig. 2.10). This mechanism prevents any sideways (lateral) movement or sliding of the joint. As with the zygapophyses of the vertebrae, ridges and grooves are an evolutionary solution to the problem of dislocation of bone joints.

Some hinge joints have little or no pronounced ridge and groove system if the risk of dislocation is minimal at that joint site. However, if the risk of dislocation is great, such as in the claws of sloths, the grooves and ridges are very pronounced (fig. 2.11). The joints in a sloth's claw move in a horizontal plane,

Fig. 2.9

Camel   *Hemiauchenia macrocephala*
Articulated Foot   Early Pleistocene

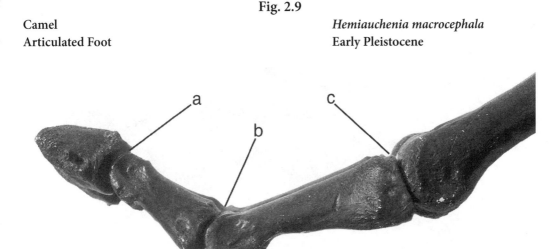

Leisey Shell Pit   Collection: R. Sinibaldi
Hillsborough County, FL   Size: 9 in.\23 cm

Fig. 2.9. A series of hinge joints in the articulated toe bones of a camel. The joints at (a), (b), and (c) can rotate in only one plane of motion.

Fig. 2.10

Horse
Toe and Cannon Bone

Equus sp.
Pleistocene

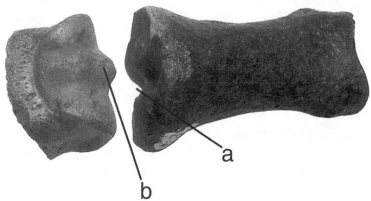

Peace River,
DeSoto County, FL

Collection: R. Sinibaldi
Size: 4.75 in.\13 cm

Fig. 2.10. The deep groove at (a) on this horse toe bone corresponds to a pronounced ridge (b) on the distal end of a juvenile cannon bone.

Fig. 2.11

Sloth
Toe Bones and Claw Core

Megalonyx jeffersonii
Pleistocene

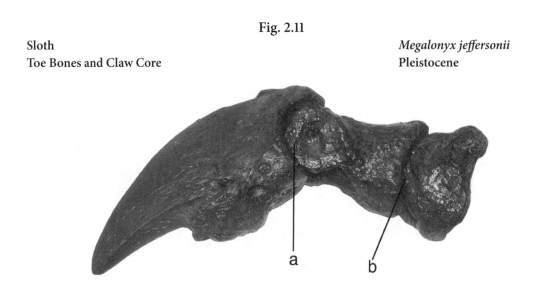

Withlacoochee River,
Marion County, FL

Collection: T. Sellari
Size: 7.5 in.\19 cm

Fig. 2.11. Sloth toe bones and claw core have evolved deep grooves and pronounced ridges at (a) and (b) to reduce dislocation of these joints.

Fig. 2.12

Saber-toothed Cat
Skull and Jaw (replica)

Xenosmilus hodsonae
Early Pleistocene

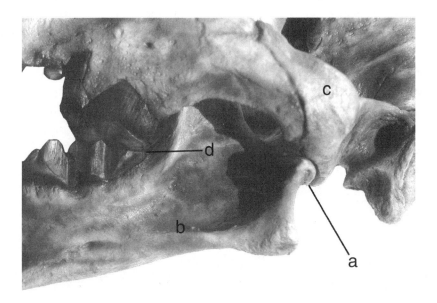

Haile Quarry,
Florida

Collection: A. Kerner
Size: 4.8 in.\12.3 cm

Fig. 2.12. The hinge joint (a) in these jaws attach the lower jaw (b) to the skull (c). Joints in jaws generally have no ridges or grooves, allowing side-to-side motion when chewing. Note that hinge joint (a) is even with the tooth level (d) in this typical carnivore mandible.

while the paw as a whole is used in a downward vertical plane to strip leaves and branches from trees for food. The deep grooves and pronounced ridges minimize dislocation in the sloth's claw joint.

Some hinge joints lack grooves and ridges and allow two types of motion: the type of rotation described above, and a side-to-side motion that is prevented in hinge joints with grooves and ridges. The jaws of many animals use both up-and-down motion (biting) and side-to-side motion (chewing). Allowing for both types of motion in a jaw increases chewing efficiency (fig. 2.15). Many herbivores have evolved this type of jaw mechanism for chewing plant materials over long periods of time. Furthermore, the location of the hinge joint in the back of the jaw can serve to differentiate carnivore from herbivore jaws, even if the teeth are missing. The articular **condyle** (a rounded process of the jaw bone that articulates with the skull) of the hinge joints of carnivores is generally even with the teeth (fig. 2.12). In herbivores, the articulation joint is generally much higher (fig. 2.15).

Ball-and-Socket Joints

Hip joints (fig. 2.13) and shoulder joints (fig. 2.14) are most commonly cited as examples of ball-and-socket joints; however, eye sockets are also a ball-and-socket joint, with bone composing the socket portion and the eye being the ball portion (fig. 2.15). A ball-and-socket joint allows movement in all three planes (forward and backward, side to side, and rotation around an axis). Any combination of the three planes of movement is also available, giving the ball-and-socket joint "universal" movement capabilities.

Scientists can study the angles of hip and shoulder sockets to determine how an extinct animal stood, walked, and ran. For many extinct mammals, an extant relative usually exists that can give scientists a clue as to how the ball-and-socket joint articulated or went together (figs. 2.16–2.17).[10] The use of extant animals to infer details of extinct animals' lives is termed the principle of behavioral fixity.

Fig. 2.13

Peccary
Femur (leg bone)
Acetabulum (pelvic bone)

Platygonus sp.
Early Pleistocene

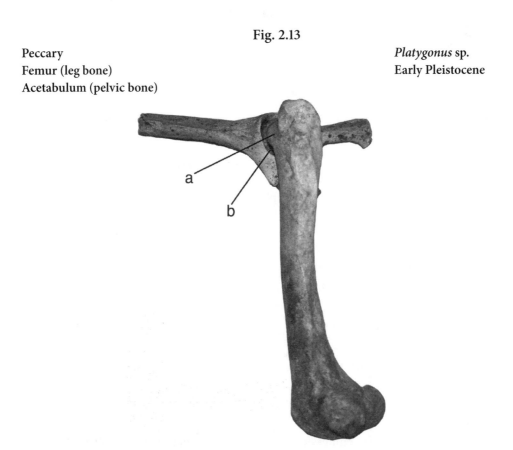

Haile XXI,
Alachua County, Florida

Collection: FLMNH
Size: 8 in.\20 cm (femur)

Fig. 2.13. The ball-shaped head of the femur (a) fits into the socket-shaped acetabulum (b) of the pelvic bone, forming a ball-and-socket joint that can move in all three planes of motion.

Fig. 2.14

Peccary
Scapula (shoulder blade)
Humerus (upper foreleg)

Platygonus sp.
Early Pleistocene

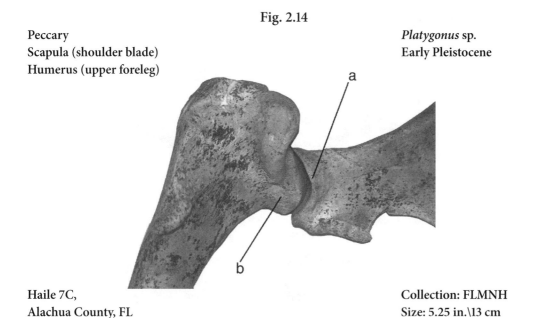

Haile 7C,
Alachua County, FL

Collection: FLMNH
Size: 5.25 in.\13 cm

Fig. 2.14. The ball-shaped head of the humerus (b) fits into the socket-shaped glenoid cavity (a) of the scapula (shoulder blade), forming a ball-and-socket joint of the shoulder area.

Fig. 2.15

Three-toed Horse
Skull

Mesohippus bairdi
Oligocene

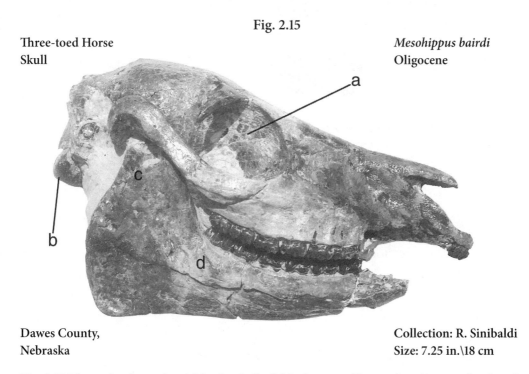

Dawes County,
Nebraska

Collection: R. Sinibaldi
Size: 7.25 in.\18 cm

Fig. 2.15. The socket formed at (a) in the skull of this three-toed horse, forming a perfect housing for the eye, another type of ball-and-socket joint. The occipital condyles are two small ball-type facets at the back of the skull (b) that articulate with the semi-socket type facets of the atlas vertebra. Together they form a ball-and-socket joint that allows skull movement in all three planes. Note that hinge joint (c) is much higher than the level of the teeth (d) in this typical herbivore mandible.

Fig. 2.16

White-tailed Deer
Femur (leg bone)
Acetabulum (pelvic bone)

Odocoileus virginianus
Pleistocene

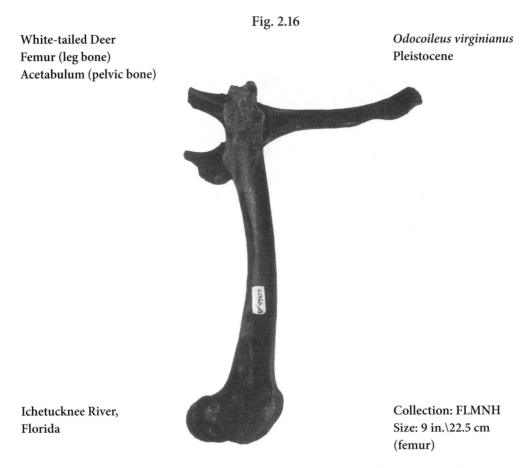

Ichetucknee River,
Florida

Collection: FLMNH
Size: 9 in.\22.5 cm
(femur)

Fig. 2.16. This fossil deer femur and pelvic bone are identical to modern analogues from a recent deer (Fig. 2.17). Their identical morphological structure informs scientists that prehistoric deer moved very similarly to modern deer.

This principle proposes that the behavior of modern phylogenetic analogues (descendants at the genus or in some cases family level) will be comparable to that of their ancestors; however, for groups such as dinosaurs that may not have many closely related descendants,[11] the hip and shoulder ball-and-socket joints can give scientists their best information on the movements of these creatures by comparison with modern animals of similar structure.

Sutures

Suture lines are a very specialized type of joint. In flat bones, such as those in the pelvis and skull, the areas where plates connect are called suture lines. These squiggly connections (fig. 2.18) are much stronger than straight connections because they increase the attachment surface area threefold or more. Suture fu-

Fig. 2.17

Key Deer   *Odocoileus virginianus clavium*
Femur (leg bone)   Recent
Acetabulum (pelvic bone)

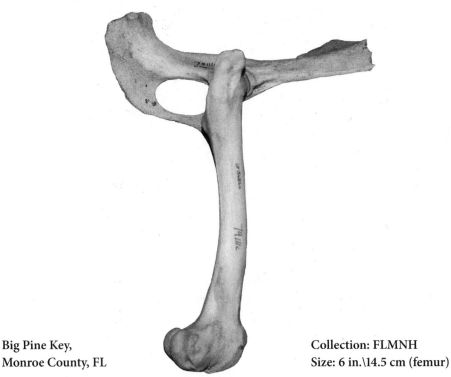

Big Pine Key,   Collection: FLMNH
Monroe County, FL   Size: 6 in.\14.5 cm (femur)

Fig. 2.17. Compared with the locomotor strategy implied by a fossil deer pelvic bone and femur (Fig. 2.16), the strategy has not changed in this modern deer. It is interesting to note that this specimen is from a Key deer, which has a reduced size resulting from restrictive island life.

sions usually form shortly after birth. Once fused in older animals, suture joints have no mobility. In young and unborn animals they allow for flexibility in the case of live birth (mammals) and quick growth in most vertebrates. **Unfused** skull or pelvis bones are generally a sign of a very young mammal (fig. 2.19). As old age approaches, the sutures become so interconnected that they no longer can be seen clearly, a stage known as obliteration.

Growth Plates and Epiphyseals

Bones do not grow larger simply by unilaterally adding more bone material to the surface. In mammals,[12] long bones such as the **femur** and **humerus** grow in girth and in length, as described below. Bone material is added to the outer surface of the long shaft area while slowly being removed from the inside of

Fig. 2.18

Cro-Magnon
Skull

Early *Homo sapiens*
Pleistocene

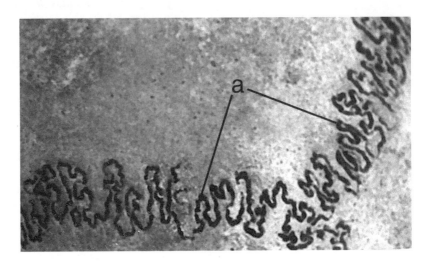

Rhine River Valley,
Germany

Private Collection
Size: 1 in.\2.5 cm

Fig. 2.18. The fused suture lines (a) of this Cro-Magnon skull allowed for growth when this person was young, then became strongly fused during adulthood.

Fig. 2.19

Peccary (juvenile)
Skull Cap

Undetermined species
Late Pleistocene

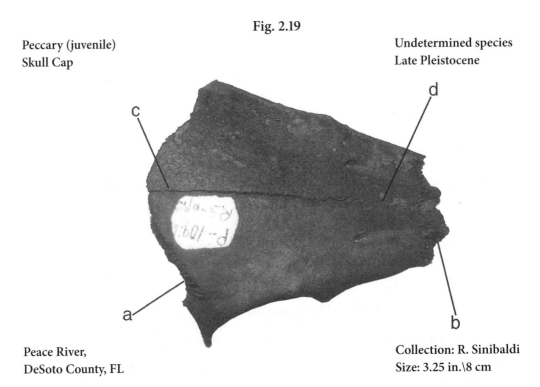

Peace River,
DeSoto County, FL

Collection: R. Sinibaldi
Size: 3.25 in.\8 cm

Fig. 2.19. This juvenile peccary skull cap exhibits unfused sutures at (a) and (b), a suture beginning to fuse at (c), and a fully fused suture at (d).

the marrow cavity. This method increases the diameter of the bone but not its length. The two joint ends of a bone must remain fully functional while an animal is growing. A growth plate just behind the articular surface at each end of a typical long bone allows the bone to grow in length.

The **growth plate** (technically called the **epiphyseal** plate) attaches the joint end of the bone (**epiphysis**) to the shaft (**diaphysis**). The end portion of the diaphysis closest to the epiphysis is called the **metaphysis**. The epiphyseal plate is the **cartilage** that fills the gap between the epiphysis and diaphysis. Until the animal is finished growing, the cartilage of the epiphyseal plate remains (fig. 2.20). The epiphysis fuses to the shaft upon termination of growth. This fusion process occurs within a somewhat regular time frame for each species and allows for estimation of age at the time of death.

The various stages of growth, and therefore age, can be determined by inspecting the ends of various long bones such as legs and toes, and also the vertebrae. In the fossils of very young animals, leg bones may be found without the ends attached to them (fig. 2.21).[13] Growth plates have a very distinct pattern that enables us to tell the difference between a fossil bone with the end broken off and a fossil bone from a juvenile missing an epiphyseal (fig. 2.22). In order to prevent the epiphysis and epiphyseal plate from sliding around and dislocat-

Figure 2.20

Dolphin Vertebra
Partially Fused Epiphysis

Undetermined species
Miocene

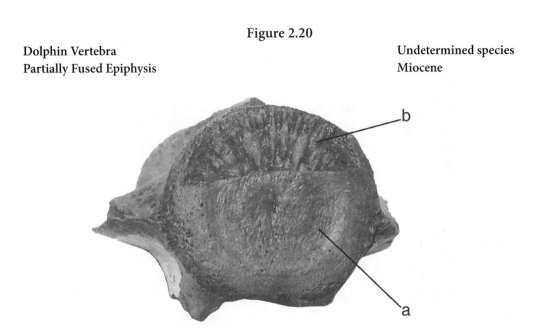

Peace River,
DeSoto County, FL

Collection: R. Sinibaldi
Size: 1.25 in.\2.5 cm

Fig. 2.20. The epiphysis on this dolphin vertebrae was almost completely fused to the vertebra centra. This is an example of an animal very close to the adult stage of life.

Fig. 2.21

White-tailed Deer
Cannon Bone (foot)

Odocoileus virginianus
Late Pleistocene

Peace River,
DeSoto County, FL

Collection: D. Sinibaldi
Size: 1.5 in.\4 cm

Fig. 2.21. This juvenile deer cannon bone has both distal epiphyses (articulating ends) missing at (a). The unfused articulating ends would have a reverse image pattern.

Fig. 2.22

Horse
Humerus (front leg)

Equus sp.
Pleistocene

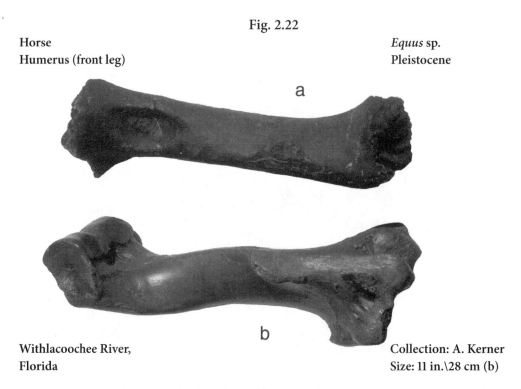

Withlacoochee River,
Florida

Collection: A. Kerner
Size: 11 in.\28 cm (b)

Fig. 2.22. Compare broken ends of this horse humerus (a) to a complete specimen (b). Also compare the broken surfaces to the distinct patterns formed by unfused epiphysis in figures 2.21, 2.23, and 2.25.

Fig. 2.23

Glyptodont
Vertebra

Glyptotherium sp.
Pleistocene

Peace River,
DeSoto County, FL

Collection: R. Sinibaldi
Size: 3.25 in.\8 cm

Fig. 2.23. The epiphysis (a) and diaphysis (b) of this glyptodont vertebra were found together. The two surfaces are exact reverse images and snap together perfectly (see fig. 2.24).

ing, a distinctive bumpy pattern forms a positive and negative relief on their articulating surfaces (fig. 2.23). It is common to find only the ends or shafts of juvenile bones. Sometimes both ends and shaft are found in close proximity and form a perfect match (fig. 2.24).

As the animal gets older but is not yet an adult (adolescence), one end of a bone may be partially or fully fused to the shaft and the other end not fused at all (fig. 2.25). The next stage one might find would entail a fossil with both ends fused but a distinct line present where the fusion took place. Finally, in a fully developed adult, little or no **fusion line** is present at the epiphyseal end of a bone (fig. 2.26).

Using this rough method, the amateur can determine the relative age of an animal: embryonic, **neonatal** (newborn), young, adolescent, and adult; however, it is extremely difficult to equate this to chronological age. Scientists, on the other hand, may have enough information from modern extant analogues to determine the chronological age of an animal. Different bones of the body fuse at different stages of life. If a scientist has enough bones from a single fossil specimen, and the corresponding extant **analogue** animal, he or she might be able to determine its chronological age. Using comparative charts for well-studied animals (horses, dogs, humans), a scientist might be able to determine within a year or better the chronological age of an animal from its unfused bones.

Fig. 2.24

Glyptodont
Vertebra

Glyptotherium floridanum
Pleistocene

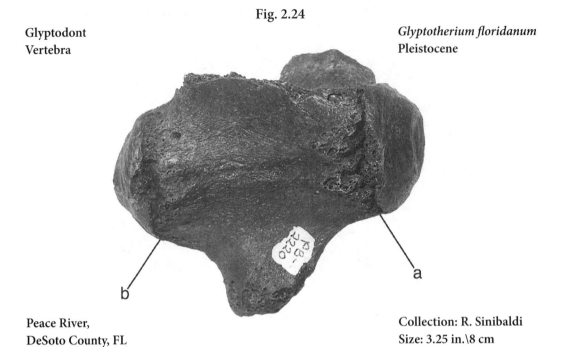

Peace River,
DeSoto County, FL

Collection: R. Sinibaldi
Size: 3.25 in.\8 cm

Fig. 2.24. The epiphysis and diaphysis shown in figure 2.23 snapped back together at (a). The other epiphysis (b) had fused sufficiently to remain in place after fossilization. Only the epiphyseal line is present at (b).

Fig. 2.25

White-tailed Deer
Radius (lower foreleg)

Odocoileus virginianus
Pleistocene

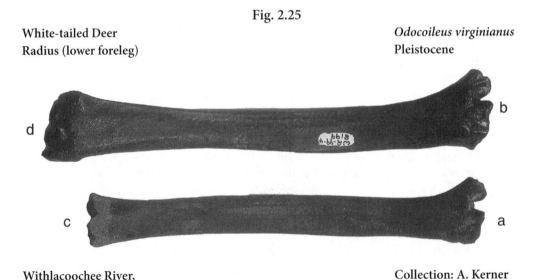

Withlacoochee River,
Florida

Collection: A. Kerner
Size: 7.75 in.\19 cm

Fig. 2.25. Note that the epiphyseal at the proximal end (a) of this juvenile deer radius is fused and nearly identical to the proximal end (b) of the adult deer radius. However, the epiphysis at the distal end (c) was not fused and is missing, when compared to the distal end at (d) of the complete adult specimen. In most mammals the epiphysis at the distal end of the radius is the last bone to completely fuse.

Fig. 2.26

Tapir
Tibia (lower rear leg)

Tapirus veroensis
Pleistocene

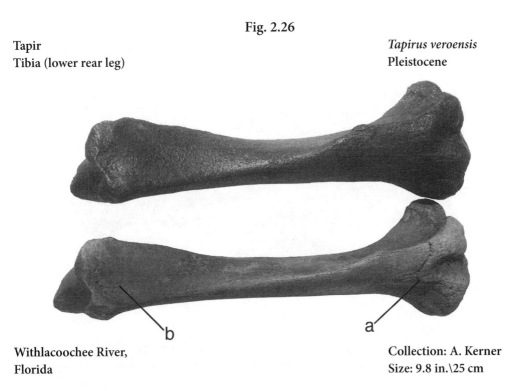

Withlacoochee River,
Florida

Collection: A. Kerner
Size: 9.8 in.\25 cm

Fig. 2.26. The lower specimen of a young adult tapir clearly shows the epiphyseal line at (a), yet it is missing at (b). Compare with the fully adult specimen above that displays no epiphyseal lines at either end of the bone.

Tendon and Ligament Attachment Scars and Processes

Technically, muscles never attach directly to bone. Muscle groups are attached to bones by tendons. Bones can be attached to each other by ligaments. Both the tendons and ligaments attach to the **periosteum**, a membrane that surrounds the cortex (outer) layer of the bone. Tendons and ligaments often leave scars on the bones at their points of attachment. That roughened area of bone, the scars or marks left by attachments of tendons and ligaments, is technically called a **rugose** surface. The size of the attachment scars, grooves, and bony processes such as ridges and crests on a bone indicate the size of the ligaments and tendons attached, and, therefore, the size of the muscles when the animal was alive (fig. 2.27).

The shape of the bone, or bony process coming off the main bone, is often an indicator of tendon and ligament attachment points. Bony processes can also form a **keel** that keeps two muscle groups separated and in place. These muscle groups often act in different directions. The shoulder blade (scapula) is a prime example in many animals (fig. 2.28), as is the sternum in birds.

Fig. 2.27

Sloth

Ulna (lower forearm)

Paramylodon harlani

Early Pleistocene

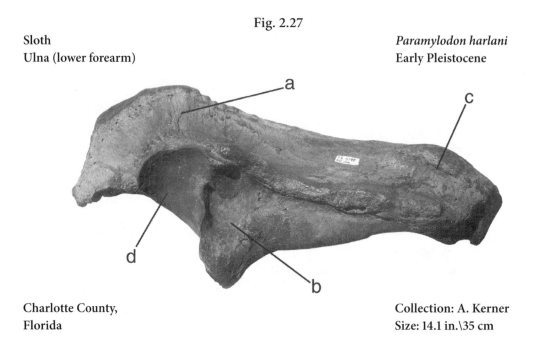

Charlotte County,

Florida

Collection: A. Kerner

Size: 14.1 in.\35 cm

Fig. 2.27. The ulna of this sloth shows the deep grooving and bone texture at (a), (b), and (c) that appears on bones where tendons and ligaments attach or insert. The socket for the humerus is at (d).

Fig. 2.28

Manatee

Scapula (shoulder blade)

Trichechus manatus

Pleistocene

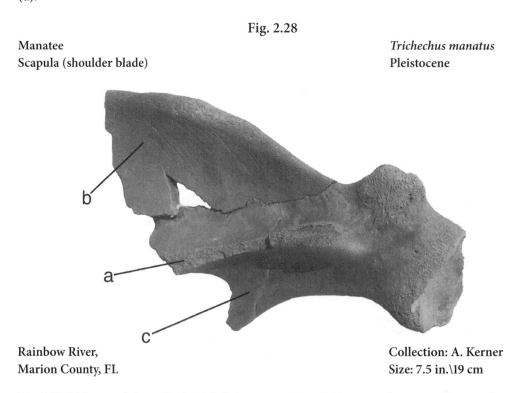

Rainbow River,

Marion County, FL

Collection: A. Kerner

Size: 7.5 in.\19 cm

Fig. 2.28. This scapula has a keel at (a) that separates two distinct muscle groups that attach at this location: the trapezius muscle at (b) and the deltoid muscle at (c).

Fig. 2.29

Hyaenodon
Skull

Hyaenodon horridus
Oligocene

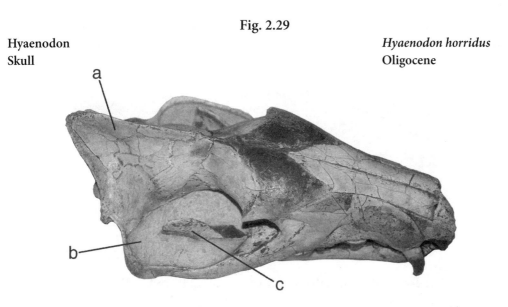

White River Formation,
South Dakota

Collection: F. Garcia
Size: no data

Fig. 2.29. The large sagittal crest at (a) provides room for large jaw muscle attachments for a powerful bite of this *Hyaenodon*. A large hole at (b), behind the zygomatic arch (cheekbone), allows the large temporalis muscle to pass through from the lower jaw (c) to attach at (a).

The size of the sagittal crest, a type of keel on top of many animal skulls, is often an indicator of bite strength. Dire wolves and saber-toothed cats are carnivores with large sagittal crests for attachment of a large muscle (**temporalis**) (fig. 2.29). Generally, carnivores have large temporalis muscles, omnivores, midsized temporalis muscles, and herbivores, smaller temporalis muscles. Many herbivores have little or no sagittal crest (fig. 2.34). The **masseter** muscle of herbivores (used for grinding and chewing) is more pronounced than their temporalis muscle. The masseter muscle, along with the **pterygoid muscle group**, attach to the outside of the lower jaw and the **zygomatic arch** (cheekbone) of the skull in such a way that side-to-side motion is produced for chewing and grinding. Horses, deer, and camels are herbivores with reduced sagittal crests but large zygomatic arches. Because of the complex nature of mammal teeth, which must align correctly to work efficiently, the pterygoid muscle group is more developed in mammals than in other animals.

A large sagittal crest on the skull is usually accompanied by large grooves on the inside of the back of the jaw bone for large muscle attachments (fig. 2.30). The zygomatic arch is usually very wide in animals with a strong bite, providing a large hole through which the temporalis muscle passes from the outside of the jaw to the skull (fig. 2.31). The temporalis muscle pulls the jaw

Fig. 2.30

Saber-toothed Cat
Mandible (lower jaw)

Smilodon fatalis
Pleistocene

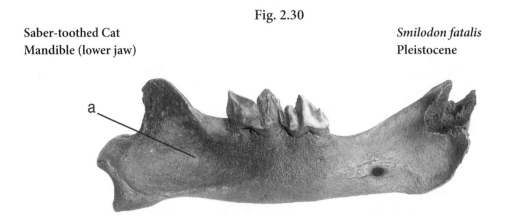

Santa Fe River,
Florida

Collection: D. Letasi
Size: 7.8 in.\19.8 cm

Fig. 2.30. Note the deep groove (a) at the outside of the back of this saber-toothed cat jaw that allows for large temporalis jaw muscle attachment, providing a powerful bite.

Fig. 2.31

Giant Oreodont
Skull

Promerycochoerus carrikeri
Miocene

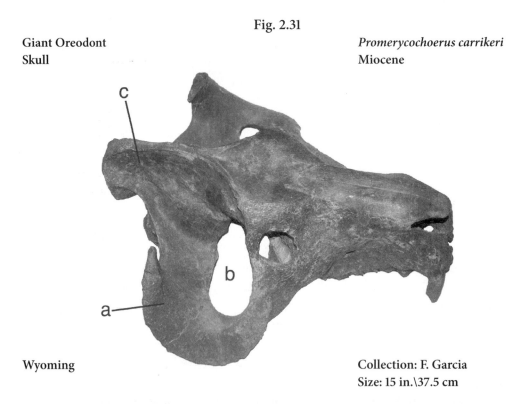

Wyoming

Collection: F. Garcia
Size: 15 in.\37.5 cm

Fig. 2.31. The extreme zygomatic arch (a) of this extinct giant oreodont allows a large temporalis muscle to pass through (b) and attach to a thick sagittal crest at (c). There is no modern analogue for this animal; however, these features indicate both strong masseter and temporalis muscles. Scientists recognize this animal as somewhat rodentlike; for a herbivore, it had an extremely powerful bite for some reason.

Fig. 2.32

Raccoon
Skull

Procyon lotor
Pleistocene

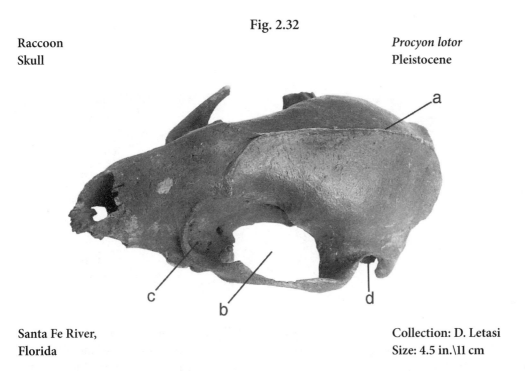

Santa Fe River,
Florida

Collection: D. Letasi
Size: 4.5 in.\11 cm

Fig. 2.32. Note the diminished sagittal crest at (a), compared with figures 2.29 and 2.31, of this raccoon skull, that of an omnivore with moderate bite strength. The skull also has a somewhat reduced zygomatic arch (b) that combines with its large eye socket (c) for good night vision. The auditory canal at (d) is large for a raccoon, compared with the size of the skull (see fig. 2.34).

up and down (open and closed); its size is an indicator of bite strength. As the temporalis muscle decreases in size, so does the sagittal crest on the top of the skull, and the hole between the zygomatic arch and the side of the skull (figs. 2.32–2.33). When a muscle contracts, its length shortens, but since the volume cannot change, there is an increase in conditional area; therefore, a wide zygomatic arch is needed to accommodate the increase in diameter of the temporalis muscle when biting.

Several other examples of tendon and ligament attachment scars and processes for various postcranial (after the skull) bones are also provided (figs. 2.34–2.37). Each attachment scar or process has its own story to tell. Scientists use comparative anatomy of extant animals to infer the ligament, tendon, and muscle sizes of extinct animals. The size of these scars and processes can confirm whether a prehistoric variation of a species was stronger or weaker, faster or slower, or more **robust** or **gracile**, than its extant relative.

Fig. 2.33

Giant Armadillo
Skull

Holmesina septentrionalis
Pleistocene

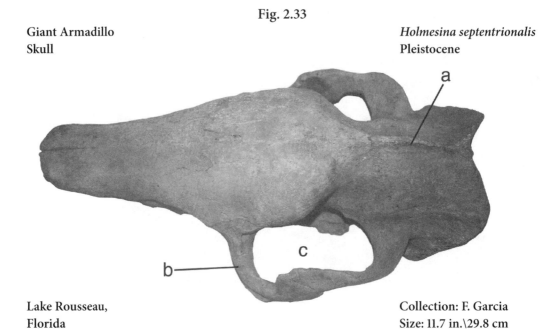

Lake Rousseau,
Florida

Collection: F. Garcia
Size: 11.7 in.\29.8 cm

Fig. 2.33. The small sagittal crest (a) on this giant armadillo leaves little room for the temporalis muscle to attach. The zygomatic arch at (b) provides a somewhat spacious area for the temporalis muscle (some of the space may also be part of the eye socket) to pass through at (c). This animal probably did not have a powerful bite.

Fig. 2.34

Tapir
Skull

Tapirus veroensis
Pleistocene

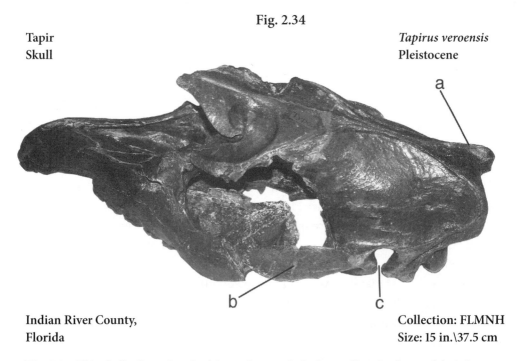

Indian River County,
Florida

Collection: FLMNH
Size: 15 in.\37.5 cm

Fig. 2.34. This skull of a tapir, a herbivore, has a relatively small sagittal crest (a) and very narrow zygomatic arches (b). Note the rectangular tag on the top of the skull denoting this particular skull as the type specimen for all *Tapirus veroensis* skulls. The auditory canal (c) of this tapir skull is comparatively small to the overall skull size (see fig. 2.32).

Fig. 2.35

Mammoth
Thoracic Vertebra

Mammuthus sp.
Pleistocene

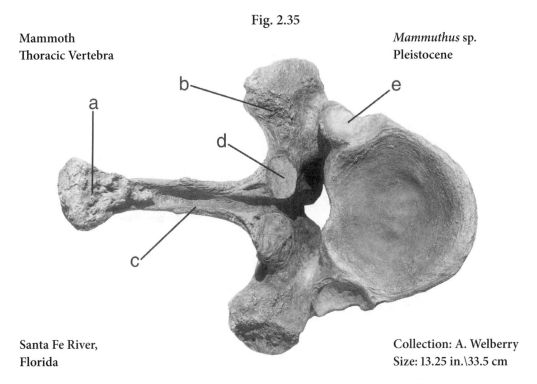

Santa Fe River,
Florida

Collection: A. Welberry
Size: 13.25 in.\33.5 cm

Fig. 2.35. Note the various rough scarring at (a), (b), and (c) for tendon and ligament attachments of the back muscles and bones of this mammoth vertebra. The smooth facet at (d) is for articulation with the next vertebra, and the facet at (e) is for articulation with a rib bone.

Fig. 2.36

Rhino
Femur (rear leg bone)

Teleoceras sp.
Early Pliocene/Late Miocene

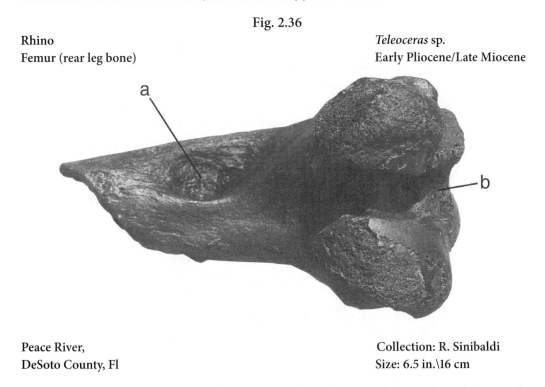

Peace River,
DeSoto County, Fl

Collection: R. Sinibaldi
Size: 6.5 in.\16 cm

Fig. 2.36. The distal end of this rhino femur shows where a large tendon would attach leg muscles at point (a), and where ligaments would attach this bone to the tibia and patella at point (b).

Fig. 2.37

Mammoth
Radius (lower foreleg)

Mammuthus sp.
Pleistocene

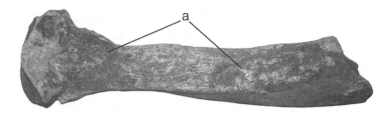

Florida

Collection: FLMNH
Size: 24 in.\60 cm

Fig. 2.37. This mammoth radius shows a large area (a) of rough bone where tendons would have attached leg muscles directly to the bone during life.

Bone Densities

Bone density can indicate a type of animal or the environment in which the animal lived. The extremely dense bones of marine mammals may have a secondary function as ballast along with their primary skeletal function.[14] Whales, dugongs (prehistoric sea cows extinct in our hemisphere but still alive in Australia), manatees, and dolphins often have extremely dense rib and skull bones (fig. 2.38). These marine mammals often dive to considerable depths with lungs filled with air. Dense bones may assist marine mammals in the same way a weight belt assists scuba divers in reaching the bottom of the ocean. Dense bones throughout the body of a marine mammal would help that animal achieve negative buoyancy, assisting in diving; however, some marine mammals, and prehistoric ichthyosaurs, that make their living by diving deep have employed the exact opposite strategy of light, spongy, less dense bone to aid in return to the surface and also in oxygen storage.[15]

At the other end of the spectrum, birds need extremely light but strong bones to escape gravity and become airborne. Bird bones are often hollow, with paper-thin reinforcing struts of bone for increased strength (fig. 2.39).[16] Many of the hollow bones in birds are also part of their very specialized respiratory system. Bats and prehistoric pterosaurs also had hollow bones with reinforcing struts. The paper-thin reinforcing struts are technically termed **diploe**. Other surprising examples of bones with honeycomb or struts are the skulls of **proboscideans** (mammoths, mastodons, elephants and gomphotheres), and the horn cores of any bovid (e.g., bison, cow). A large proboscidean skull constructed of solid

Fig. 2.38

Manatee   *Trichechus* sp.
Rib Bone   Pleistocene

Rainbow River,   Collection: R. Sinibaldi
Marion County, FL   Size: 5 in.\12.5 cm

Fig. 2.38. Note the lack of a marrow cavity at (a) of this cross section of manatee rib bone. These dense bones assist manatees and other aquatic mammals (whales, dolphins) to dive when their lungs are filled with air.

Fig. 2.39

Bird   Undetermined species
Leg Bone   Pleistocene

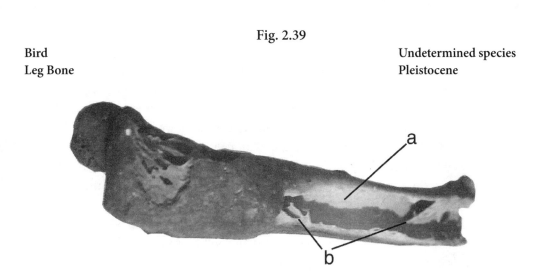

Rainbow River,   Collection: R. Sinibaldi
Marion County, FL   Size: 2 in.\5 cm

Fig. 2.39. Bird bones are generally hollow (a) with reinforcing struts (b), providing light yet strong bones for flight. Some bird bones are also connected to the respiratory system.

Fig. 2.40

Mammoth
Skull Material

Mammuthus sp.
Pleistocene

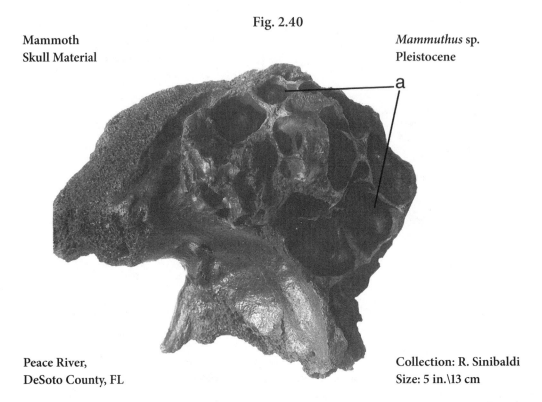

Peace River,
DeSoto County, FL

Collection: R. Sinibaldi
Size: 5 in.\13 cm

Fig. 2.40. Large animals with heavy heads evolved skulls with pneumatized bone air pockets. Note the large and small air pockets at (a). Honeycombed bone is another evolutionary solution to the problem of light yet strong bones.

bone would be too heavy to carry around; therefore, a light but strong honeycomb construction of skull bone material with trapped air pockets, technically known as **pneumatized bone**, with thin bone structures termed diploe, evolved as the animals gained size (fig. 2.40). The skull structures of other large-skulled animals such as giraffe and bison also comprise pneumatized bone.[17]

Between the dense bones of aquatic mammals and the hollow bones with struts and honeycombs of birds and extremely large animals fall the moderately dense bones of most terrestrial animals. Long bones, such as those of the legs, toes, and ribs, usually have a hollow cavity filled with marrow (fig. 2.41) and are of various diameters. The thicker the bone, the more weight it can bear. Generally, long bones with a thin diameter and large hollow cavity represent lighter animals per unit height, compared with a similar bone of the same length with thick diameter and narrow central cavity (fig. 2.42).

Bone density also plays a major role in determining which bones survive the various fossilization processes. The bones of young animals tend to be less dense and are therefore underrepresented in the fossil record compared with adult bones of the same animal. Likewise, the brittle bones of most birds tend

Fig. 2.41

Sloth
Partial Radius

Paramylodon harlani
Pleistocene

Peace River,
DeSoto County, FL

Collection: R. Sinibaldi
Size: 9 in.\23 cm

Fig. 2.41. This naturally split sloth radius has well-preserved spongy (cancellous) bone common to most terrestrial (land) mammals.

Fig. 2.42

(a) Bison Leg Bone
(b) Camel Leg Bone

(a) *Bison antiquus*
(b) *Paleolama mirifica*
Pleistocene

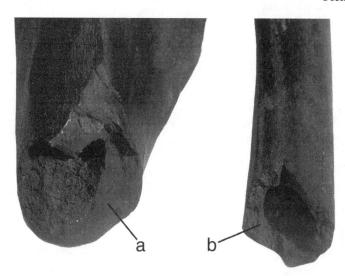

Withlacoochee River,
Florida

Collection: A. Kerner
Size: 2.8 in.\7.2 cm (Diameter of [a])

Fig. 2.42. Compare the difference between the robust, heavy diaphysis of the bison leg bone (a) on the right and the relatively light and narrow camel leg (b) on the left. These bone morphologies reflect the different lifestyles and body morphologies of the respective animals.

to be relatively scarce in the fossil record. On the opposite end of the spectrum, the bones of larger animals not only tend to survive better through the millennia, but are also noticed (and therefore collected and reported) more often than those of smaller animals.

Vision

The placement and size of the orbits, or eye sockets, in a skull can help scientists determine whether a prehistoric animal had **monocular** or **binocular** vision, was **nocturnal** or **diurnal**, and was terrestrial or **semiaquatic**, or the position of the animal in the food chain. Each type of vision has its own advantages and disadvantages that suit the needs of each animal.[18]

Monocular versus Binocular Vision

Placement of the eye sockets on the sides of the skull allows for very wide **peripheral vision,** actually extending behind the animal (fig. 2.43). For large ani-

Fig. 2.43

Oreodont
Skull

Merycoidodon culbertsoni
Oligocene

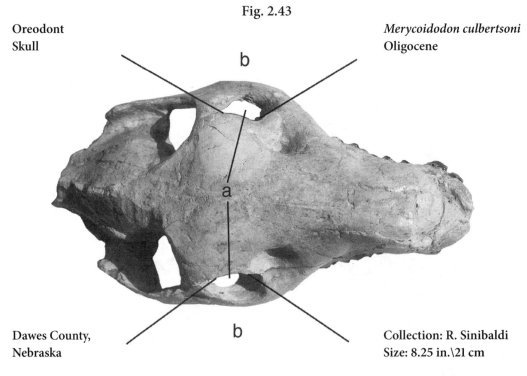

Dawes County,
Nebraska

Collection: R. Sinibaldi
Size: 8.25 in.\21 cm

Fig. 2.43. The eye sockets (a) of this oreodont are rotated all the way to the sides of the skull. The projected visual range, indicated by lines (b), demonstrates no overlapping vision between the eyes. This lack of stereoscopic vision was a trade-off for an extremely wide range of vision that allowed this herbivore to detect predators from a very wide angle of attack.

Fig. 2.44

European Cave Bear
Skull

Ursus spelaeus
Pleistocene

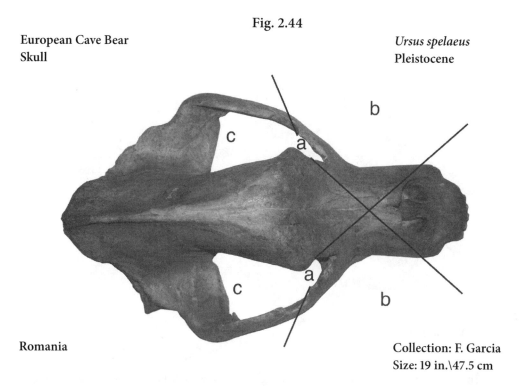

Romania

Collection: F. Garcia
Size: 19 in.\47.5 cm

Fig. 2.44. The eye sockets (a) of this cave bear are rotated almost fully forward. The projected overlapping vision, indicated by lines (b), shows this animal had good stereoscopic vision. The large holes at (c) are for the temporalis muscle to pass from the lower jaw to the skull and run directly behind the eye sockets.

mals (bison, rhino, elephants, and others) this type of vision is advantageous for seeing predators approaching from the rear or sides; however, monocular vision does not allow for **depth perception**, an advantage for animals that spend a great portion of their lives with their heads down, grazing. Each eye sees a different picture.

Orbits rotated toward the front of the skull allow the brain to see the same image from two angles. The brain then integrates these images into a three-dimensional picture that allows the animal to judge depth or distance of objects (fig. 2.44). Carnivores need excellent depth perception to engage in an attack. Their limited peripheral vision is usually not a problem since they themselves are rarely attacked.

Most omnivores also have the capability of some degree of binocular vision. Fast-moving herbivores such as deer and horses have orbits rotated slightly forward, giving them some degree of binocular vision to assist in judging distances when fleeing at high speed (fig. 2.45). In figures 2.43–2.45, the visual fields of each animal are indicated with lines.

Fig. 2.45

Giant Pig
Skull

Archaeotherium mortini
Oligocene

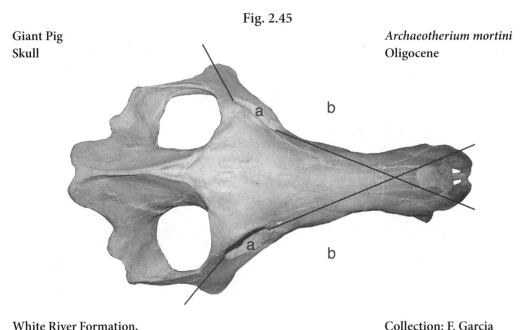

White River Formation,
Nebraska

Collection: F. Garcia
Size: 26 in.\67.5 cm

Fig. 2.45. The eye sockets (a) of the giant pig are rotated somewhat forward, providing this animal with minimal stereoscopic vision, indicated by lines (b).

Nocturnal versus Diurnal Vision

Many animals have evolved a nocturnal lifestyle, feeding at night, requiring relatively larger eye sockets to accommodate larger eyes that gather more light for night vision (fig. 2.32). Larger eye sockets generally enable the animal to get more light into the eye to be detected by the optical nerves. Before the information detected by the eye is relayed to the brain, many modifications have been made to the eye itself to control the amount of light and information to be processed.[19] Diurnal animals, those that feed primarily during daylight hours, have smaller eye sockets in proportion to skull size (fig. 2.44). Some animals have developed a **crepuscular** lifestyle and are active only in the early morning or early evening.

Terrestrial versus Semiaquatic Lifestyle

Animals that spend a good portion of their life in the water have evolved skulls with eye sockets near the top. In animals such as alligators, turtles (fig. 2.46), otters (fig. 2.47), hippos, and beavers, the eye sockets are on or near the top of the skull. The skulls of semiaquatic animals tend to be somewhat flattened or streamlined for swimming efficiency. In addition, the nostrils of alligators, crocodiles, turtles, and other semiaquatic animals are located near the top of

Fig. 2.46

Florida Snapper
Skull

Chelydra serpentina osceola
Late Pleistocene

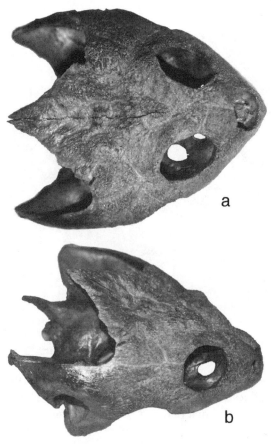

a

b

Santa Fe River
Florida

Collection: A. Kerner
Size: 4 in.\10 cm

Fig. 2.46. Note the streamlined shape of this Florida snapping turtle skull evolved for efficient underwater swimming. View (a) is dorsal and (b) a lateral view of the skull.

the skull. Location of eyes and nostrils on the top of the skull gives the animal the ability to watch for predators and search for food while remaining semi-submerged and still capable of breathing air. Compare the position of the eye sockets in semiaquatic skull shapes with other eye socket placements and skull shapes pictured in figures 2.43–2.45.

Many animals have a bone inside their eye called the sclerotic ring. Mammals' prehistoric ancestors lost this adaptation; however, many animals still retain this bone, embedded in their eyeball. This bone is usually shaped like a doughnut and may help the eyeball maintain its shape, especially in animals that spend time deep underwater.

Figure 2.47

Giant Otter Skull   *Enhydritherium terraenovae*
Aquatic Mammal   Late Miocene/Early Pliocene

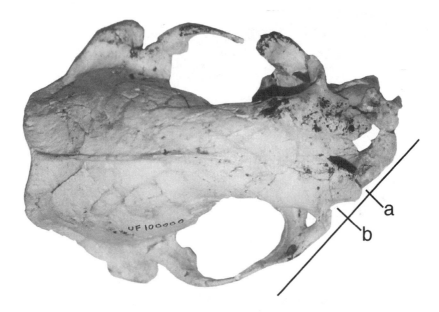

Moss Acres Racetrack   Collection: FLMNH
Marion County, FL   Size: 5 in.\12 cm

Fig. 2.47. Note the streamlined shape of this otter skull. Compare the very small facial curves at (a) and (b) of the otter to the facial features on the skulls pictured in 2.43, 2.44, and 2.45. Note the similarity in shape of the otter skull to that of the turtle skull in figure 2.46.

Bones as Armor

Some forms of bones are used as armor or protection for the animal. Turtle shell comes to mind and is abundant in the fossil record. Turtle shells evolved from a set of fused rib plates to provide protection for the animal's body. Each species of turtle has a shell with its own distinct pattern. These patterns enable the collector to identify turtle species from even small fragmentary pieces (fig. 2.48). Giant armadillos, technically called pampatheres, and glyptodonts (a distant cousin of the giant armadillo) are other types of prehistoric animals that had protective **carapaces** (shells) covering most or all of their bodies (figs. 2.49–2.50), as do today's smaller armadillos. The pattern on each osteoderm or **scute** (portion of bony armor) often reflects the skin pattern directly covering the scute. The purpose of the holes penetrating the central polygon of the glyptodont scute in figure 2.50 is to accommodate the bulbs of hair follicles and the blood vessels and nerves that travel to the skin on the outer side of the bony

Fig. 2.48

(a) Giant Land Tortoise
(b) Giant Land Tortoise
(c) Soft Shelled Turtle
(d) Pond Turtle

(a) *Hesperotestudo* sp.
(b) *Hesperotestudo* sp.
(c) *Apalone ferox*
(d) *Trachemys scripta*
Pleistocene

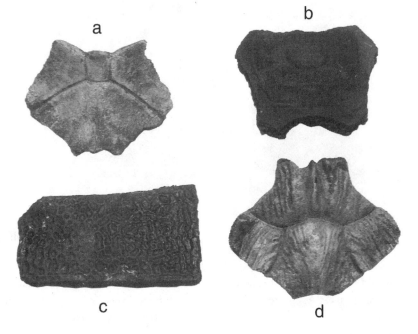

Peace River,
DeSoto County, FL

Collection: R. Sinibaldi
Size: 2 in.\5 cm (c)

Fig. 2.48. Each of these four turtle shell pieces has its own distinct patterns that enable identification. The grooved lines on (a) and (d) delineate the boundaries of epidermal scutes that attached directly to the bony shell during life.

armor. Even most turtles have a layer of skin (technically a horny scale) covering their shells. Individual scutes are very common finds (fig. 2.51), but an intact, entirely articulated carapace of an armadillo or glyptodont is very rare. In some fossil deposits, articulated turtle carapaces and plastrons (top and bottom of the shell) are quite common and exquisitely preserved (fig. 2.52). Finally, alligators and crocodiles also have dermal scutes under their skin for protection. It is believed that the dermals scutes of alligators and crocodiles are also efficient conductors of solar energy, an important function in cold-blooded animals (fig. 2.53). Turtle shell may also serve as a thermal conductor of solar energy. In addition, **subcutaneous** dermal plates in rays and sharks are forms of bony armor (fig. 2.54). Another rare form of subcutaneous scute used as armor is found in the fossil remains of the giant mylodont ground sloths (fig. 2.55). Other bones

Fig. 2.49

Giant Armadillo
Osteoderm (scute)

a

b

Holmesina floridanus
Late Pliocene

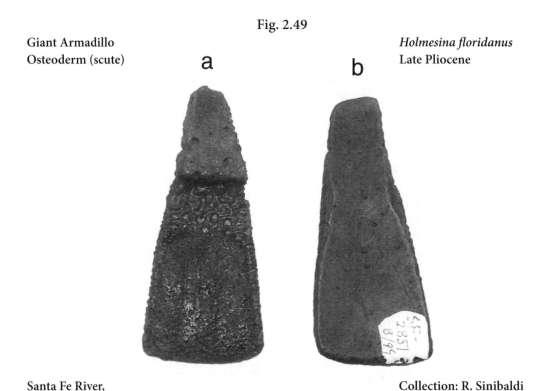

Santa Fe River,
Florida

Collection: R. Sinibaldi
Size: 3 in.\7.5 cm

Fig. 2.49. The upper side (a) of this giant armadillo scute bears the pattern of attachments points of the animal's skin and scales directly to the bone. The underside (b) is smooth, where muscle would have run under the animal's protective armor. These osteoderms are from the movable portion of the armadillo's band.

Fig. 2.50

Glyptodont
Osteoderm (scute)

Glyptotherium floridanum
Pleistocene

Peace River,
DeSoto County, FL

Collection: R. Sinibaldi
Size: 2.37 in.\6 cm

Fig. 2.50. Although related to the giant armadillo (fig. 2.49), the glyptodont had a distinctive pattern on its osteoderms, or scutes.

Giant Armadillo
Osteoderms (scutes)

Holmesina septentrionalis
Pleistocene

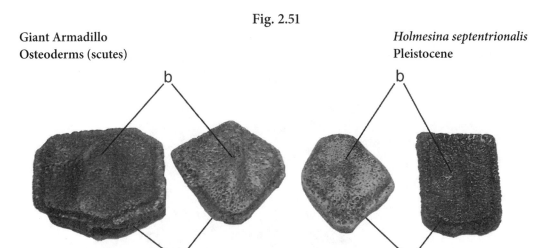

Peace River,
DeSoto County, FL

Collection: R. Sinibaldi
Size: 2 in.\5 cm (largest)

Fig. 2.51. Osteoderms of various animals are common finds that may have different shapes for the same species. These four giant armadillo scutes are all shaped differently but have the same distinct identifying ridges at (a) and vertical protuberances at (b). Although shaped differently, these diagnostic markings allow identification from the same genus. These osteoderms are from the immovable portion of the armadillo's carapace.

Fig. 2.52

Tortoise
Carapace (shell)

Stylemys nebrascensis
Oligocene

Dawes County,
Nebraska

Collection: D. Sinibaldi
Size: 10 in.\25.5 cm

Fig. 2.52. In some areas of the White River Formation of Nebraska, complete and well-preserved tortoise carapaces are a common find.

Fig. 2.53

Alligator   *Alligator mississippiensis*
Osteoderm (scute)   Pleistocene

Peace River,   Collection: D. Sinibaldi
DeSoto County, FL   Size: 2.75 in.\7 cm

Fig. 2.53. It is believed that the osteoderms (scutes) of alligators (and crocodiles, fig. 2.59) act not only as armored protection, but also as solar heat conductors in these cold-blooded reptiles.

Fig. 2.54

Stingray   Undetermined species
Osteoderms   Miocene–Early Pliocene

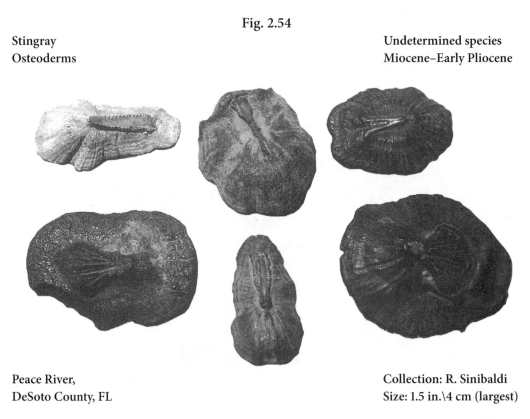

Peace River,   Collection: R. Sinibaldi
DeSoto County, FL   Size: 1.5 in.\4 cm (largest)

Fig. 2.54. These stingray dermal plates protected the animal. Although they are found in a variety of shapes and sizes, their uplifted barbed ridge pattern is unmistakable.

Fig. 2.55

Giant Ground Sloth   *Paramylodon harlani*
Osteoderms (dermal scutes)   Pleistocene

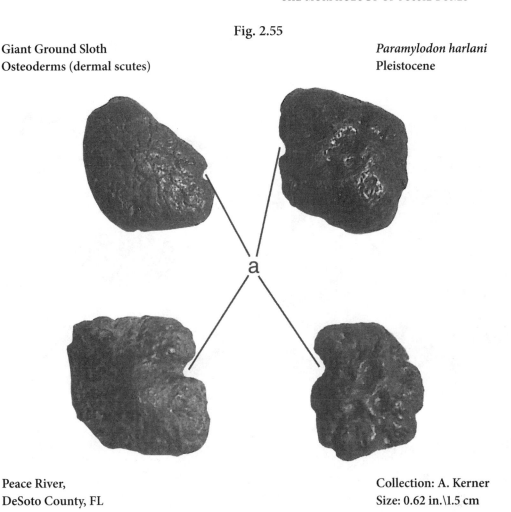

Peace River,   Collection: A. Kerner
DeSoto County, FL   Size: 0.62 in.\1.5 cm

Fig. 2.55. These indistinct and often overlooked subcutaneous dermal scutes of the large extinct ground sloth, *Paramylodon*, may have protected this slow-moving animal from large predators. Note the diagnostic notches at (a).

with skin patterns are covered in the next section. Armor with attack or bite marks is discussed in chapter 5.

The leg spurs and foot pads of giant land tortoises may have also served as protective armor when the animal retreated into its shell. Many turtles today have very small forms of these spurs that line up on the outside of the leg when the animal is retracted into its shell. The leg spurs of the giant land tortoise may have even had a dual purpose of affording the extremely heavy land reptile additional traction as it carried its gigantic body across the prehistoric terrain (fig. 2.56).

Fig. 2.56

Giant Land Tortoise
(a) Foot Pads
(b) Leg Spurs

Hesperotestudo species
Early Pleistocene

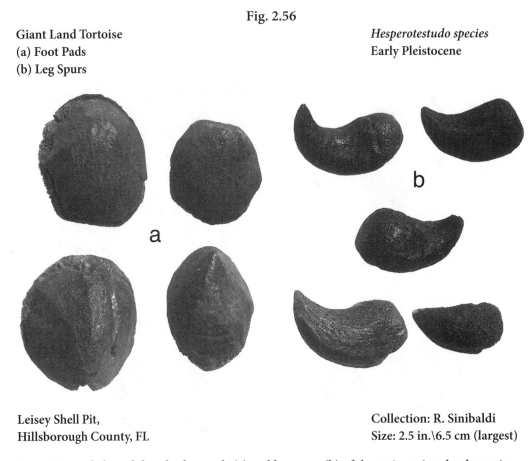

Leisey Shell Pit,
Hillsborough County, FL

Collection: R. Sinibaldi
Size: 2.5 in.\6.5 cm (largest)

Fig. 2.56. It is believed that the foot pads (a) and leg spurs (b) of the extinct giant land tortoise served the dual purpose of traction during locomotion and armor when the animal retreated into its shell.

Skin Attachment Scars

Alligator skull material provides an excellent example of skin attachment scars on bone. In those places where skin has directly attached to the bone, a deep repetitive grooved or pitted pattern often exists (fig. 2.57). The repetitive patterns of skin attachment scars presented in this section contrast with the non-repetitive attachment scars of tendons and ligaments described earlier (figs. 2.35–2.37). Where muscles run between the bone and the skin in an alligator skull, the bone is smooth (fig. 2.58). Alligator and crocodile dermal scutes, used as armor and for solar conduction, as discussed in the previous section, exhibit these same patterns (fig. 2.59).

Another common example in the fossil record of a skin attachment scar is the pattern at the base of a deer antler (fig. 2.60). In fact, most horned animals

Fig. 2.57

Alligator
Skull Fragments

Alligator mississippiensis
Pleistocene

Peace River,
DeSoto County, FL

Collection: R. Sinibaldi
Size: 3.5 in.\9 cm (largest)

Fig. 2.57. Alligator bone material bears a specific pattern where the skin attached directly to the bone. Compare this pattern to the pattern on the alligator osteoderms (fig. 2.53, 2.59).

Fig. 2.58

Alligator
Skull

Alligator mississippiensis
Recent

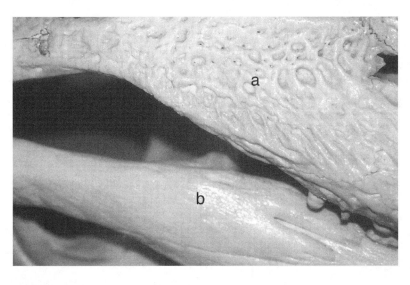

Pinellas County,
Florida

Collection: F. Garcia
Size: 10 in.\25 cm

Fig. 2.58. The pitted areas of the skull and jaws (a) indicate skin attachments directly to the bone of the alligator. Where the muscle runs between the bone and the skin, the bone is smooth (b).

Fig. 2.59

Crocodile
Osteoderm (scute)

Undetermined species
Eocene

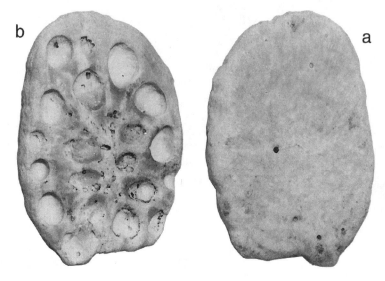

Rainbow River,
Marion County, FL

Collection: D. Sinibaldi
Size: 2 in.\5 cm

Fig. 2.59. Note the smooth surface (a) on the underside of this crocodile scute, where it came into contact with muscle tissue. The pitted surface (b) is from the upper side of the scute, where the skin directly attached to the bone. Compare this crocodile scute, which has no central ridge, to an alligator scute (fig. 2.53), which usually has a prominent central ridge.

Fig. 2.60

White-tailed Deer
Antler Base

Odocoileus virginianus
Pleistocene

Peace River,
DeSoto County, FL

Collection: R. Sinibaldi
Size: 3 in.\7.5 cm

Fig. 2.60. This deer antler base (c) displays the distinct markings (b) where the skin gathered and attached around the base. A portion of the skull (a) is still attached to this antler core, indicating this antler was not shed when the animal died.

Fig. 2.61

Bison
Horn Core and Skull

Bison bonasus schoenhaupti
Pleistocene

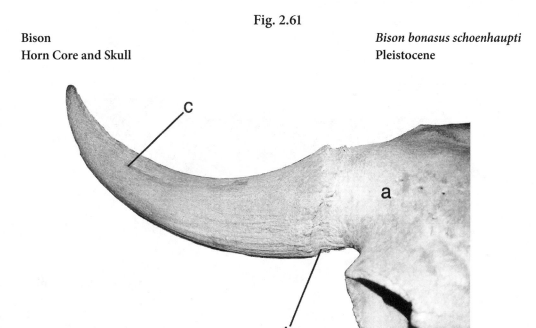

Rhine River,
Germany

Collection: A. Kerner
Size: 15 in.\37.5 cm

Fig. 2.61. This bison skull (a) and horn (c) display the distinct markings where the skin attached to the bone at (c). See figure 2.60 for comparison with deer antler.

(bison, fig. 2.61,[20] bovids) have a skin attachment scar at the base of their horns or antlers similar to that of a deer. The skin covering a deer antler is called velvet. In addition to identifying an animal by the pattern of antler or horn attachments, fragments of skull with or without antlers attached can indicate the time of year an animal died, as antlers are shed and replaced seasonally.

Skin attachment scars also form on fish jaws (fig. 2.62) and turtle and glyptodont/armadillo scutes or carapaces.

Markings Left by Nerves and Blood Vessels

Many times, nerves and blood vessels travel through bones to get from one point to another. This is often the shortest route, but more importantly, the nerves are protectively surrounded by bone en route to their destinations. The jaws of mammals often have holes, technically called foramina (singular,

Fig. 2.62

Garfish
Maxilla

Atractosteus sp.
Pleistocene

Peace River,
DeSoto County, FL

Collection: R. Sinibaldi
Size: 2 in.\5 cm

Fig. 2.62. Compare the pattern on this garfish maxilla with the patterns on figures 2.48–2.61. Each animal has a distinctive skin attachment pattern.

Fig. 2.63

Tapir
Jaw

Tapirus veroensis
Pleistocene

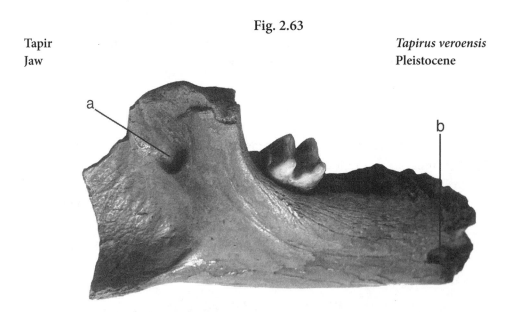

Peace River,
DeSoto County, FL

Collection: R. Sinibaldi
Size: 7.25 in.\18 cm

Fig. 2.63. This tapir jaw displays a prominent foramen or hole at (a) where the nerves and blood supply traveled through the jaw, under the roots of the teeth, to the front of the jaw (b).

Fig. 2.64

Camel
Sacrum

Family *Camelidae*
Pleistocene

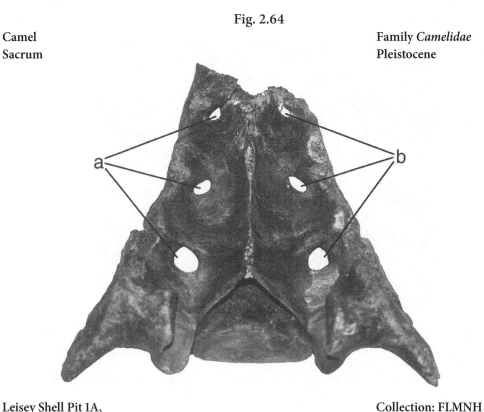

Leisey Shell Pit 1A,
Hillsborough County, FL

Collection: FLMNH
Size: 5.5 in.\14 cm (v)

Fig. 2.64. This camel sacrum has identical nerve holes on both sides at (a) and (b) where the nerves exited the spinal cord and traveled to the lower extremities of the body.

foramen), running from the back of the jaw, under the teeth, and toward the front of the mouth (fig. 2.63). These holes supply the route for both nerves and blood vessels of the teeth. Vertebral processes, especially at the sacrum (fig. 2.64), also exhibit pronounced holes through which nerves pass. Also see figure 2.50, the bony armor of a glyptodont that has visible foramina for the accommodation of nerves, blood vessels, and hair follicles.

In rare instances, blood vessels running along the side of bones leave impressions on the bone surfaces. If this occurs, the impressions are generally on the skull or jaws of an animal, usually the inside (figs. 2.65–2.66). Many times plant roots leave markings on the surface of bones that may closely resemble blood vessel markings, a subject covered in chapter 4 (fig. 4.1).

Fig. 2.65

Cro-Magnon
Skull (interior view)

Early *Homo sapiens*
Pleistocene

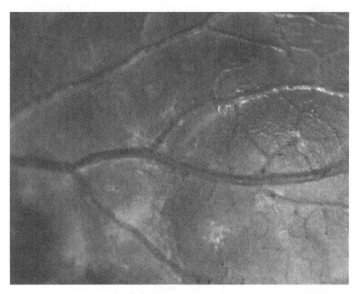

Rhine River,
Germany

Private Collection
Size: 1 in.\2.5 cm

Fig. 2.65. A close-up of the interior of this Cro-Magnon human skull clearly shows markings left by blood vessels on the bone.

Fig. 2.66

Mammoth
Tusk Socket

Mammuthus sp.
Pleistocene

Origin Unknown

Collection: B. Fite
Size: 13 in.\32.5 cm

Fig. 2.66. The tusk socket of this mammoth displays the markings where blood vessels ran between the tusks and the bone of the skull.

Auditory Bones

Over long periods of time, many solutions to the problems of hearing have evolved. Fish have solved the problem one way, marine mammals another way, and terrestrial vertebrates still a different way. Each solution to the need for auditory capabilities has left its own auditory-type bones in the fossil record.

Fish must detect sound traveling through water, a medium denser than air. They have developed **otoliths**, bones within a cavity in their skull, for this purpose. These tiny lumps of bones are very dense and vibrate at a rate different from that of the surrounding water. Sense organs in the fish's skull transmit these vibrations to the brain to decipher. Otoliths, because of their density, fossilize well; however, they are often overlooked because of their size and their generally nondescript shape (fig. 2.67).[21]

Marine mammals first developed hearing as terrestrial animals in their evolutionary past, then evolved apparatus for underwater auditory processing. The ear bones of whales,[22] dolphins, and manatees are very dense for detecting sound underwater. As discussed above, sound does not travel as well underwater as in the air, and the auditory apparatus of marine mammals must be refined to be efficient. Because of their dense nature, the ear bones of marine mam-

Fig. 2.67

Fish	*Corvina gemma*
Otoliths (ear bones)	Oligocene

Vicksburg,	Collection: FLMNH
Mississippi	Size: 0.35 in.\1 cm

Fig. 2.67. These small, nondescript fish otoliths (bones within the inner ear) are often overlooked as pebbles or rocks. They are extremely dense, enabling fish to hear under water.

Fig. 2.68

Whale
Ear Bones

Undetermined species
Miocene

Peace River,
DeSoto County, FL

Collection: R. Sinibaldi
Size: 3.5 in.\9 cm

Fig. 2.68. These whale ear bones are extremely dense (like fish otoliths, fig. 2.67), enabling the animal to hear in a dense medium (water). Although a little more recognizable and considerably larger than fish otoliths, these bones are also often overlooked. The petrosal bone (inner ear) is on the left and the auditory bulla (middle ear) bone is on the right.

mals fossilize well (the same way fish otoliths do) and are very common finds. As with otoliths, they are also mistaken for rocks by the inexperienced fossil hunter. The most commonly found marine mammal ear bones are the **petrosal** bone (bony part of the skull where the inner ear is located) and the **auditory bulla** (bone surrounding the middle ear) (fig. 2.68).

Most land mammals have an auditory anatomy that we would recognize as inner, middle, and outer ear. The outer ear is composed of skin and cartilage and usually does not fossilize. The middle ear processes are embedded in the auditory bulla and attached to the mastoid and petrous portions of the temporal bones of the skull. Some mammals, such as cats, have an external auditory bulla, whereas others, including humans, have the bulla housed in the base of the skull. The location of the auditory bulla may determine the interrelatedness of various fossil species.[23] Parts of the inner and middle ear are composed of bone and bony canals that often fossilize well. The middle ear contains the auditory bones of the malleus, incus, and stapes, which are housed in the auditory bulla. The inner ear contains the labyrinth (semicircular canals) and cochlea.

Fig. 2.69

Horse   *Equus* sp.
Petrosal (ear bone)   Early Pleistocene

Leisey Shell Pit,   Collection: R. Sinibaldi
Hillsborough County, FL   Size: 2 in.\5 cm

Fig. 2.69. These horse ear bones are embedded in skull material (the petrous portion of the temporal bone). The ear bones of terrestrial mammals often look like nondescript skull fragments and are often overlooked.

Many times inner ear bones, technically called petrosal bones, look like indiscriminate chunks of skull bone; however, upon further inspection, the ear canal, eardrum, cochlea, and various nerve holes of the ear bones can often be identified in well-preserved specimens (figs. 2.69–2.70).

When a skull is completely intact, comparative size of the auditory canals can give a clue to the degree to which an animal depended on its hearing; comparatively larger auditory processes indicate better hearing. The auditory bones of the middle ear are housed in a boxlike chamber covered with bone, forming what is known as the auditory bulla. Carnivores rely on acute hearing for hunting and characteristically possess a large auditory bulla. Though herbivores need their auditory senses to detect predators, they have a much smaller auditory bulla since they feed primarily during the day and depend more on vision. Furthermore, nocturnal animals generally rely more heavily on their auditory capabilities than diurnal animals. Compare the size of the auditory canal in a raccoon skull (fig. 2.32) with that in a tapir skull (fig. 2.34). The size of the auditory bulla can best be examined by viewing the underside of the skull.

Fig. 2.70

White-tailed Deer   *Odocoileus virginianus*
Petrosal (inner ear bone)   Pleistocene

Santa Fe River,   Collection: R. Sinibaldi
Florida   Size: 1.25 in.\3.3 cm

Fig. 2.70. This inner ear bone from a deer has come free from its surrounding skull material. Compare with figure 2.69, which still has surrounding skull material.

The Braincase

The inside of the skull can offer scientists tremendous amounts of information on the intelligence and sensory abilities of animals. Scientists have studied braincases from prehistoric humans in depth to compare intelligence, language abilities, and human development.[24] Specific lobes of the brain correspond to specific abilities, as in Broca's area with language abilities in early humans.[25] Other lobes correspond to olfactory senses (smell), auditory abilities (hearing), sight, and other senses. Roughly, it is believed that the more lobe convolutions or folds in the brain, the "higher" the intelligence of the animal. The human brain contains more convolutions for its size than that of any other animal (fig. 2.71). Overall brain size is not an indicator of overall intelligence; the brain-to-body-size ratio is the best indicator of comparative intelligence.[26]

A fossil collector may find two types of braincases from prehistoric animals: the actual skull case (technically termed the **calvarium**) or a brain cast (**endocranial cast**). In mammals, the brain completely fills the braincase; therefore, the actual skull case in mammals will show the impressions of the brain convolutions and can assist scientists in determining an animal's sensory abilities. The brains of mammals, however, are surrounded by three very thin layers of protective tissue and some cerebral spinal fluid, meaning the impression of the brain will not be perfectly exact. Furthermore, if the skull is complete and empty, the scientist can fill it with sand, measure the volume it holds, and determine the brain size (usually designated in milliliters). Most amateurs not trained in

Fig. 2.71

Cro-Magnon
Skull (interior view)

Early *Homo sapiens*
Pleistocene

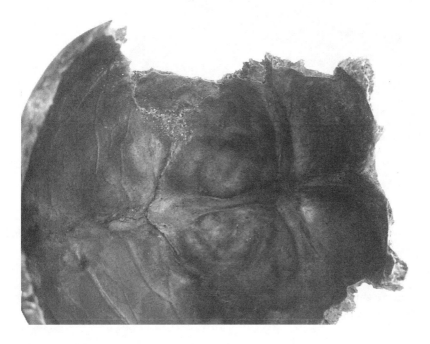

Rhine River,
Germany

Private Collection
Size: 4 in.\10 cm

Fig. 2.71. This partial braincase shows some of the folds of an early human's brain. Scientists can study these impressions to compare the organization of the brains of our ancestors with that of the brains of modern humans.

brain morphology will be limited to looking at the size and number of lobe impressions. As previously stated, the more convoluted, the more specialized/organized the brain of the animal (fig. 2.72).

A brain cast, if it is well preserved, can give almost the same information as the skull case. Many times, after an animal dies and the brain is completely decayed, the cavity will fill up with sediment that will then harden and fossilize (fig. 2.73). A well-preserved endocranial cast (also called an **endocast**) will be a positive image of the brain the way it looked during life. Scientists will sometimes deliberately make casts of the cavity in order to visualize and study a positive image of the brain; the process of pouring a rubber cast and extracting it does not damage the skull and therefore preserves the fossil specimen. In other animals, such as fish, reptiles, and dinosaurs, the brain does not completely fill the braincase, and a fossil endocranial cast will not give a good impression of the actual brain size or shape in life.

Fig. 2.72

Peccary
Skull Cap

Undetermined species
Late Pleistocene

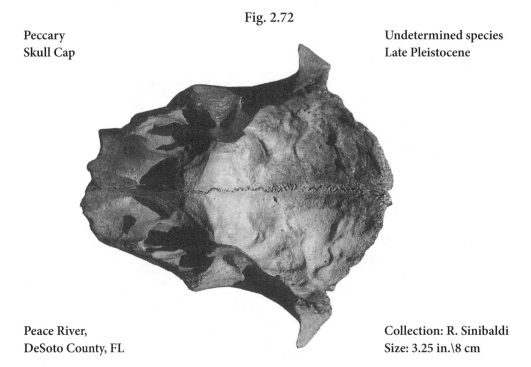

Peace River,
DeSoto County, FL

Collection: R. Sinibaldi
Size: 3.25 in.\8 cm

Fig. 2.72. The braincase of this juvenile peccary also demonstrates impressions from the lobes of its brain. Scientists can study the organization of extinct animals (to some extent) by looking at these impressions.

Fig. 2.73

Oreodont
Braincast

Merycoidodontidae species.
Oligocene

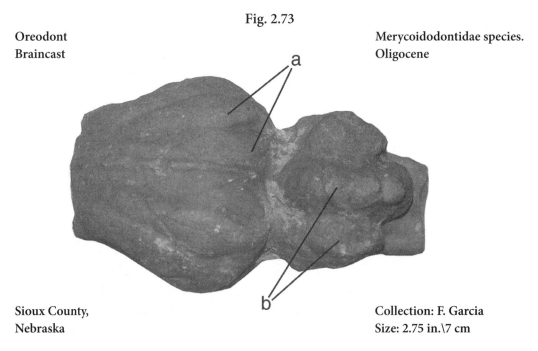

Sioux County,
Nebraska

Collection: F. Garcia
Size: 2.75 in.\7 cm

Fig. 2.73. The endocranial cast of the brain of an oreodont was formed after the brain material decomposed and was replaced by sediment in the skull cavity. Note the primitive pattern of folds at (a) and (b).

CHAPTER 3

The Morphology of Fossil Teeth

Dentition is destiny, at least to some degree. You can deduce much about an animal's diet, ecology, and behavior from its dental morphology.

David Quammen

Introduction

As stated in chapter 2, bones and teeth are the hardest parts of a vertebrate animal's anatomy. Of the two, teeth are considerably harder than bone; therefore, of all anatomical features that have the potential to fossilize, teeth have the best chance.[1] The fossil record supports this premise, with many species of prehistoric animals known only by the remains of their fossilized teeth.[2]

Teeth are generally made of three types of materials; enamel, dentine, and cementum. **Enamel** is the hardest of the three elements of teeth and wears the most slowly. **Dentine** and **cementum** wear considerably faster. The uneven wear rate in the three elements of teeth allows the tooth surface usually to maintain some semblance of the ridge, bump, or cusp system with which it began to enhance chewing efficiency, a feature that is especially important in herbivores (plant eaters), which spend the majority of their day chewing.[3] The three materials that make up most mammal teeth are very similar to bone; however, bone material contains cell spaces within them and tooth material does not. The cells that produced the tooth material moved away from the site and are not trapped in the structure as they are in general bone material. This lack of cell spaces also increases the strength of tooth material.

In addition to their hardness, teeth have another advantage over other anatomical parts that make them more likely to be discovered as fossils: greater quantity. Most animals produce only one of each bone (two if you count left and right), but it is very common for most mammals to produce two sets of upper and lower teeth. Some animals, such as proboscideans (mammoths, mastodons, gomphotheres) and **sirenia** (manatees and dugongs), produce six or more sets of teeth. Their teeth enter from the back of the jaw and travel forward until worn out, then exit through the front of the jaw. Reptiles, such as alligators and crocodiles, continuously replace worn teeth from underneath, but the big winners in tooth production are sharks. Some individual sharks can produce as many as 40,000 teeth during their lifetimes. All of this tooth production leaves a skewed fossil record in favor of teeth over bone.[4]

There is a plus side to the prominence of teeth in the fossil record: tooth morphology can probably tell us more about an extinct animal than any other single anatomical item, especially in the case of mammals. Tooth morphology can tell us if an animal was a carnivore (meat eater), herbivore (plant eater), or omnivore (plant and meat eater); furthermore, careful examination of teeth can divide herbivores into grazers and browsers.

Note that the terms carnivore, herbivore, and omnivore are not **taxonomic classifications**. These three terms confer a general lifestyle classification that may not coincide with scientific taxonomic rankings such as order, family, genus, and **species**.[5] However, for investigating the information in bones and teeth, the terms carnivore, herbivore, and omnivore are far more descriptive of lifestyle than some obscure scientific terms.

For most mammals, tooth morphology can tell an animal's approximate age (variation due to age is technically called **ontogenetic variation**). The size and wear patterns on teeth are extremely accurate indicators of age, especially for herbivores. A total lack of wear pattern usually indicates an unerupted tooth of a newborn. Fossil teeth are often worn down to or even below the gum line, representative of extreme old age; however, in some carnivores, very little tooth wear may be seen, even in old teeth, if they ate mostly meat. Other carnivores that scavenged a good portion of their dietary intake, combining bone with meat, may have fairly worn teeth even as juveniles. Furthermore, pathological teeth, covered in chapter 6, can inform about diseases and injuries in prehistoric animal populations. For reptiles and sharks, size may be more indicative of age than a wear pattern.

In large samples of fossilized teeth, paleontologists are able to detect **sexual dimorphism** (different forms for male and female).[6] Generally, in mammals, male teeth are larger. The males in some species, such as horses, have canine teeth, whereas the females' canines are reduced or missing completely. Furthermore, in large samples, paleontologists can determine geographic variation in a species, called clines. Very small, but fairly consistent variations in the structure of enamel folds, cusps, and other details in teeth from the same species may show up in geographically different regions.[7] In the fossil record, these variations may lead to debate over the question of a possible new species versus slight variation indicative of a subspecies or race (variety).

General Mammalian Tooth Morphology

Most mammal teeth contain the same components. Some exceptions to the rules will be covered separately. Entire books have been devoted to the evolution of hominid (human) teeth alone; therefore, consider the following merely a brief overview of tooth morphology.

Teeth are located either in the upper jaw, or **maxilla** and **premaxilla** (fig. 3.1), or in the lower jaw or **mandible**[8] (fig. 3.2) and are referred to as maxillary (upper) or mandibular (lower) teeth, respectively. The section of a tooth anchored in the jaw is called the root. The part of the tooth above the jaw is called the crown (fig. 3.3). In the center of most teeth is the **pulp chamber**, containing soft tissue: pulp, nerves, and blood supply. When a fossilized tooth is viewed from the bottom or roots, the holes that can be seen are the pulp cavities (fig. 3.4). Since pulp, nerves, and blood vessels don't fossilize, they generally leave a hole where each nerve entered the tooth. Broken teeth often clearly exhibit the pulp chamber as a hollow cavity (fig. 3.5).

As mentioned, most teeth are composed of three materials: enamel, dentine, and cementum. Cementum anchors teeth in their sockets (technically called **alveoli**). Some complex teeth may have a cementum layer covering the entire tooth, or have cementum enfolded in enamel and/or dentine. Cementum is very similar to bone and wears more quickly than dentine and enamel.

Enamel consists of 97% mineral (hydroxyapatite, composed of crystallized phosphate and calcium) and is extremely dense and very brittle. No cells exist in the enamel portion of a tooth; therefore, damage to the enamel portion of a tooth cannot be repaired by the body. Dentine is only 75% mineral and is, therefore, softer than enamel (yet harder than cementum). Dentine has some ability to repair minor defects. Many mammals have evolved various solutions to creating an "advanced" tooth surface (called the occlusal surface) that brings all three elements (enamel, dentine, and cementum) to the chewing surface.[9] More primitive types of teeth may bring only one or two of the elements to the

Fig. 3.1

Oreodont
Maxilla (upper jaw)

Merycoidodon culbertsoni
Oligocene

Dawes County,
Nebraska

Collection: R. Sinibaldi
Size: 4.75 in.\12 cm

Fig. 3.1. The upper palate or maxilla of this oreodont has a full complement of teeth: incisors (a), canine (b), premolars (c), and molars (d).

Fig. 3.2

Tapir
Lower Jaw Section with 2 Teeth

Tapirus haysii
Early Pleistocene

Leisey Shell Pit,
Hillsborough County, FL

Collection: R. Sinibaldi
Size: 3.5 in.\9 cm

Fig. 3.2. This lower jaw fragment (mandible) of a tapir displays two lower molars, with the roots still embedded in the bone.

Fig. 3.3

Tapir
Lower Premolar

Tapirus veroensis
Pleistocene

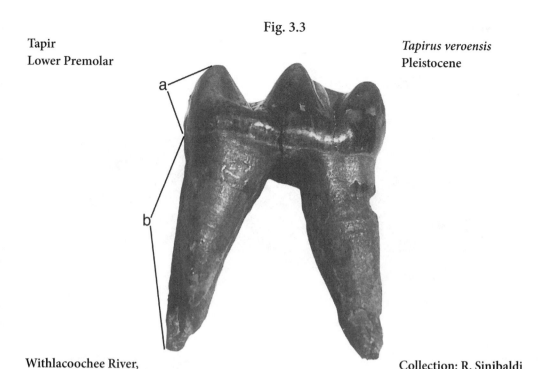

Withlacoochee River,
Marion County, FL

Collection: R. Sinibaldi
Size: 1 in.\2.3 cm

Fig. 3.3. This tapir premolar clearly demonstrates the crown (a) section and the root (b) section of the tooth.

Fig. 3.4

Horse
Upper Molar

Equus sp.
Pleistocene

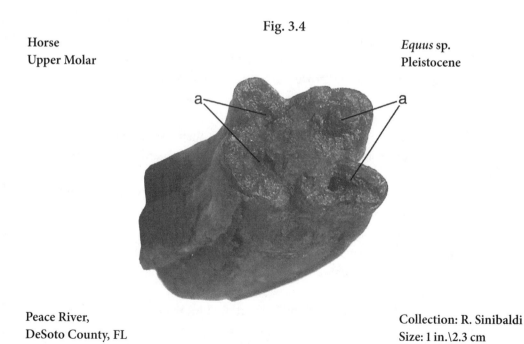

Peace River,
DeSoto County, FL

Collection: R. Sinibaldi
Size: 1 in.\2.3 cm

Fig. 3.4. The four holes (a) viewed from the bottom of this horse molar are pulp cavities that allow blood and nerve endings to enter the tooth. In technical literature this view of a tooth would be termed the radical aspect of the tooth.

Fig. 3.5

Tapir
Upper Molar

Tapirus veroensis
Pleistocene

Withlacoochee River,
Marion County, FL

Collection: R. Sinibaldi
Size: 1.63 in.\4 cm

Fig. 3.5. This tapir molar split in half after fossilizing, clearly exposing the pulp cavity (a). The tooth is rotated sideways; the crown (b) should be facing down as this is an upper tooth.

occlusal surface. Human teeth are a good example of primitive teeth, with only enamel exposed at the occlusal surface.

The various types of folds, cusps, ridges, and combinations of these evolved to enable different animals to process different dietary material efficiently. Scientists use these various tooth morphologies as diagnostic tools to identify species and infer the paleo diets of extinct animals.

Generally, mammals have four types of teeth in their **dental battery: incisors, canines, premolars, and molars** (fig. 3.6). The standard dental pattern for mammals is three incisors, one canine, four premolars, and three molars on each side of both the upper and lower jaws; however, many variations have evolved from this standard pattern to suit the needs of each species. Furthermore, most mammals have a set of "baby" teeth (**deciduous teeth**) that usually vary greatly in number, size, and sometimes form from their adult (permanent) teeth. All but the molars are replaced by adult teeth (there are no deciduous molars).

Finally, a quick note on the scientific shorthand for dental formulae. Teeth may be specified in several different ways in the literature. Upper or maxillary teeth may be designated with an uppercase letter, while mandibular teeth are designated with a lowercase letter (for example, "I" for an upper incisor and "i" for a lower incisor). Another common formula uses a superscript number to

Fig. 3.6

Giant Pig
Maxilla

Archaeotherium sp.
Oligocene

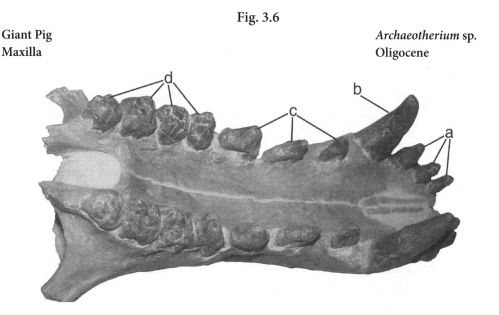

Sioux County,
Nebraska

Collection: F. Garcia
Size: 17 in.\42.5 cm

Fig. 3.6. The upper jaw of this giant pig has a full battery of mammalian dentition: (a) incisors, (b) canines, (c) premolars, and (d) molars.

designate upper teeth, for example, I^3, C^1, P^4, and M^3 (the third upper incisor, upper canine, fourth upper premolar, and the third upper molar, respectively). Mandibular teeth would be written i_3, c_1, p_4, and m_3 (with a subscript number). In the case of deciduous (baby) teeth, a "d" would appear before the letter and subscript number (such as dpm_1, designating the deciduous first lower premolar).

The entire dental battery of one side could be written two ways:

i 1/0, c 0/0, p 3/3, m 3/3

or

$$\frac{1\ 0\ 3\ 3}{0\ 0\ 3\ 3}$$

This is the dental formula for mammoths. Mammoths had one upper incisor (the tusk), no canines, three upper and lower premolars, and three upper and lower molars on each side of the skull.

Furthermore, teeth can be described as being left or right of the median **sagittal plane** (an imaginary line splitting the skull into right and left halves). Becoming familiar with this scientific notation for teeth will assist amateurs in reading scientific articles and books.

Herbivores

Grazers

Herbivores are animals whose diet consists of plant material. Through the pressures of **natural selection** (the force driving evolution), herbivores have developed very specific types of dentitions. Because of the variety of plants available to eat, herbivores can be further classified as **grazers** or **browsers**. Again, each group has evolved very specific types of dentition in order to efficiently process the various plants they consume.

Mammalian grazers are herbivores that eat primarily, if not only, various grasses. Grasses are a geologically recent development on earth. Because of the relatively low nutrient value of grasses and their high abrasive **silica** content, grazers have developed high-crowned (**hypsodont**) teeth (fig. 3.7). The relatively low nutritional value of grasses requires the animal to eat, and therefore chew, substantial amounts each day. This excessive chewing can cause extreme tooth wear. The silica in grasses also works as an abrasive on the tooth's crown, compounding wear on the occlusal surface.

The "evolutionary solution" to grazing is a high-crowned tooth that continues to push up and grow at a rate somewhat even with the rate of wear on the occlusal surface. Hypsodont teeth grow continuously for a long portion of the animal's life but eventually form roots and stop growing. At some stage in old age, the crown wears down to, or below, the gum line. At this point the animal can no longer feed. Age determination by wear pattern is covered later in this

Fig. 3.7

Horse
Upper Molar

Equus sp.
Pleistocene

Peace River,
DeSoto County, FL

Collection: R. Sinibaldi
Size: 3.5 in.\9 cm

Fig. 3.7. Horses, notorious grazers, evolved high-crowned (hypsodont) teeth as an evolutionary solution to eating grasses containing high amounts of silica, which tends to wear teeth down.

Fig. 3.8

Horse
Upper Molar

Equus sp.
Pleistocene

Peace River,
DeSoto County, FL

Collection: R. Sinibaldi
Size: 1 in.\2.4 cm

Fig. 3.8. A view of the occlusal (chewing) surface of this horse upper molar displays the complex folding of enamel, dentine, and cementum. The different wear rates of each material caused continuous ridges to form on the occlusal surface of the tooth.

chapter. Horses, mammoths, rabbits, and some rodents are just a few examples of animals that are or were grazers with high-crowned teeth.

Both horses and mammoths developed hypsodont teeth (both are/were grazers). The slow evolution of horse teeth from browsing type to grazing type is well documented. Horses (the most recent evolutionary genus stage called *Equus*) have evolved high-crowned teeth that fold enamel, cementum, and dentine into complex patterns and present them at the occlusal surface (fig. 3.8). As previously stated, this configuration results in an uneven wear pattern, allowing for sharp surface edges to be present at all times (the tooth will never wear completely flat until extreme old age). The complex folding also increases the surface area of the enamel, the hardest part of the tooth. The visible tooth protruding from the gum of a young horse is only 10–15 percent of the entire tooth.[10]

Mammoths also evolved a high-crowned tooth. The folds of enamel, cementum, and dentine formed into simple plates running sideways in the jaw (fig. 3.9). Unlike most mammals that chew from side to side, mammoths used a back-and-forth motion (inferred from both elephant eating habits and microwear patterns on fossil teeth), making horizontal plate formation very efficient. As in horses, the enamel, dentine, and cementum are present at the

Fig. 3.9

Mammoth Tooth
Polished slice prepared by T. Estevez

Mammuthus sp.
Pleistocene

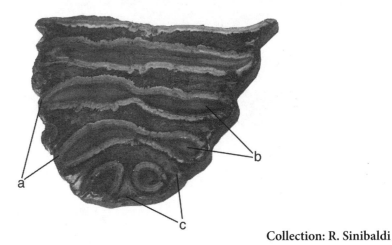

Peace River,
DeSoto County, FL

Collection: R. Sinibaldi
Size: 2.5 in.\6.5 cm

Fig. 3.9. A sliced and polished cross section of a mammoth tooth (not complete) clearly displays the enamel plates (a) filled with dentine (b) and held together with cementum (c).

occlusal surface, again ensuring some type of surface ridges to make chewing efficient for mammoths.

Horses have two distinct sets of teeth during their lives, deciduous (baby) and permanent (adult). Although mammoths have the same number of premolars and molars as horses, they produce their sets of teeth differently, in a conveyorlike fashion. Mammoth teeth erupt from the back of the jaw and move forward one at a time. The difference in size between a horse's two sets of teeth is minimal (fig. 3.10), especially at the occlusal surface. A huge size difference exists, however, between the first set of milk or baby teeth of mammoths and their final set of adult teeth (fig. 3.11). After having a set of three deciduous teeth on each side of the jaw, horses simultaneously have a set of three premolars and a set of three molars in their mouths as adults (a total of six cheek teeth on each side of the jaw, upper and lower). After producing three sets of deciduous teeth, mammoths and other proboscideans produce three sets of premolars and three sets of molars as adults; however, as mentioned, they erupt in conveyor-belt fashion from the back of the jaw and travel forward. Therefore, mammoths and other proboscideans never have the full complement of teeth in their jaws at the same time. Mammoths generally had between one and three teeth per jaw

Fig. 3.10

Horse
(a) Deciduous Tooth
(b) Adult Tooth (m3)

Equus sp.
Pleistocene

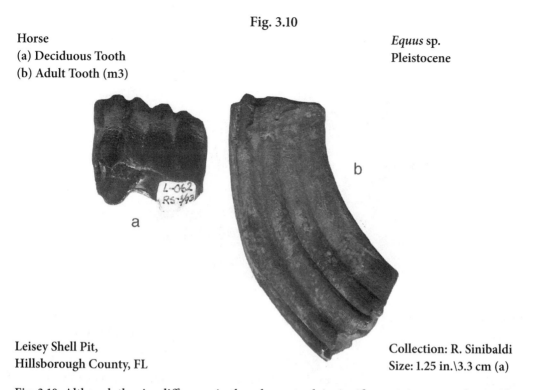

Leisey Shell Pit,
Hillsborough County, FL

Collection: R. Sinibaldi
Size: 1.25 in.\3.3 cm (a)

Fig. 3.10. Although the size difference in these horse teeth is significant, it is not as substantial as the difference in size of proboscidean teeth (fig. 3.11). Note that the occlusal surface is very similar in both teeth, and the baby tooth has a much shorter root as it is not meant to last as long as the adult tooth.

quadrant at once in the wear position, depending on age. Mastodons, which were browsers, may have had two or more teeth per jaw quadrant in use at a time, but they still erupted in conveyor-belt fashion. Age determinations by size and wear differences are covered later in this chapter. A horse may need to eat up to 14 pounds of food a day, a mammoth, up to 650 pounds[11] of grasses, leaves, and twigs (along with about 175 pints of water). Each evolved its own efficient solution to processing food intake.

It should be noted that when silica-rich grasses evolved, those grasses shifted to producing a first carbon photosynthetic product in a set of reactions referred to as a C4 metabolic pathway. This pathway utilizes four carbon atoms in the first product of photosynthesis. Plants using the C4 metabolic pathway also have a distinct type of carbon isotope, C-13, in their structure. This distinct carbon isotope pattern is reinforced in the minerals in the bones and teeth of animals that eat them. Most primitive grasses, as well as other plants, have a first product photosynthesis of three carbon atoms, referred to as a C3 metabolic pathway, producing a distinct C-12 carbon isotope trace; therefore, modern grazers will

Fig. 3.11

Mammoth
(a) Deciduous Tooth
(b) Adult Tooth

Mammuthus sp.
Pleistocene

(a) Suwannee River, FL
(b) Peace River, FL

Collection: A. Kerner
Collection: L. Jefferson
Size: 13 in.\32.5 cm

Fig. 3.11. A significant size difference can be seen between the deciduous (baby) tooth (a), and the adult tooth (b) of a mammoth. Proboscidean teeth present a special case and are presented in figures 3.45, 3.54, and 3.60.

have a distinct C4 carbon signal in their teeth when compared with browsers, who will have a distinct C3 carbon signal in their teeth from eating other plants. Scientists can use these carbon signals to infer paleo diets for extinct species, as well as climate changes (C4 grasses are more adapted to arid climates and C3 grasses to cold climates) and flora changes in paleo ecosystems. The change from C3 ecosystems to C4 ecosystems occurred somewhere between 5 and 7 million years ago. It should also be noted here that dividing all herbivores into a dichotomy of browsers and grazers is a very simplistic view. Many species may be mixed feeders, eating both grasses and leaves as a result of stresses in the environment, or because they are in an evolutionary stage of moving from browser to grazer.[12] Mixed feeders will therefore have a ratio of C4 to C3 carbon signals in their teeth corresponding to the various proportions of leaves and grasses they eat. C4 and C3 metabolic pathways still exist in plants.[13]

Browsers

Browsers evolved teeth for better processing of leaves, twigs, bark, and other plant materials not directly on the ground. Although common sense suggests that items such as twigs and bark are tougher than grass, this is not true. Twigs,

Fig. 3.12

Camel
Lower Molar

Paleolama mirifica
Pleistocene

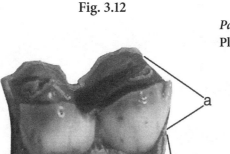

Rainbow River,
Marion County, FL

Collection: R. Sinibaldi
Size: 0.75 in.\2 cm

Fig. 3.12. The crown (a) of this camel tooth, a browser, is relatively low compared with teeth of grazers, which have a higher degree of hypsodonty (see fig. 3.7). The root (b) is substantially longer than the crown in this older animal.

bark, and other plant materials that are far above ground generally do not contain the silica found in grasses or low-lying plants; therefore, browsers' teeth do not wear as quickly as the teeth of grazers, and they develop a different occlusal surface pattern.

Instead of high-crowned (hypsodont) teeth, most mammalian browsers have a lower degree of hypsodonty. The degree of hypsodonty compares the crown height to the length of the root (fig. 3.12). Teeth that are low crowned developmentally (as opposed to high-crowned teeth that are simply worn down) are generally termed **brachydont**.

In addition to the crown height of the tooth, tooth design at the occlusal surface of browsers has evolved into a variety of solutions for processing food. Some browsers have **selenodont** teeth, which are molars and premolars with crescent-shaped cusps at the occlusal surface (fig. 3.13). **Lophodont, bilophodont**, and **bunodont** teeth are also evolutionary solutions to tooth design for browsers. Lophodont teeth are molars and premolars with cusps that have fused into ridges (fig. 3.14). Bilophodont teeth have two sets of cusps that have fused into ridges (fig. 3.15). Bunodont teeth are molars and premolars with rounded cusps (fig. 3.16). A search of the extensive fossil record reveals many

Fig. 3.13

Camel
Upper Molar

Hemiauchenia macrocephala
Pleistocene

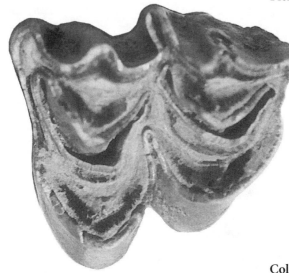

Apollo Beach,
Hillsborough County, FL

Collection: R. Sinibaldi
Size: 0.9 in.\2.4 cm

Fig. 3.13. The occlusal view of this camel tooth displays its crescent-shaped morphology, termed selenodont.

Fig. 3.14

Rhino
Upper Molar

Teleoceras hicksi
Miocene

Peace River,
DeSoto County, FL

Collection: R. Sinibaldi
Size: 2.75 in.\7 cm

Fig. 3.14. The occlusal view of this rhino upper molar displays fused ridge morphology, termed lophodont. Note the diagnostic pi shape of the occlusal surface of rhino teeth.

Fig. 3.15

Tapir
Upper Molar

Tapirus veroensis
Pleistocene

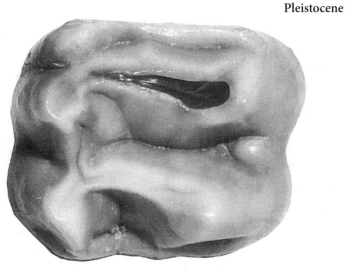

Rainbow River Springs,
Marion County, FL

Collection: R. Sinibaldi
Size: 1 in.\2.4 cm

Fig. 3.15. The occlusal view of this tapir upper molar displays the pair of fused ridges termed bilophodont.

Fig. 3.16

Peccary
Lower Molar

Mylohyus nasutus
Late Pleistocene

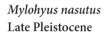

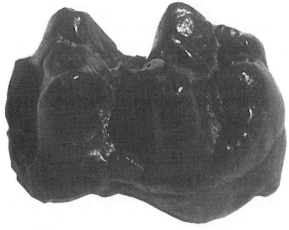

Peace River,
DeSoto County, FL

Collection: R. Sinibaldi
Size: 0.75 in.\2 cm

Fig. 3.16. This peccary tooth has a rounded cusp morphology termed bunodont. Human molars and mastodon teeth (see fig. 6.1) are also considered bunodont.

Fig. 3.17

Woolly Rhino
Mandible (lower jaw)

Coelodonta antiquitatis
Pleistocene

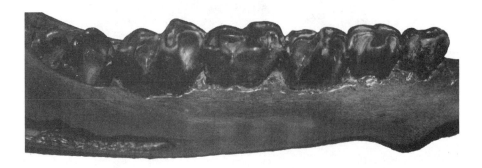

Rhine River,
Germany

Collection: A. Kerner
Size: 11 in.\28 cm

Fig. 3.17. Browsers have a distinctive wear pattern, demonstrated by this woolly rhino jaw, with relatively simple cusps, lophs, and ridges covered in enamel.

combinations of the various tooth morphologies, combining differing levels of hypsodonty with various aspects of occlusal surface configurations.

So, which browsers have which teeth? Generally, deer, antelope, camels, llamas, and bison have selenodont premolar and molar teeth.[14] Rhinoceros have lophodont teeth. Tapirs and some peccaries have bilophodont teeth. Mastodons, humans, pigs, and some peccaries have bunodont molars and premolars.

The brachydont teeth of some browsers do not continue to grow during most of the animals' life (unlike the hypsodont teeth of most grazers). In general, adult mammalian browsers, like adult grazers, also have sets of three premolars and three molars in their mouth at the same time; however, mastodons, like mammoths, utilized a conveyor-belt system of tooth eruption.[15] Even though the vegetation eaten by browsers is less abrasive than a grazer's diet, browsers' teeth still produce distinctive wear patterns (fig. 3.17). As with grazers, browsers' teeth can be used to determine age by looking at the amount of wear on the premolars and molars (fig. 3.18).

It is interesting to note that before they were grazers, early horses were browsers and had low-crowned lopho-selenodont teeth before grasses evolved. Over millions of years, as horses evolved from browsers to grazers, their teeth went through some dramatic changes. Horse teeth moved from brachydont to hypsodont as they also added multiple folds of enamel, cementum, and dentine (fig. 3.19). All these changes helped them cope with the high silica content of grasses. Horse teeth are only one example of evolving teeth. All the browsers'

Fig. 3.18

White-tailed Deer   *Odocoileus virginianus*
Ramus (lower jaw)   Pleistocene

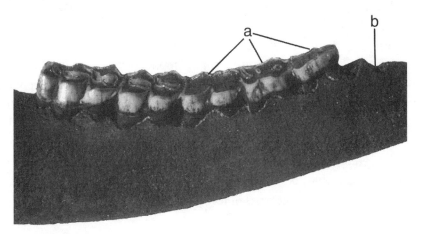

Withlacoochee River,   Collection: A. Kerner
Florida   Size: 4 in.\10 cm

Fig. 3.18. This deer jaw displays the extreme wear of an older animal. Note the extreme wear of the 3rd and 4th premolar and the 1st molar at (a). The second premolar is missing at (b), probably lost during the fossilization process.

Fig. 3.19

(a) Horse Upper Molar   (a) *Equus* sp.
(b) Three-toed Horse Upper Molar   (b) *Mesohippus* sp.
Pleistocene
Oligocene

(a) Peace River, DeSoto County, FL   Collection: R. Sinibaldi
(b) Dawes County, Nebraska   Size: 1 in.\2.4 cm (a)

Fig. 3.19. Compare the complex occlusal surface of the hypsodont *Equus* tooth (a) of the late Pleistocene (a grazer) with the relatively simple lophs in the occlusal surface of a *Mesohippus* tooth (b) of the Oligocene (a browser). It took more than 35 million years of evolution to move from (b) to (a).

and grazers' teeth described in the last two sections are examples of highly evolved (specialized) teeth; the example of horse tooth evolution is perhaps the best documented and researched in the fossil record.[16]

It is also noteworthy that the teeth of most proboscideans underwent a similar evolution. Early proboscideans such as gomphotheres and mastodons had low-crowned teeth. Their evolutionary relatives, the mammoths, and elephants to some degree, have high-crowned teeth; however, all proboscideans exhibited the conveyer-belt tooth replacement system discussed above for mammoths. The proboscidean evolutionary tree is well documented, with many taxa overlapping in geological time as they split off into various genera and species. These overlaps were possible because proboscideans were able to exploit diverse ecological niches with different types of teeth.

Carnivores

Predators and Scavengers

The teeth of carnivores are among their most distinguishing anatomical features. Almost all carnivorous mammals have carnassial teeth (fig. 3.20), which work in a scissorlike fashion, with upper and lower premolar and/or molar teeth meeting to shear through flesh (fig 3.21). Carnivores do not chew their food; they bite off chunks and swallow them whole. Some carnassial teeth are very robust and also used for crushing bone.

Many carnivores have very pronounced canine teeth. These large fangs evolved to puncture the skin and hide of prey in order to hold and eventually kill the animal (fig. 3.22). Not all canines evolved to the level of those found in the well-known saber-toothed cats, though (fig. 3.23). Paleontologists are still debating exactly how saber-toothed cats used their enormous canines. No living analogues exist of saber-toothed cats (most of which are not even true cats), which means the debate may go on indefinitely. Broken sabers are fairly common in the fossil record and are covered in chapter 6.

The dental battery in many carnivores is greatly reduced. In the fossil record generally, incisors are present but very reduced, and canine teeth are pronounced. The number of premolars and molars is usually reduced to two or three teeth each in the upper and lower jaws. Other premolars or molars are either absent or vestigial (too small to be significant, left over from an earlier evolutionary stage; fig. 3.24). The highest-crowned tooth is usually referred to as the carnassial and is the dominant shearing tooth in a carnivore's dental battery.

Carnivore teeth are relatively rare in the fossil record. Reports of animal biomass range from 1 to 3 percent for carnivores, a figure inferred from the

Fig. 3.20

Catlike Carnivore
Mandible with 2 Teeth

Nimravides thinobates
Miocene

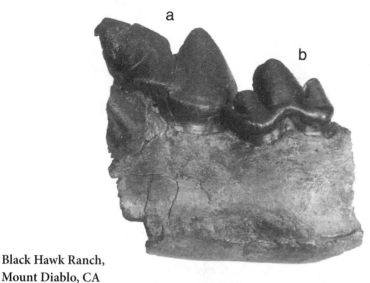

Black Hawk Ranch,
Mount Diablo, CA

Collection: D. Letasi
Size: 2.37 in.\5.5 cm

Fig. 3.20. A typically shaped carnassial tooth (a) of this large prehistoric catlike animal. The premolar (b) is equally sharp and similarly shaped.

Fig. 3.21

Hyaenodon
Skull

Hyaenodon horridus
Oligocene

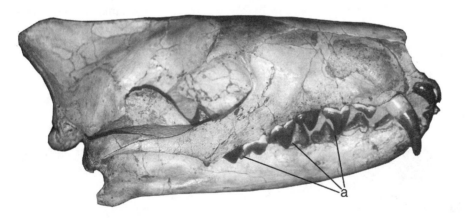

White River Formation,
South Dakota

Collection: F. Garcia
Size: no data

Fig. 3.21. The scissors-like carnassial teeth of both the upper and lower jaws of this hyaenodon meet at multiple points (a) to shear meat before swallowing.

Fig. 3.22

Saber-toothed Cat
Complete Upper Dentition

Smilodon gracilis
Pleistocene

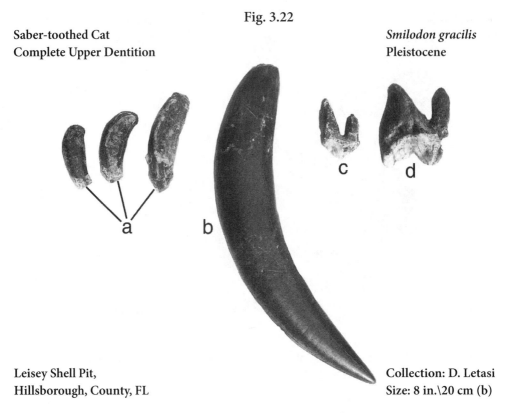

Leisey Shell Pit,
Hillsborough, County, FL

Collection: D. Letasi
Size: 8 in.\20 cm (b)

Fig. 3.22. The complete upper dentition of this saber-toothed cat shows the pronounced development of its canine (saber) (b) compared with its incisors (a), premolar (c), and carnassial (d).

Fig. 3.23

Jaguar
Upper Canine

Panthera onca (augusta)
Pleistocene

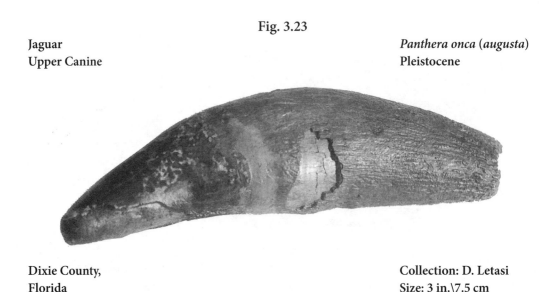

Dixie County,
Florida

Collection: D. Letasi
Size: 3 in.\7.5 cm

Fig. 3.23. The large canine of this jaguar is formidable, but not as pronounced as that of the saber-toothed cats (see fig. 3.22).

Fig. 3.24

Dire Wolf   *Canis dirus*
Mandible   Pleistocene

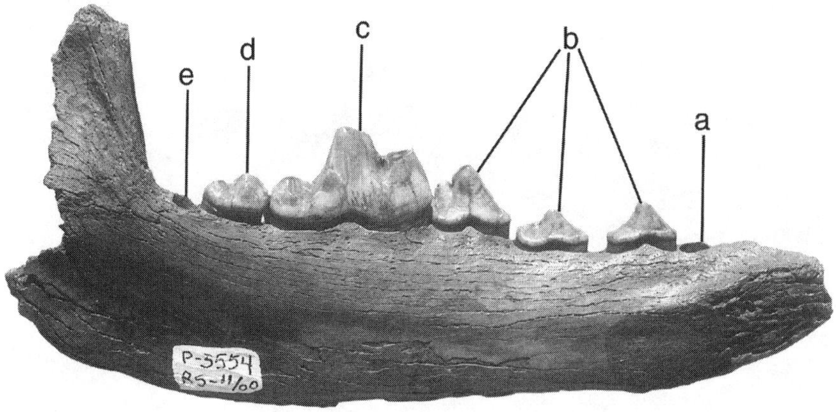

Peace River,   Collection: R. Sinibaldi
DeSoto County, FL   Size: 7.25 in.\18.5 cm

Fig. 3.24. Compare the very large carnassial (c) to the second molar (d) and the very small hole for the missing m3 at (e). Three premolars are located at (b); the small hole at (a) is for a very small missing pm1.

present-day carnivore-to-herbivore ratio. The fossil record tends to support this number. The La Brea Tar Pits are a well-known exception to this rule, because of their unique situation of preservation of many, many dire wolves and saber-toothed cats.

The behavior of most prehistoric carnivores is also inferred from extant descendants or related species, for example, dire wolf behavior from today's wolves, saber-toothed cat behavior from today's big cats (although they are not direct descendants). If a prehistoric animal has no contemporary counterpart, it may not be possible to infer whether the animal was a pure predator or also scavenged carrion (dead meat) for part of its diet. If no contemporary animal is available for comparison, scientists will often debate whether the animal was a predator or a scavenger. The feeding behavior of T-Rex is a great example of scientific debate in this area. In general, today's big carnivores do scavenge available meat at times, and this probably held true for the big carnivores of the past.

Finally, insectivores are very small carnivores that eat primarily insects (fig. 3.25). Their shearing carnassials are very efficient at biting through the exoskeleton of insects. Insectivores are generally grouped with carnivores in nonscien-

Fig. 3.25

Insectivore
Mandible

Undetermined species
Oligocene

Dawes County,
Nebraska

Collection: R. Sinibaldi
Size: 1.5 in.\4 cm

Fig. 3.25. This very small jaw, less than 2 inches, from an insectivore, has a dental battery very similar to that of many larger carnivores (compare with fig. 3.24).

tific publications; however, scientifically, they usually have a distinct taxonomic identification and classification designation. It is believed that insectivore teeth are the most primitive teeth of all mammals, and that all other types of mammal teeth evolved from insectivore teeth; therefore, many of today's larger carnivores may have evolved directly from insectivorous ancestors.

Before leaving carnivores, it should be noted that carnivores have a higher ratio of nitrogen-15 to nitrogen-14 in their bones and teeth than herbivores and omnivores. Using this ratio, scientists can often determine whether an animal was a carnivore or herbivore if the actual morphology of the animal's bones and teeth do not have a modern analogue or do not give a clear indication of the animal's lifestyle. The short-faced bears[17] of the Pleistocene were of this type, where scientists could not tell from the fossil evidence whether the animal was a carnivore or herbivore. Today's bears are predominantly omnivores, but the short-faced bear was proven to be mainly a carnivore by its very high nitrogen-15 to nitrogen-14 ratio.

Omnivores

Omnivores are animals that eat both plants and meat (including fish). The most common omnivores are bears (except polar bears), raccoons, skunks, otters, pigs, opossums, foxes, various rodents, and humans. Although many of these

Fig. 3.26

Short-faced Bear   *Tremarctos floridanus*
Maxilla   Pleistocene

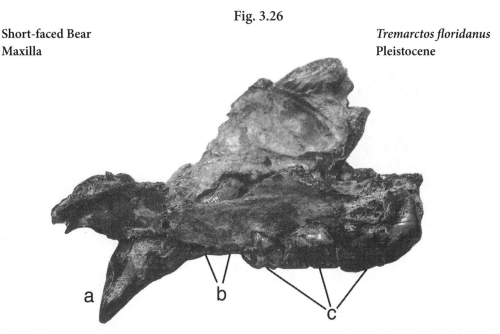

Peace River,   Collection: R. Sinibaldi
DeSoto County, FL   Size: 5 in.\12.5 cm

Fig. 3.26. Modern bears are notorious for their diversity. Black bears are omnivores, brown bears are more carnivorous, and polar bears are true carnivores. This extinct short-faced bear was probably an omnivore. It has a pronounced canine (a), and relatively flat molars (c). At least two premolars are missing at (b) in this specimen. However, new evidence may classify *T. floridanus* as more of a carnivore, while the modern South American *Tremarctos ornatus* is a herbivore!

animals are omnivores, many of their scientific designations put them technically in the order Carnivora (bears, raccoons, skunks, otters, and foxes), and some, such as skunks, otters, and foxes, may fulfill the majority of their diet as carnivores. Some omnivores have pronounced canines and some do not. Their premolars and molars are generally broader and lower crowned than the carnassials of strict carnivores (fig. 3.26). Omnivores lack teeth with the pure shearing ability of the pronounced carnassials found in full-time carnivores.

Many omnivores scavenge the majority of their meat instead of hunting it. Extant bears, skunks, raccoons, opossums, and rodents are notorious scavengers. We can infer from this behavior that their fossil relatives were probably similar. Unlike carnivorous scavengers, omnivores also supplement their diets with plant materials (seeds, nuts, fruits, roots, tubers, etc.). Wide, lower-crowned teeth are better for processing such a diet.

Omnivores generally have a more extensive dental battery than strict carnivores (fig. 3.27), usually with a full complement of incisors, canines, premolars, and molars. Scientists must often use dental morphology to infer an omnivo-

Fig. 3.27

Raccoon
Mandible

Procyon lotor
Recent

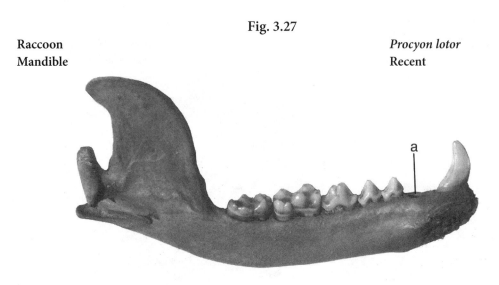

Santa Fe River,
Florida

Collection: J. Tatum
Size: 3.25 in.\8.5 cm

Fig. 3.27. Compare the dental battery of this raccoon, an omnivore that eats a diverse diet of plant material and meat/fish, with the dental battery of a true carnivore (fig. 3.22). A premolar is missing at (a).

rous lifestyle for an extinct animal. This inference may require a jaw with a full complement of teeth, as one tooth can be misleading (fig. 3.28). Skeletal remains are poor predictors of omnivorous behavior. Omnivore skeletons may possess characteristics of carnivores or herbivores or both.

Foxes are omnivores that are more predator than scavenger. Some of their premolars and molars have retained the carnassial shape, while their rear molars have flat occlusal (grinding) surfaces. This enables foxes to truly survive in a variety of environments and condition (fig. 3.29).

A final note on herbivores, carnivores, and omnivores: aside from variation in the dental batteries of these animals, scientists can determine whether an extinct animal was a carnivore, herbivore, or omnivore by the ratio of two types of nitrogen isotopes in their bones. A low ratio of nitrogen-15 to nitrogen-14 in animal bones means an animal was herbivorous; a high ratio means the animal was carnivorous. Ratios in the middle generally indicate omnivorous animals. These nitrogen isotope ratios, along with tooth and bone structure, can also help determine whether an animal scavenged or hunted for its food.

Fig. 3.28

Short-faced Bear
Lower Canine

Tremarctos floridanus
Pleistocene

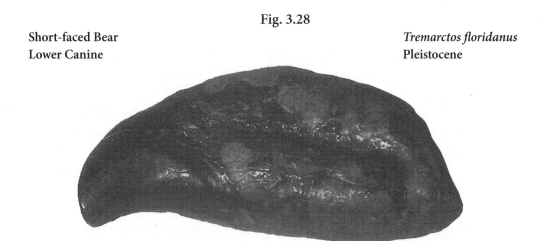

Peace River,
DeSoto County, FL

Collection: R. Sinibaldi
Size: 2.25 in.\6 cm

Fig. 3.28. Finding a single large canine, such as this lower canine from a bear, may mislead one into thinking the animal was a true carnivore (see fig. 3.26).

Fig. 3.29

Gray Fox
Mandible

Urocyon sp.
Pleistocene

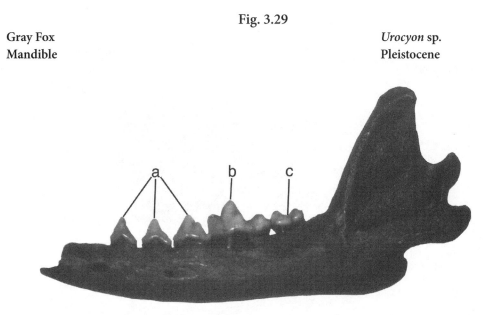

Devils Den,
Levy County, FL

Collection: FLMNH
Size: 3.5 in.\8.5 cm

Fig. 3.29. The fox has a dentition that indicates the lifestyle of more of a predator than an omnivore, with carnassial-shaped premolars (a) and molars (b), and only a small flat surface from the back of the carnassial to the last molar at (c).

Special Cases of Mammalian Teeth

Many examples can be found of mammal teeth that fall outside the usual morphological forms previously covered. Because they are a common fossil find, tusks will first be described as examples of a highly specialized tooth form. In addition, the dentition of the entire mammalian order **Xenarthra** will be described as an example of dental patterns not conforming to those of mammals in general.

The tusks of proboscideans (mammoths, mastodons, gomphotheres, and elephants) are actually a highly specialized form of incisor. Ivory from tusk material is also highly prized for its special properties that make it "workable" by humans into various objects.[18] Tusks are composed primarily of dentinal tubules (a type of dentine) covered with a thin layer of enamel and an even thinner layer of cementum. The cementum wears away quickly at the exposed surfaces (the portion of the tusk outside the socket). The dentinal tubules, called ivory, have a very distinct pattern (fig. 3.30). This pattern, termed a **Schreger pattern**, makes identifying even a small piece of ivory possible.

Schreger patterns are made up of left and right spiraling elements or bands of light and dark materials. These left and right spirals intersect at different angles

Fig. 3.30

Mastodon
Tusk Cross Section

Mammut americanum
Pleistocene

Peace River,
DeSoto County, FL

Collection: R. Sinibaldi
Size: 2.75 in.\7 cm

Fig. 3.30. The angle of the Schreger pattern (cross-hatching) in this ivory tusk fragment is approximately 125 degrees, identifying it as coming from a mastodon.

Fig. 3.31

Mastodon
Lower Tusk Cross Section

Mammut americanum
Early Pleistocene

Leisey Shell Pit
Hillsborough County, FL

Collection: R. Sinibaldi
Size: 1.9 in.\4.8 cm

Fig. 3.31. Some mastodons had lower tusks during the North American Pleistocene period. The angle of the Schreger pattern on this specimen is almost 125 degrees.

in ivory specimens from different proboscideans. By measuring the angles of intersection, one can determine whether a piece of ivory (even a fairly small piece) is from a mastodon or a mammoth. The Schreger pattern angle for mastodons is approximately 125 degrees (fig. 3.31). The pattern angle for mammoths is approximately 87 degrees (fig. 3.32).[19] Schreger patterns are now also used by U.S. Customs agents to determine whether imported ivory is legal. The ivory of both mammoths and mastodonts is legal to import and possess; however, the ivory of extant elephants, with a distinct Schreger pattern, is illegal either to possess or to import without appropriate legal permits and documentation.[20]

Tusks continue to grow throughout the animal's life with the addition of successive cones of dentine at the base (within the socket); however, the growth patterns of male and female tusks are slightly different. Female tusks, after sexual maturity, continue to grow in length only. Male tusks grow in both length and circumference throughout their lives; in addition, the pulp cavity in male tusks continues to grow throughout the male's life. Therefore, long slim tusks with minimal or no pulp cavity are generally female. Male tusks are more robust in circumference and contain a pronounced pulp cavity in most of the specimen (figs. 3.33–3.34).

Fig. 3.32

Columbian Mammoth   *Mammuthus columbi*
Tusk Cross Section   Pleistocene

Wekiva River,   Collection: FLMNH
Seminole County, FL   Size: 2 in.\5 cm

Fig. 3.32. The cross-hatched Schreger pattern on this mammoth ivory is at almost 90 degrees (almost square).

Fig. 3.33

American Mastodon   *Mammut americanum*
Tusk Pulp Cavity   Pleistocene

Wekiva River,   Collection: FLMNH
Seminole County, FL   Size: 7.5 in.\18.5 cm

Fig. 3.33. The pulp cavity of this mastodon tusk is very large at the alveolar margin, where the tusk is anchored into the skull.

Fig. 3.34

American Mastodon
Tusk Pulp Cavity

Mammut americanum
Pleistocene

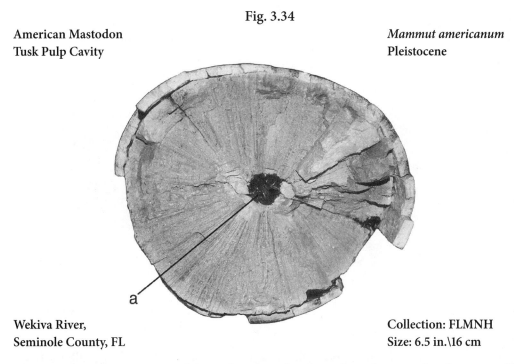

Wekiva River,
Seminole County, FL

Collection: FLMNH
Size: 6.5 in.\16 cm

Fig. 3.34. This is a cross-sectional view taken three feet down the tusk pictured in figure 3.33. The pulp cavity has narrowed considerably but is still well defined. It has been filled with a stabilizing material by the preparator.

In well-preserved specimens, the growth cones can be recognized (fig. 3.35). These cones represent periods coinciding with good and bad seasons (they are not annual growth rings like those in trees, but similar).[21] Furthermore, the base of the tusk has a distinct concave shape where growth takes place (fig. 3.36). Scientists study the rings of growth cones and correlate them to the seasons of the ice ages. Thinner layers are indicative of winter months (food scarcity) and thicker layers correlate with summer months (and eating well). The innermost ring, closest to the socket, represents the season of the animal's death. In addition, the rings on the tusks of females can help determine how often they gave birth and the length of intervals between births. When a female is pregnant, the rings on the tusks are very narrow, because a large portion of calcium and other nutrients go to the fetus. The gestation period among elephants and their prehistoric relatives is close to two years.

Almost all proboscideans had upper tusks, and some had lower tusks as well. Generally, the upper tusks are extremely large, and the lower tusks much smaller. The composition of both upper and lower tusks is identical, as previously described; however, the function of upper and lower tusks was considerably different. Large upper tusks served several functions: attracting a mate, defense,

Fig. 3.35

Mammoth
Tusk

Mammuthus columbi
Pleistocene

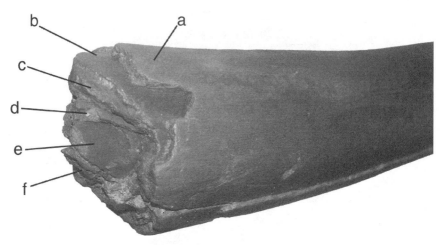

Hendry County,
Florida

Collection: FLMNH
Size: 9 in.\22.5 cm

Fig. 3.35. The growth cones on this mammoth tusk are clearly seen in layers (a–f). Although they are of differing widths, representing good and bad times of growth, they do not represent annual rings like those found in trees.

Fig. 3.36

Mastodon
Alveolar Margin of Tusk

Mammut americanum
Pleistocene

Leisey Shell Pit,
Hillsborough County, FL

Collection: R. Sinibaldi
Size: 1.9 in.\4.8 cm

Fig. 3.36. The broken-off alveolar margin of this lower mastodon tusk is equivalent to the root section of this specialized tooth.

Fig. 3.37

Mastodon
Lower Tusks

Mammut americanum
Pleistocene

Leisey Shell Pit,
Hillsborough County, FL

Collection: R. Sinibaldi
Size: 8.5 in.\21.5 cm

Fig. 3.37. These lower tusks from a mastodon may have been used for foraging in the ground. Section (a) was found by the author six months before sections (b), (c), and (d).

and possible clearing of snow for the mammoth. Lower tusks are believed to have been used for foraging food from the ground or marshy areas (fig. 3.37). Modern elephants have upper tusks only and provide us with an example of the use of upper tusks in extinct species. No modern phylogenetic analogue exists to infer the use of lower tusks in extinct proboscidean species. Note that some extinct female mastodons had no lower tusks, and some extant female elephants have no tusks at all. Another interesting note is that modern elephants have a "sidedness," just as humans are either right or left handed. Elephants have a tusk side preference that leaves that tusk, the master tusk, shorter and more worn, and usually rounder at the tip. Enough complete fossil proboscidean specimens have been found to confirm that this phenomenon is also true for extinct species.

The order Xenarthra comprises armadillos, giant armadillos, glyptodonts, sloths, and anteaters. Their dental morphology is unlike the general mammal dental pattern. The order Xenarthra, therefore, provides an excellent example of unusual dental morphology. Generally, their teeth are rootless and contain no enamel. They are peglike in shape and continue to grow in circumference and size (height) throughout the animal's life (fig. 3.38). Most species do not produce deciduous teeth.

Fig. 3.38

Sloth
Molariform Tooth

Paramylodon harlani
Early Pleistocene

Leisey Shell Pit,
Hillsborough County, FL

Collection: R. Sinibaldi
Size: 1.12 in.\3 cm

Fig. 3.38. This peglike sloth tooth had no true enamel and continued to grow throughout the animal's life.

Fig. 3.39

Sloth
Molariform Tooth

Megalonyx jeffersonii
Pleistocene

Santa Fe River,
Florida

Collection: R. Sinibaldi
Size: 1.25 in.\3.3 cm

Fig. 3.39. The outer dentine (a) wore more slowly than the inner dentine (b) on this sloth upper molariform tooth, creating ridges for an efficient chewing (occlusal) surface.

Fig. 3.40

Sloth
Molariform Tooth

Paramylodon harlani
Pleistocene

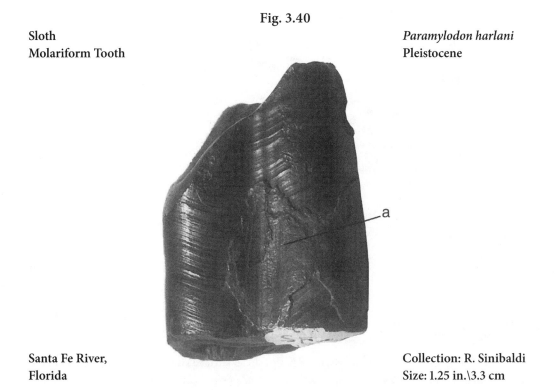

a

Santa Fe River,
Florida

Collection: R. Sinibaldi
Size: 1.25 in.\3.3 cm

Fig. 3.40. Very little is left of the fragile cementum layer that would have covered the entire outer surface of this sloth tooth, anchoring it into the socket.

The teeth of Xenarthra are composed of two types of dentine. The inner dentine (**vasodentine**) is relatively soft and wears quickly. The outer dentine (**osteodentine**) is harder and wears more slowly than the inner dentine (fig. 3.39). Consistent with the principles of other mammal teeth, the uneven wear rate of the two types of dentines leaves a ridge that aids the occlusal surface in processing food. The entire tooth is covered in a thin layer of cementum that is very fragile when fossilized (fig. 3.40). As in other mammal teeth, the cementum of Xenarthra teeth anchors them into the jaw.

Animals in the Xenarthra order are herbivores, omnivores, or insectivores. Most Xenarthrans have teeth and their teeth are considered either **molariform** (fig. 3.41) or **caniniform** (fig. 3.42) as they do not follow the general format of incisor, canine, premolar, molar of most mammals. Amateurs often refer to sloth teeth as being composed of ivory. Sloth teeth are composed of dentine, as are elephant tusks, so there is probably some truth to this statement, but the types of dentine found in sloth teeth and proboscidean tusks vary considerably. Sloth and armadillo teeth generally exhibit a ringed or striated pattern (fig. 3.43), as opposed to the cross-hatched Schreger pattern of ivory in proboscidean tusks.

Fig. 3.41

Sloth   *Paramylodon harlani*
Molariform Tooth   Early Pleistocene

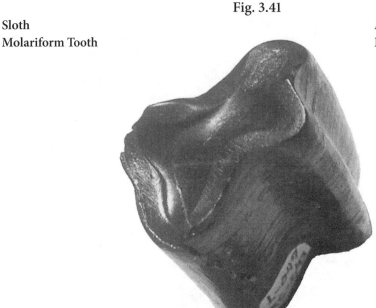

Leisey Shell Pit,   Collection: R. Sinibaldi
Hillsborough County, FL   Size: 1.5 in.\3.5 cm

Fig. 3.41. Molariform teeth in sloths provide a flat occlusal surface similar to that in molars and premolars in other herbivores. Compare with figure 3.42, a sloth caniniform tooth.

Fig. 3.42

Sloth   *Megalonyx* sp.
Caniniform Tooth   Pleistocene

Horse Creek,   Collection: R. Sinibaldi
DeSoto County, FL   Size: 1 in.\2.5 cm

Fig. 3.42. This upper caniniform tooth from the front of a sloth jaw may have served a purpose similar to that of canines in other herbivores; however, it still has a relatively flat occlusal surface. Compare with molariform teeth in figures 3.39 and 3.41.

Fig. 3.43

Sloth
Molariform Tooth

Paramylodon harlani
Pleistocene

Silver River,
Florida

Collection: A. Kerner
Size: 3.5 in.\8.5 cm
(jaw section)

Fig. 3.43. Note the multiple striations on the sides of this sloth tooth. These are growth rings, but they probably do not correspond directly to years the way rings in a tree do.

Rodent teeth present another special case. Most rodents have incisors that grow throughout the life of the animal (fig. 3.44). The scientific literature refers to teeth that continuously grow throughout an animal's life as **hypselodont**. Hypselodont teeth do not form true roots. The proximal ends of the incisors of rodent teeth are open, allowing for continual growth. The incisors are more or less triangular in cross section, having enamel only on the front surface. This configuration allows the softer underlying dentine to wear faster and keeps a chisel-shaped cutting edge on the occlusal surface of the tooth. In this way, the gnawing lifestyle of the rodent can be maintained with an unending supply of incisor tooth surface. In good times, when food is plentiful and easy to obtain, rodents will gnaw just to keep their incisors at a manageable size (see chapter 5 for figures of items gnawed by rodents).

Age Determination/Stages of Development

Age determination of an animal by size and morphological features of fossil teeth may not be as straightforward as many suggest. If using size as a factor to determine age, cne must be careful not to confuse teeth from various species

Fig. 3.44

Giant Beaver
Mandible

Castoroides leiseyorum
Early Pleistocene

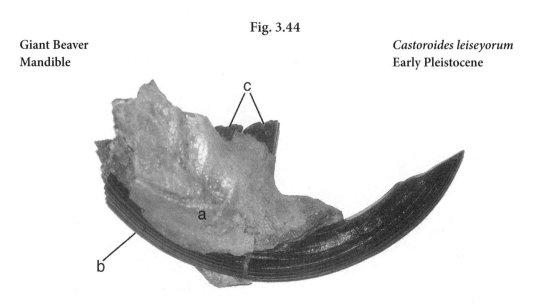

Caloosa Shell Pit,
Hillsborough County, FL

Collection: F. Garcia
Size: 8 in.\20.5 cm

Fig. 3.44. The damage to this giant beaver jaw at (a) allows a view of perpetually growing incisor at (b) that runs the entire length of the jaw, under all the other molars (c).

with teeth of a single species at different stages of development. In addition, most mammal teeth do not grow as the animal grows larger. The same holds true for morphological features; one must determine whether a specimen is a deciduous tooth with a different morphology from adult teeth from that species, or truly a tooth from a different species. An identification book is usually needed for these determinations. In extremely difficult cases, a comparative collection from a museum or university may be needed. In the past these similarities have occasionally caused tooth specimens from one fossil species to be misidentified as belonging to more than one species.

The following, therefore, are general points about age determination of animals by use of fossil teeth. These points are meant to give the reader a feel for the relative age of the animal from which a tooth came. Because of many factors related to wear on teeth (covered throughout this section) it is more prudent to discuss stages of development than age in number of years. The following section will describe the stages of development from prenatal through old age. Generally, the younger an animal, the greater the chance of accurately determining its age. As various teeth erupt at different stages of an animals' early life, age determinations can be made with some confidence; however, once all the adult teeth have erupted, various diets may differentially affect the wear patterns on the teeth, making it difficult to assess age accurately.

Fig. 3.45

Gomphothere
Maxilla

Platybelodon sp.
Miocene

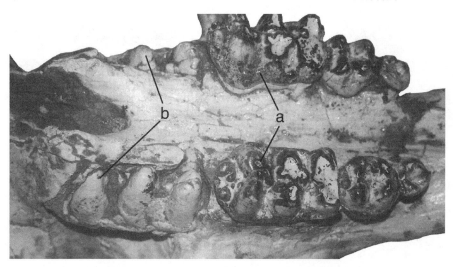

China

Collection: F. Garcia
Size: 12 in.\30 cm

Fig. 3.45. The maxilla of this shovel-tusk gomphothere has both erupted teeth (a) showing some wear, and unerupted teeth (b) that have not moved into position for use.

Unerupted teeth are new teeth that have not broken through the surface of the gum; therefore, they have no wear pattern on the occlusal surface (fig. 3.45). Additionally, unerupted teeth will have either no roots, or incompletely formed roots. Two types of unerupted teeth occur: unerupted deciduous teeth and unerupted adult teeth. Deciduous teeth tend to be smaller and usually morphologically different from adult teeth (fig. 3.46). A fossilized unerupted deciduous tooth indicates that the animal was either prenatal (not born yet) or neonatal (newborn) at the time of death. The animal would have had to die with the tooth in its mouth, because unerupted teeth cannot be **exfoliated**. After the deciduous tooth erupts, it will begin to wear, developing a pattern; obviously, the pattern can begin forming only after the animal is born and begins feeding (fig. 3.47). Deciduous teeth found fossilized in a jaw mean the animal died as a baby or young juvenile (fig. 3.48). The entire deciduous dentition may contain significantly fewer or morphologically different teeth compared with the adult dentition of the same species (fig. 3.49). Deciduous teeth found in isolation could have been replaced by adult teeth, or the animal could have died at a very young age and the jaw **disarticulated** after death (fig. 3.50). Many deciduous teeth occur together with adult teeth in the jaw as the animal goes through various stages of development leading to adulthood.

Fig. 3.46

Horse
Partial Upper Dentition

Equus sp.
Pleistocene

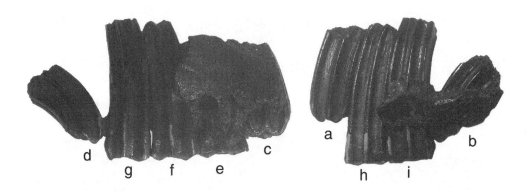

Suwannee River,
Florida

Collection: A. Kerner
Size: 4 in.\10 cm (a–b)

Fig. 3.46. The partial upper dentition of this horse has four unerupted teeth at (a), (b), (c), and (d) with no wear pattern, and one very worn deciduous tooth (e). The remaining four teeth are young adult teeth that have begun to wear.

Fig. 3.47

Horse
Deciduous Tooth

Equus sp.
Early Pleistocene

Leisey Shell Pit,
Hillsborough County, FL

Collection: R. Sinibaldi
Size: 1.37 in.\3.5 cm

Fig. 3.47. This deciduous (baby) horse tooth has erupted and shows signs of wear (a). Compare with the occlusal surface of unerupted deciduous horse teeth in figure 3.51.

Fig. 3.48

Giant Pig
Maxilla

Archaeotherium sp.
Oligocene

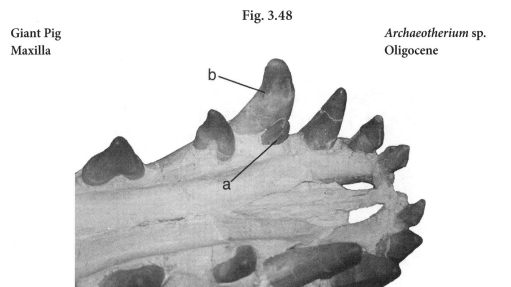

White River Formation,
Nebraska

Collection: F. Garcia
Size: 9 in.\22.5 cm

Fig. 3.48. The upper jaw of this extinct giant pig has both the deciduous (baby) canine teeth (b) and the newly erupting adult canines (a). This animal had not made it into full adulthood before it died.

Fig. 3.49

Tapir
(a) Adult Lower Jaw
(b) Juvenile Lower Jaw

Tapirus veroensis
Pleistocene

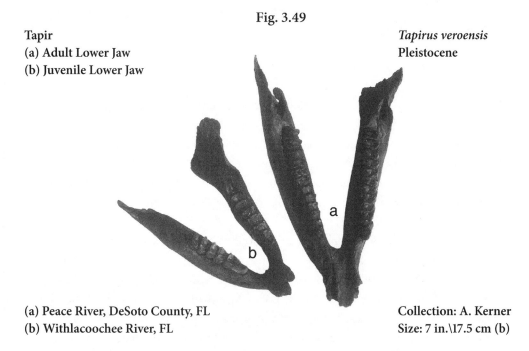

(a) Peace River, DeSoto County, FL
(b) Withlacoochee River, FL

Collection: A. Kerner
Size: 7 in.\17.5 cm (b)

Fig. 3.49. Six teeth are found on each side of this adult tapir jaw (a), whereas only three teeth appear on each side of the juvenile tapir jaw (b). Note that the teeth are morphologically similar in this case.

Fig. 3.50

Camel
Lower Deciduous Tooth

Hemiauchenia macrocephala
Pleistocene

Withlacoochee River,
Marion County, FL

Collection: A. Kerner
Size: 1.6 in.\4.1 cm

Fig. 3.50. This deciduous molar from a camel has three crescent-shaped cusps. It would have been replaced by two adult teeth, one with two crescent shaped-cusps, and a premolar with one crescent-shaped cusp. The fact that this baby tooth has jawbone still attached to it reveals that this camel died as a juvenile.

The next stage of development, adolescence, is marked by unerupted adult teeth. In most mammals the premolars erupt first, and then the molars, progressing from the front to the back of the jaw. In some animals the order of eruption varies, leaving what look like impacted teeth (discussed in chapter 6). Unerupted adult teeth found in isolation (fig. 3.51) or in a jaw mean the animal died as a juvenile. It is not uncommon to find a jaw with the last one or two molars unerupted (fig. 3.52).

Crown height and wear pattern can help determine the age or stage of development in adult teeth. In hypsodont teeth (high crowned), those of horses and mammoths, there can be a great amount of crown height variation (figs. 3.53–3.54). In brachydont teeth (low crowned), as in tapirs, mastodons, peccaries (a type of prehistoric pig), and humans, wear pattern and crown height may not vary as dramatically as in hypsodont and hypselodont teeth; however, careful inspection will show differences in the wear of brachydont teeth (fig. 3.55). These variations represent different stages of adulthood.

Fig. 3.51

Horse
Unerupted Adult Upper Molars

Equus sp.
Pleistocene

Caloosa Shell Pit,
Hillsborough County, FL

Collection: R. Sinibaldi
Size: 0.9 in.\2.3 cm (1st)

Fig. 3.51. These unerupted adult teeth from a horse indicate that the animal died as a young adult.

Fig. 3.52

Three-toed Horse
Mandible

Mesohippus bairdi
Oligocene

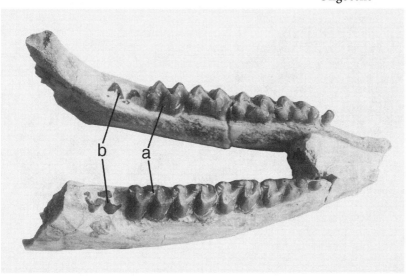

South Dakota

Collection: D. Letasi
Size: 3.5 in.\9 cm

Fig. 3.52. In this juvenile three-toed horse jaw, the last molar on each side (b) is just erupting. Note that little or no wear appears on the previous molar on each side (a). This animal also died as a young adult.

Fig. 3.53

Horse
Upper Molars

Equus sp.
Pleistocene

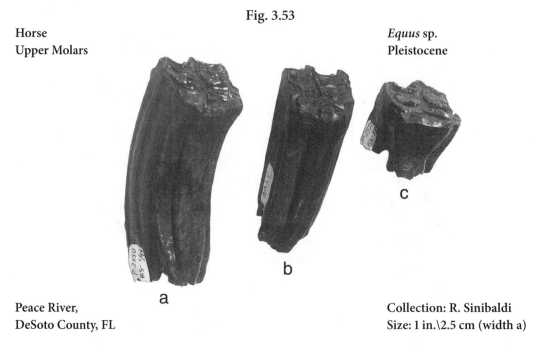

Peace River,
DeSoto County, FL

Collection: R. Sinibaldi
Size: 1 in.\2.5 cm (width a)

Fig. 3.53. These high-crowned hypsodont teeth from three different horses display crown height variation associated with age. The tallest tooth (a) is from the youngest animal, the medium-sized tooth (b) is from a somewhat older animal, and the shortest tooth (c) is from a very old animal.

Fig. 3.54

Mammoth
Teeth

Mammuthus sp.
Pleistocene

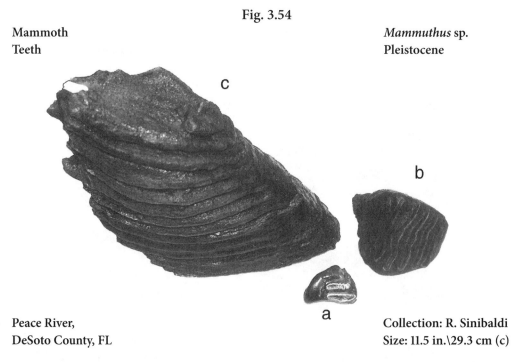

Peace River,
DeSoto County, FL

Collection: R. Sinibaldi
Size: 11.5 in.\29.3 cm (c)

Fig. 3.54. A considerable difference can be seen in the size of mammoth teeth depending on the animal's age. Tooth (a) is from a juvenile, (b) is from a young adult, and (c) is from a full-grown adult. Note that (a) and (b) were both spit or exfoliated teeth, and (c), with several plates missing, is not even a full tooth.

Fig. 3.55

Oreodont
Skull (displaying maxilla)

Merycoidodon culbertsoni
Oligocene

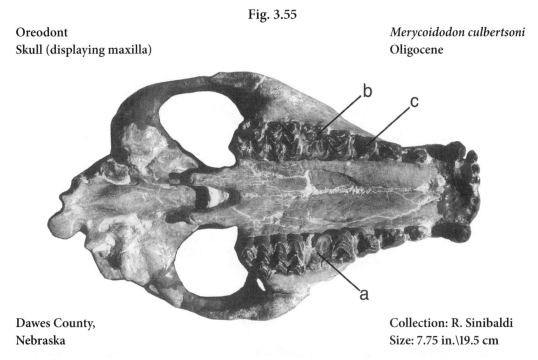

Dawes County,
Nebraska

Collection: R. Sinibaldi
Size: 7.75 in.\19.5 cm

Fig. 3.55. The low-crowned (brachydont) teeth of this oreodont have distinct and extreme wear at (a), (b), and (c). The last two molars still have most of their occlusal surface, indicating a mature adult animal.

In extreme old age, the teeth will wear down to, and sometimes below, the gum line. The gum line is usually visible in well-preserved teeth (figs. 3.56–3.57).[22] In the last tooth on the right in figure 3.57 it can be seen that in extreme old age, the enamel folds completely wear out in horse teeth. Extremely worn teeth (fig. 3.58) usually mean the animal lived a full life cycle and died in old age. Most amateurs attribute death to starvation resulting from inability to process food when they find an extremely worn tooth. Although starvation may happen, especially among elephants, many predators also focus on aging or weak animals, and the presence of extremely worn teeth alone cannot lead to a true diagnosis of the cause of death.

Modern horse teeth, which are very similar to their extinct Pleistocene counterparts, are well documented as to stage of development and age. Today's horse veterinarians are often called upon to determine the age of a horse (along with its health status) before sale or trade. It is interesting to note that veterinary guides use horse incisors, not molars, to determine approximate age.[23] Presented in figure 3.59 is a comparison of incisors similar to that used by today's veterinarians to determine age.[24] It should be noted that types of foods, amounts of silica in different environments, and other factors may affect a direct correlation

Fig. 3.56

Horse
Partial Ramus (lower jaw)

Equus sp.
Pleistocene

Caloosa Shell Pit,
Hillsborough County, FL

Collection: R. Sinibaldi
Size: 6 in.\15.3 cm

Fig. 3.56. The partial jaw of this very old horse has two teeth at (a) and (d) that are worn down to and perhaps below the estimated gum line (*arrows*). Tooth (b) was still somewhat above the gum line, and tooth (c) has a minimal amount of enamel showing above the projected gum line.

Fig. 3.57

Horse
Partial Maxilla

Equus sp.
Pleistocene

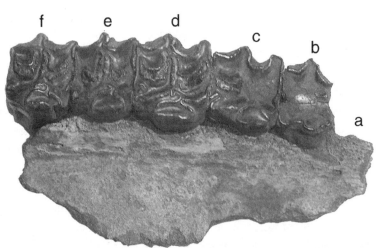

Withlacoochee River,
Marion County, FL

Collection: R. Sinibaldi
Size: 4.5 in.\11.5 cm

Fig. 3.57. The premolar, technically p2 at location (a), is missing in this horse maxilla. The next two premolars, at (b) and (c), display extreme wear from old age. Molars at (d), (e) and (f) are worn down but still have full occlusal surfaces.

Fig. 3.58

American Mastodon
Molar

Mammut americanum
Pleistocene

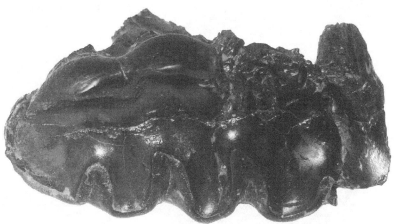

Suwannee River,
Florida

Collection: T. Sellari
Size: 5.5 in.\13.7 cm

Fig. 3.58. The extreme wear on this large rear molar of a mastodon is evidence that this animal lived into old age (possibly 60 to 70 years). Compare with young mastodon teeth in figures 3.45 and 6.1.

Fig. 3.59

Horse
Incisors (aged 2–17 years)

Equus sp.
Early Pleistocene

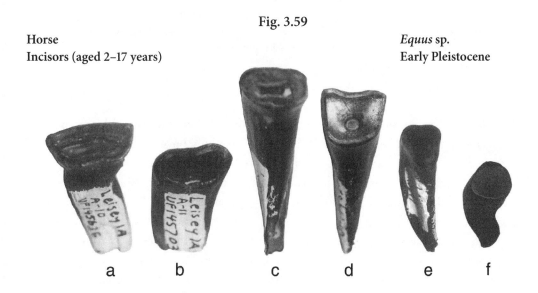

Leisey Shell Pit 1A,
Hillsborough County, FL

Collection: FLMNH
Size: 0.5 in.\1.25 cm (c)

Fig. 3.59. (a) is a worn deciduous incisor from a horse 2–2.5 years old; (b) is a newly erupted adult incisor, 2.5–3 years; (c) is a central incisor from a 6–8-year-old horse; (d) is an incisor from a 10–12-year-old animal; (e) is an incisor from a 14–17-year-old horse; and (f) is from an animal more than 20 years old. These ages were roughly estimated from modern-day veterinary charts used to determine the age of living horses.

Fig. 3.60

Mammoth   *Mammuthus* sp.
Spit Tooth   Pleistocene

Peace River,   Collection: R. Sinibaldi
DeSoto County, FL   Size: 3.5 in.\9 cm

Fig. 3.60. The occlusal surface of this mammoth spit tooth is at (a). The roots have been digested or eroded away at (b) by a special gland in the front of the jaw. A concave wear pattern occurs at (c) from the next tooth pushing this tooth forward in the jaw. In this specialized manner, mammoths produced six sets of progressively larger teeth per quadrant during their lifetimes.

between features of today's horses and those of Pleistocene horses of the recent geological past. The teeth of a Pleistocene horse may have worn much more quickly or slowly than those of a domesticated horse of today.

Problems that scientists face when determining ages of fossil populations from teeth include the fact that the chemical composition of fossil teeth may differ from that of modern analogues, affecting wear rate, a modern phylogenetic analogue for comparison may be lacking (as with dinosaurs), different amounts of silica may occur in the food of herbivores from different geographically or chronologically different eras, and sexual dimorphism (covered in next section) may affect tooth size. Therefore, as previously stated, it is always much safer to discuss stages of development rather than exact ages of extinct species.

As discussed in the section on grazers, proboscideans (mammoths, mastodons, gomphotheres, and today's elephants) may produce six or seven sets of teeth. Teeth erupt in the rear of their jaws and move forward into position for chewing. As teeth get older they continue to move toward the front of the jaw, where a special gland digests the roots of the worn tooth so it can be exfoliated. Many amateurs refer to these teeth as **spit teeth** (fig. 3.60). Spit teeth are very distinct in that the roots are generally missing, the rear of the tooth has a concave wear pattern from the next tooth pushing it forward, and the tooth appears to be only "half" there. Spit teeth increase in size as the animal gets older.

Sexual Dimorphism

Determining an animal's sex by use of its teeth is possible on rare occasions with mammals. Animals that do exhibit **sexual dimorphism** in their dental battery, different morphological features between males and females, have the biggest differences generally in their canine teeth. In some mammals, canines exist in the males and not in the females (fig. 3.61). In other mammals the canines may be up to 40 percent larger in males than in females (fig. 3.62). The majority of mammals, however, do not exhibit sexual dimorphism in teeth to such a degree that dimorphism can be diagnostic for nonexperts. Experts with large sample

Fig. 3.61

Horse   *Hipparion* sp.
Male Maxilla   Early Pliocene

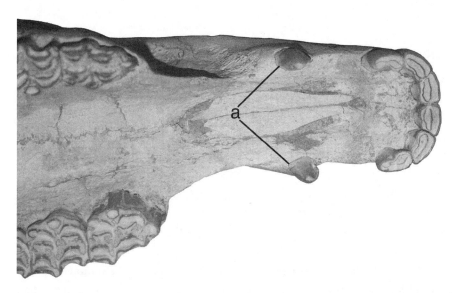

Gansu Province,   Collection: F. Garcia
China   Size: 8.5 in.\21.5 cm

Fig. 3.61. The canine teeth (a) in the upper jaw of this horse identify it as a male. **Female horses have few or no canines (see fig. 3.63).**

Fig. 3.62

Peccary
Lower Canines

Platygonus sp.
Pleistocene

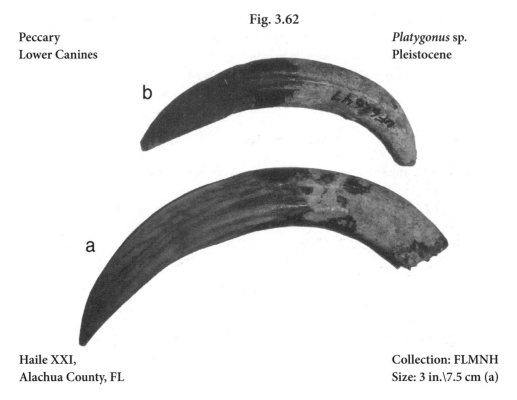

Haile XXI,
Alachua County, FL

Collection: FLMNH
Size: 3 in.\7.5 cm (a)

Fig. 3.62. These adult canines from a pair of peccaries display sexual dimorphism in the larger male (a) and smaller female (b).

sizes and knowledge of geological age to account for evolutionary changes may be able to attribute sexual differences to various teeth, including molars.

Horses, once again, are one of the more well-documented examples of sexual dimorphism in the fossil record. Males generally have much larger canines than females; many females lack canine teeth altogether (fig. 3.63). The molar or cheek teeth do not have enough size variation to be diagnostic. Horses late in the fossil record have modern phylogenetic analogues that have helped scientists determine sexual dimorphism in extinct species. Sexual dimorphism has been determined in older, more "primitive" species of horses through the study of large quarry samples of fossils known to be of the same species and from the same geological time period.

Determining sexual dimorphism using size as a factor runs into two problems. First, small males and large females of the same species very often overlap. Second, in many species, the female may have evolved to be larger than the male. Large comparative collections, along with scientific expertise, is often the only way to determine whether a tooth was from a female or male. Even then, most scientists will be cautious about designating gender to an individual on

Fig. 3.63

Horse
Female Mandible

Equus sp.
Pleistocene

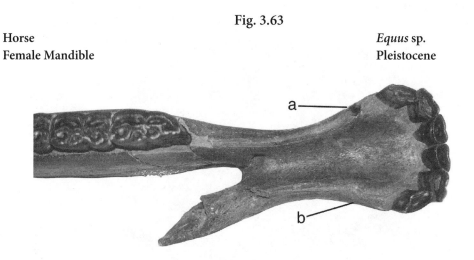

Leisey Shell Pit,
Hillsborough County, FL

Collection: FLMNH
Size: 7.5 in.\19 cm

Fig. 3.63. This female horse jaw is an example of both a very reduced canine (a) and no canine at all (b). Compare with the pronounced canines of a male horse in figure 3.61.

the basis of teeth. Fossil species showing a great deal of sexual dimorphism may be considered two different species by scientists who lack sufficient evidence to combine the fossils under one scientific designation.

Little is known about sexual dimorphism in extinct sharks; however, at least one extant species has been shown to exhibit sexual dimorphism in its teeth. It is believed that some extinct sharks also exhibited sexual dimorphism in the teeth of males and females. It must be remembered that the skeletons of sharks are composed mostly of cartilaginous materials that do not fossilize well; thus, without additional remains, it is extremely difficult to attribute sexual dimorphism to various shark species.

Note that sexual dimorphism in mammoth tusks was discussed in the previous section on special cases of mammal teeth in this chapter.

Shark Tooth Morphology

Other than a shark's teeth, its skeletal composition is only lightly **calcified** (primarily cartilage) and rarely fossilizes. Fossilized vertebral disks (**centra**), **dermal denticles** (**brambles**), and **coprolites**[25] (fossilized feces) are occasionally found (figs. 3.64–3.66), especially from the Tertiary period, when shark remains were preserved in loose sand, gravel, and clay. In older deposits of shale and limestone, much finer preservation is often possible, with skin, fins,

Fig. 3.64

Extinct Salmon Shark
Vertebral Disk

Otodus obliquus
Upper Paleocene to
Eocene

Khouribga,
Morocco

Collection: G. Hubbell
Size: 2.25 in.\6 cm

Fig. 3.64. Although the vertebral disks in sharks are only lightly calcified, they are often preserved if the conditions are right.

Fig. 3.65

Ray or Skate
Dermal Denticle or Bramble

Undetermined species
Miocene

Cargill Phosphate Mine,
Polk County, FL

Collection: R. Sinibaldi
Size: 0.87 in.\2.2 cm

Fig. 3.65. Some prehistoric species of sharks and rays had large dermal denticles embedded in their skin for protection. These are among the few nondental items that fossilized from prehistoric sharks and rays. Some scientists believe that the first teeth evolved from these specialized bones.

Fig. 3.66

Shark
Coprolite

Undetermined species
Miocene

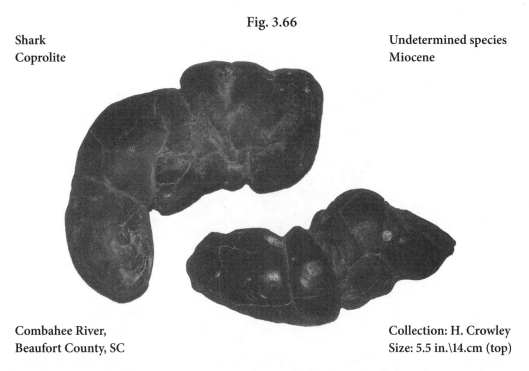

Combahee River,
Beaufort County, SC

Collection: H. Crowley
Size: 5.5 in.\14.cm (top)

Fig. 3.66. Coprolites, fossilized feces, are a common find in many localities. These coprolites, found in a deposit with hundreds of megalodon teeth, have been labeled as shark coprolites; in reality, however, it is extremely difficult to attribute coprolites to any specific species.

and other fine parts completely fossilized; however, as mentioned at the beginning of this chapter, individual sharks may produce up to 40,000 teeth in their lifetime that are very durable and leave an extensive fossil record.

Similar to mammal teeth, shark teeth have a crown and a type of root called the base. The crown is the exposed feeding surface, and the base anchors the tooth in the jaw (fig. 3.67). Beyond this superficial similarity, shark and mammal dentitions are very different.

The outer surface of a shark tooth is covered with a thin layer of **enameloid**, a substance similar to, but not considered true enamel (fig. 3.68).[26] Under the enameloid surface are two layers of dentine (**pallial dentine** and **orthodentine**). Some shark teeth have a pulp cavity (fig. 3.69); some do not. The base is composed of orthodentine. Aside from anchoring the tooth in the jaw, the orthodentine carries the blood supply to the tooth while it is forming. Small entrance holes, foramina, for the passage of nerves and blood supply can be seen in the base of the tooth (fig. 3.70). The base does not fully form until the tooth is ready to move into the feeding position. Shark teeth that are not fully formed are often hollow and sometimes mistaken for teeth broken off at the gum line (fig. 3.71).

Fig. 3.67

Mackerel Shark
Tooth

Serratolamna twiggsensis
Eocene

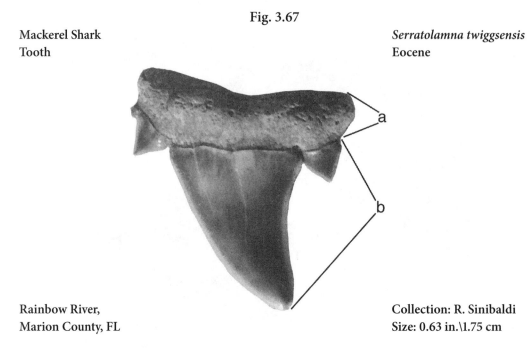

Rainbow River,
Marion County, FL

Collection: R. Sinibaldi
Size: 0.63 in.\1.75 cm

Fig. 3.67. This mackerel shark tooth displays the root (a) and crown (b) typical of most shark teeth.

Fig. 3.68

Extinct White Shark
Upper Tooth

Carcharocles megalodon
Miocene

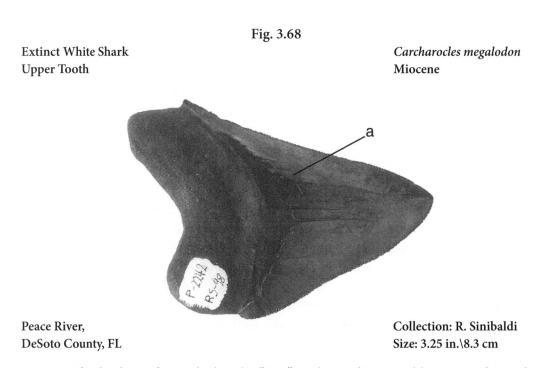

Peace River,
DeSoto County, FL

Collection: R. Sinibaldi
Size: 3.25 in.\8.3 cm

Fig. 3.68. The thin layer of enameloid on this "Meg" tooth is peeling away (a) to expose the much heavier layer of dentine.

Fig. 3.69

Dusky Shark
Split Tooth

Carcharhinus obscurus
Pliocene

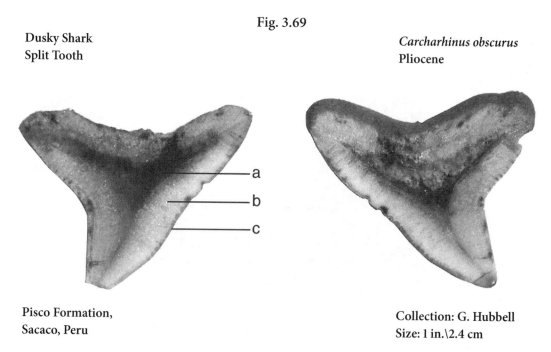

Pisco Formation,
Sacaco, Peru

Collection: G. Hubbell
Size: 1 in.\2.4 cm

Fig. 3.69. This dusky shark tooth split in half naturally, exposing its pulp cavity (a) and thick dentine layer (b). The cross section shows how thin the enameloid surface (c) truly is.

Fig. 3.70

Narrow-toothed Mako Shark
Lower Tooth

Isurus oxyrhinchus
Miocene

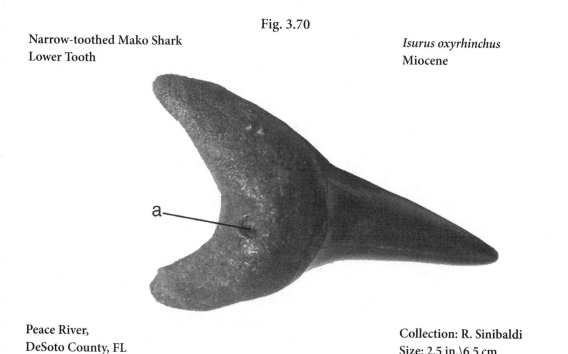

Peace River,
DeSoto County, FL

Collection: R. Sinibaldi
Size: 2.5 in.\6.5 cm

Fig. 3.70. This well-preserved Mako tooth has a prominent foramen or hole (a) for nerve and blood supply to the pulp cavity.

Fig. 3.71

Mako Shark
Undeveloped Tooth

Isurus hastalis
Middle Miocene

Sacaco,
Peru

Collection: G. Hubbell
Size: 1.25 in.\3 cm

Fig. 3.71. Teeth farther back in the file lack a fully formed root. They are often hollow and mistaken for broken teeth. This tooth was six rows back in the file (see fig. 3.73).

A shark's mouth contains rows of teeth as well as **files of teeth**. The first row of teeth is in the feeding position. As many as twelve or thirteen more rows of teeth in various stages of development lie behind the first row (fig. 3.72). Each row farther back is less developed. A file of teeth comprises all the teeth in the same position in the jaw. The configuration of each tooth in a file is exactly the same as the one in front of it. When a tooth is exfoliated, the next tooth in the file moves forward to replace it (fig. 3.73). Studies of the modern great white shark (*Carcharodon carcharias*) show that roughly one-third of its slots for teeth are in transition at any given time. Because of the violent feeding nature of sharks, this system of tooth replacement ensures that serviceable teeth are ready to replace damaged or lost ones at all times.

Scientists have used phylogenetic analogues to re-create the dentitions of extinct sharks; this way, a museum or university can mount an entire jaw full of teeth. These jaws are usually composites of teeth from many individuals (fig. 3.74). Since the jaws of sharks are not composed of bone, it is very rare that articulated sets of teeth are found together. On rare occasions a set of teeth is found in close proximity or, better yet, in the shape of the mouth. On more than one occasion, finding teeth in place has led scientists to rethink how extinct

Fig. 3.72

Mako Shark
Front Row, Lower Right Articulated Set

Isurus hastalis
Miocene

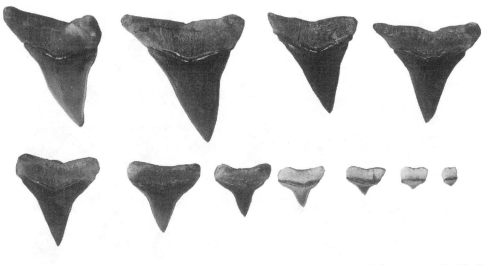

Sacaco,
Peru

Collection: G. Hubbell
Size: 1.8 in.\4 cm (largest)

Fig. 3.72. On rare occasions, entire dentitions are found associated. These enable experts to assemble complete rows (above) and files (fig. 3.73) of teeth.

Fig. 3.73

Mako Shark
File #2, Lower Right

Isurus hastalis
Miocene

Sacaco,
Peru

Collection: G. Hubbell
Size: 1.8 in.\4 cm (largest)

Fig. 3.73. A complete file from the lower jaw of a Mako shark. Note the almost complete development of the first three teeth (a), all of which may come into contact with prey when feeding. The last four teeth (b) are progressively less developed, and would continue to develop as they moved forward in the file.

Fig. 3.74

Mako Shark
Associated Complete Dentition
(right side)

Isurus hastalis
Miocene

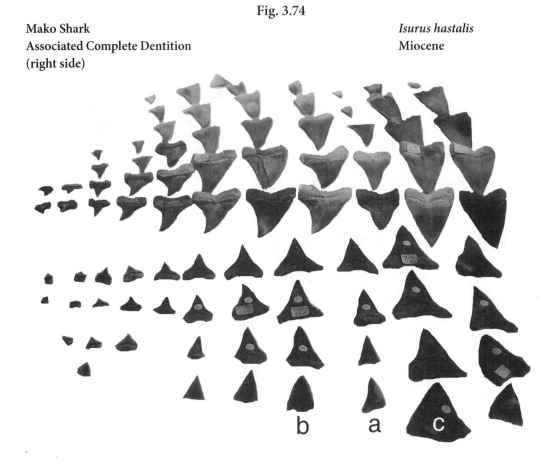

Sacaco,
Peru

Collection: G. Hubbell
Size: 1.8 in.\4 cm (largest)

Fig. 3.74. This almost complete dentition was found associated. By use of a modern phylogenetic analogue of the extinct Mako, the smaller teeth at file (a) were placed between files (b) and (c) instead of at the back of the jaw.

teeth fit into the jaw as a previously re-created jaw using a modern analogue proved to be incorrect (fig. 3.75).[27]

Shark teeth can be divided by their function into four types: cutting, grasping, clutching, and crushing. Cutting teeth are used for gouging large chunks of flesh from prey (fig. 3.76). Grasping teeth are used to impale and hold active prey (fig. 3.77). Clutching teeth are also used to impale prey, like grasping teeth, but may also be used to crush prey (fig. 3.78). Crushing teeth are able to withstand tremendous forces while crushing armored prey (such as shellfish). Crushing teeth are most common in skates and rays, close relatives to sharks (fig. 3.79).

Fig. 3.75

Great White Shark
Articulated Upper and Lower Jaws

Carcharodon carcharias
Pliocene

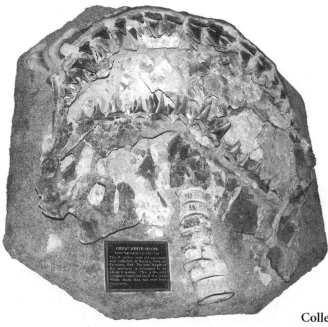

Sacaco,
Peru

Collection: G. Hubbell
Size: 24 in.\59 cm

Fig. 3.75. In extremely rare instances, a completely articulated fossilized jaw with all teeth in place is found. This eliminates any speculation about where individual teeth belong in a row or file (see fig. 3.74).

Fig. 3.76

Great White Shark
Cutting Tooth (upper)

Carcharodon carcharias
Pliocene

Sacaco,
Peru

Collection: G. Hubbell
Size: 2 in.\5 cm

Fig. 3.76. Cutting teeth may or may not be serrated, but they are always triangular in shape, very sharp, and generally robust.

Fig. 3.77

Sand Tiger Shark
Grasping Tooth

Carcharias taurus
Miocene

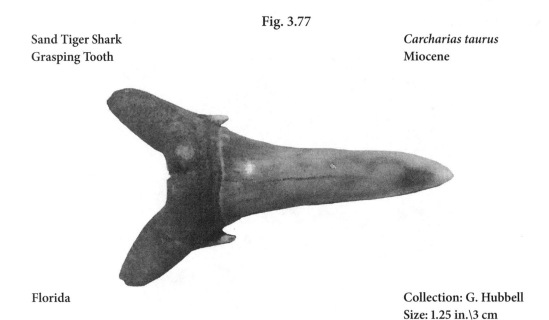

Florida

Collection: G. Hubbell
Size: 1.25 in.\3 cm

Fig. 3.77. The narrower morphology and small side cusps of grasping teeth lead scientists to believe these teeth are used to grasp active prey.

Fig. 3.78

Shark
Clutching Tooth

Cretolamna sp.
Cretaceous

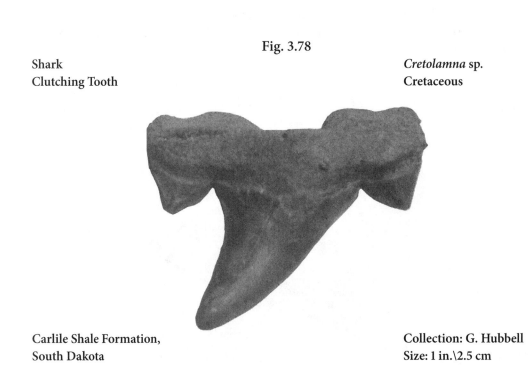

Carlile Shale Formation,
South Dakota

Collection: G. Hubbell
Size: 1 in.\2.5 cm

Fig. 3.78. Clutching teeth were used to grasp prey, but their robust morphology (compare with fig. 3.77) may have also allowed them to crush prey.

Fig. 3.79

Clam Crushing Shark
Crushing Tooth

Ptychodus sp.
Cretaceous

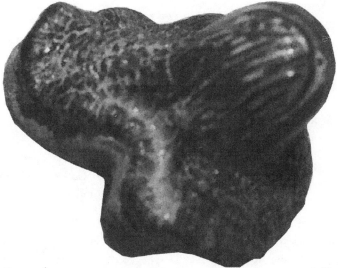

Carlile Shale Formation,
South Dakota

Collection: G. Hubbell
Size: 0.5 in.\1.25 cm

Fig. 3.79. Crushing teeth such as this one evolved to crush shellfish and crustaceans. Rays and skates, closely related to sharks, also have crushing-type dentitions.

Different sharks have different dentition patterns that may range from simple to complex. **Simple dentitions** have only one type of tooth in both upper and lower jaws. The teeth may remain the same size throughout the jaw or get progressively smaller toward the back of the jaw (see fig. 3.74).

Complex dentitions comprise two or more types of teeth. Complex dentitions fall into two basic categories: **monognathic heterodont dentition** and **dignathic heterodont dentition**. In monognathic heterodont dentition, two or more types of teeth occur in each jaw, changing from front to back (fig. 3.80). In dignathic heterodont dentition (fig. 3.81), the teeth of the upper jaw are of a different type from those of the lower jaw (such as cutting teeth in one jaw and grasping teeth in the other).

Some very early shark teeth defy classification (fig. 3.82). Not enough is known about the complete dentition or body plan of the shark to determine why the teeth evolved in various bizarre forms. Finally, this note of caution to amateurs[28] and interested collectors about embedded shark's teeth: these are almost always fakes (fig. 3.83), although true specimens have been found. A "real" or "true" embedded shark tooth in a bone will always be considered scientifi-

Fig. 3.80

Port Jackson's Shark
Lower Jaw

Heterodontus portusjacksoni
Recent

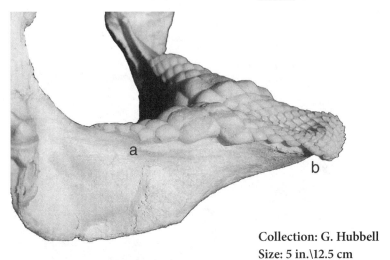

Western Australia

Collection: G. Hubbell
Size: 5 in.\12.5 cm

Fig. 3.80. This recent Port Jackson's shark has two distinct types of teeth in the same jaw (monognathic heterodont dentition): crushing teeth (a) in the rear of the jaw, and clutching teeth (b) in the front of the jaw.

Fig. 3.81

Snaggletooth Shark
Dignathic Heterodont Teeth
(a) upper
(b) lower

Hemipristis serra
Middle Miocene

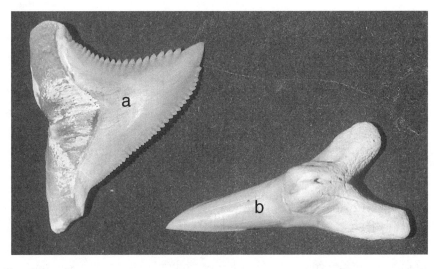

Bone Valley Formation,
Polk County, FL

Collection: G. Hubbell
Size: 1.5 in.\4 cm (a)

Fig. 3.81. The types of teeth in a snaggletooth shark are completely different between the upper jaw (a) and lower jaw (b). All the upper teeth are of the cutting type and all the lower teeth are of the grasping type.

Fig. 3.82

Whorl Tooth Shark
9 fused teeth

Edestus heinrichi
Pennsylvanian

Pennsylvania

Collection: G. Hubbell
Size: 3 in.\7.5 cm

Fig. 3.82. These bizarre fused teeth were specialized for a reason that still eludes scientists. The 300-million-year-old *Edestus* genus has no modern analogue with which to compare it.

Fig. 3.83

Fake Embedded Tooth
Shark Tooth in a Vertebra

Current Fake Using
Miocene Tooth

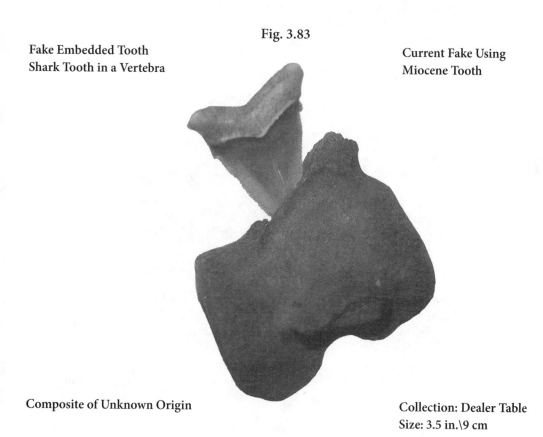

Composite of Unknown Origin

Collection: Dealer Table
Size: 3.5 in.\9 cm

Fig. 3.83. This tooth embedded in a vertebra was being sold at a fossil fair as a fake. The problem is that once these fakes get into circulation, they are often passed on as "real" to unsuspecting collectors.

cally relevant. Finding one would be like finding the "smoking gun"; it would be concrete proof that a certain species of shark fed on a particular species of prey. These rare finds are usually only a tip of the tooth that has broken off in the bone.

Reptile and Fish Teeth

The relatively simple dentitions of fishes and reptiles, with disposable teeth that are continually replaced, are not very specialized. Most fishes and reptiles do not process their food in their mouth, but gulp their prey. Unlike mammals, most fish and reptile species continue to grow throughout their lives, continuously replacing their teeth with ever larger ones in their constantly growing jaws.

The dentition of most reptiles is considered **homodont** (all teeth similar). Reptiles like alligators and crocodiles have evolved simple cone-shaped teeth (fig. 3.84). Today's Komodo dragons also have homodont dentitions, except that their teeth are shaped like triangular blades for attacking and eating prey.

Figs. 3.84

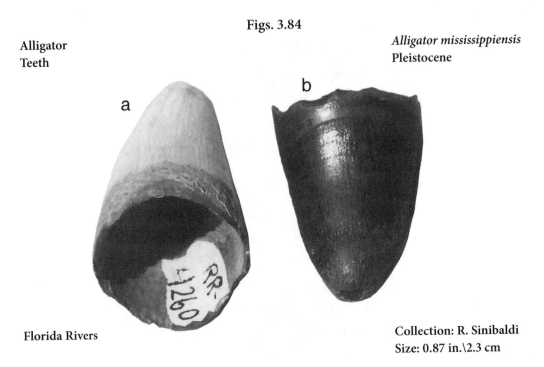

Alligator
Teeth

Alligator mississippiensis
Pleistocene

a

b

Florida Rivers

Collection: R. Sinibaldi
Size: 0.87 in.\2.3 cm

Fig. 3.84. Note the simple cone shape of these alligator teeth. View (a) shows the root side of the tooth, and view (b) the occlusal surface.

Fig. 3.85

Alligator   *Alligator mississippiensis*
Partial Jaws without Dentition   Pleistocene

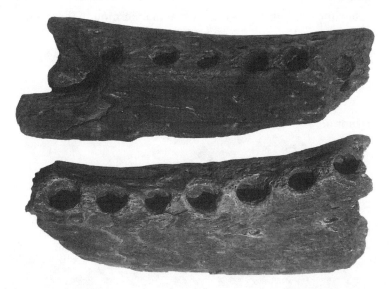

Peace River   Collection: R. Sinibaldi
DeSoto County, FL   Size: 3.75 in.\9.5 cm

Fig. 3.85. The tooth sockets in these alligator jaws are all identical, the sign of homodont dentition.

Reptile teeth may vary in size, but the sockets in the jaw are all the same shape.
This means that if a jaw is found without any teeth present, if the tooth sockets are all similar in shape, it is probably a reptile jaw (fig. 3.85) or fish jaw.[29]
Mammal jaws have a variety of socket shapes to accommodate canines, incisors, premolars, molars, and various other specialized forms of teeth (tusks and
carnassials, for example). Similar to sharks, reptiles continuously replace their
teeth;[30] therefore, no tooth has a well-defined root like that of a mammal's tooth
(fig. 3.86). The underside of each tooth will bear the shape of the next tooth
developing underneath it (fig. 3.87). Reptile jaws may come in a variety of sizes
and shapes but generally contain homodont dentition (fig. 3.88). Turtles do not
have teeth, and some have evolved another solution to obtaining and processing food (fig. 3.89). Their maxilla and mandible have developed sets of opposing
ridges that turtles use to crop or grasp food and process it before swallowing.

The dentitions of fishes also present various evolutionary solutions to obtaining food. Fish, like reptiles and amphibians, continuously replace their teeth;
however, unlike the teeth of reptiles, those of fish may be found in a great variety of shapes. Generally, no matter what the shape of their teeth, most fish have
homodont dentitions (fig. 3.90). Most fishes, similar to sharks, use their teeth to

cut, grasp, clutch, and crush their prey. Some fishes have teeth that do not line up neatly on the sides of the jaws like those of mammals; instead, some of their teeth are located in bony plates back inside the throat as well as in their mouth. Since fish breathe through their gills, located in their mouth, they cannot chew food and breathe at the same time, and here the solution was to evolve a food processing apparatus inside the throat and behind the gill plates (fig. 3.91).

Fig. 3.86

Alligator
Jaw with Broken Dentition

Alligator mississippiensis
Pleistocene

Rainbow River,
Marion County, FL

Collection: D. Sinibaldi
Size: 3.5 in.\9 cm

Fig. 3.86. Without well-developed roots, alligator teeth easily fall out of the jaw during the fossilization process. A replacement tooth (a) can be seen nested inside the remains of a tooth root.

Fig. 3.87

Alligator
Nested Teeth

Alligator mississippiensis
Pleistocene

Florida Rivers

Collection: R. Sinibaldi
Size: 2.5 in.\6.5 cm

Fig. 3.87. Note how the concave tip of one tooth fits into the convex root of the tooth it will replace.

Fig. 3.88

Mosasaur Jaw Section   Undetermined species
Homodont Dentition   Cretaceous

Morocco   Collection: F. Garcia
                                              Size: 22 in.\55 cm

Fig. 3.88. This mosasaur jaw section displays 5 teeth, all the same shape and size. This mosasaur was a prehistoric aquatic reptile from 85 to 90 million years ago. Most early reptiles had homodont dentition.

Fig. 3.89

Giant Tortoise   *Hesperotestudo crassiscutata*
Jaw   Late Pliocene

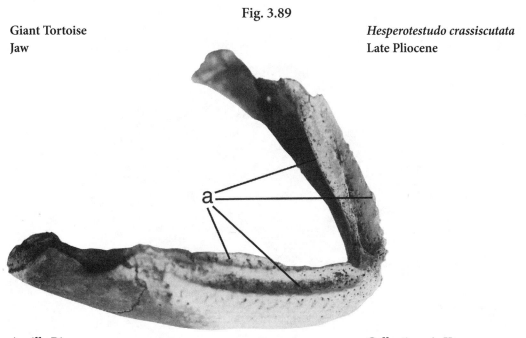

Aucilla River,   Collection: A. Kerner
Florida   Size: 4.2 in.\10.8 cm (across)

Fig. 3.89. This giant tortoise jaw exhibits developed ridges (a) in place of dentition. The upper jaw would have corresponding ridges for efficient cropping of plant material.

Fig. 3.90

Garfish Jaw
Homodont Dentition

Lepisosteus sp.
Pleistocene

La Belle Highway Pit
Hendry County, FL

Collection: FLMNH
Size: 3.5 in.\9 cm

Fig. 3.90. Although the teeth in this garfish jaw vary in size, their general morphology is the same. As needed, teeth are continuously replaced in the jaw from below to maintain a full complement of teeth.

Fig. 3.91

Black Drum Fish
Dentition

Pogonias cromis
Pleistocene

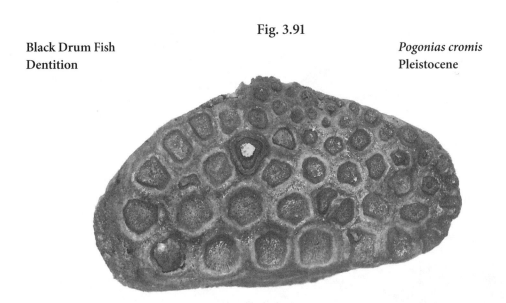

Suwannee River
Florida

Collection: A. Kerner
Size: 3.4 in.\8.8 cm

Fig. 3.91. Drum fish evolved a type of dentition located back in the throat. These plates, which would contain small undifferentiated teeth in life, are an evolutionary adaptation for processing ingested food since fish cannot chew.

CHAPTER 4

Natural Alterations to Fossils

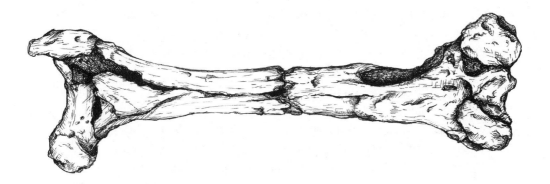

My good friend the paleontologist is in greater danger than he realizes when he leaves description and attempts explanation. He has no way to check up on his speculations and it is notorious that the human mind without control has a bad habit of wandering.

Thomas H. Morgan

Introduction

Common alterations to bones that occur naturally after the animal is dead are often mistaken for pathologies or cultural modifications. Therefore, before pathological or culturally modified bone is considered, this chapter will describe possible natural alterations to bones occurring before, during, or after fossilization.[1] Although many specimens presented in this chapter (and the following three chapters) may not be considered "museum quality," each has an important story to tell.[2]

Natural alterations to bones can be divided into four categories: biological alterations, geological alterations, hydrological alterations, and atmospheric alterations.[3] These alterations are far more common than pathologies and cultural modifications to bones. **Biological alterations** include but are not limited to root markings or etchings, worm or insect holes, disarticulation, and trampling. **Geological alterations** include pressure, acid alterations, split line cracks, and chemical alterations. **Hydrological alterations** include tumbling in ocean surf, polishing in river currents, and dissolution. Finally, fading, delamination, and weathering are **atmospheric alterations** to bones.

Other biological alterations such as gnawing and attack marks are covered in chapters 5 and 6 under the subject of pseudopathologies. These are truly biological alterations, and could have been placed in this chapter, but placing those anomalies in the chapters about healed attacks will give the reader a clearer comparison of the differences between pathologies and pseudopathologies.

Beginning with chapter 4, many of the subjects covered could fall under the study of taphonomy. **Taphonomy**, defined simply, is the study of everything that can happen to a bone assemblage between the death of an animal and its discovery. It focuses on the processes that affect both completeness and composition of skeletal remains. In the technical literature, the term diagenesis refers to alterations to bones and teeth that continue after they are buried. When looking at a bone, one should always look for the simplest and most common explanation for unusual markings; these are, first, natural alterations, second, pathological explanations, and, finally, cultural modifications by Paleo-Indians or later Native Americans. Natural processes often mimic[4] the effects of pathologies or cultural modification and can be very misleading. Cautious explanations should be given for any bone exhibiting alterations of any kind: natural, pathological, or cultural.[5] All bones and teeth pass through some form of taphonomic filter[6] that in most cases reduces the amount of original information about the specimen.

It should be noted that the paleontological record can become distorted for many reasons. Taphonomic study of bison skulls, for example, revealed roughly ten male skulls to every one female skull discovered, as reported by Guthrie (2005). This distorted ratio puzzled scientists, because today's male bison do not outnumber females by even two to one. It turned out that "bullheadedness" is the cause of the preservation bias. Male bison compete for females by violently butting each other in the head, requiring males to have far more robust skulls and horn cores. That very robustness leads to a better chance of preservation in the fossil record and therefore a biased male-to-female ratio of preserved skulls. These taphonomic distortions occur for other animals as well.[7] In addition, a sampling bias can occur in the case of immature and mature bones. Immature bones tend to be less dense and generally smaller. Their ability to resist attritional factors throughout long periods of time is therefore lower, often biasing the fossil record toward mature adults. Scientists must therefore look at as many taphonomic factors as possible before drawing any conclusions about bone assemblages or even single specimens.

Biological Alterations

Biological alterations to bones are caused by other living organisms after an animal has died and the bones have been deposited. They include, but are not limited to, root markings, worm holes, disarticulation, and **trampling**. All four of these processes are excellent mimics of other pathological or cultural alterations to bones. Bite marks and gnawing are covered in chapter 5. Biologically produced alterations to bones and teeth that are not caused by vertebrates are technically termed bioerosion. Bioerosion includes root etchings, insect damage, damage caused by other invertebrates (e.g., worms, marine life), and damage by microorganisms such as fungi and bacteria.

Root Markings

Bones and teeth near the surface after burial may be subject to biological alteration attributed to the roots of plants sometimes referred to as root etching or root imprints. The roots of many plants contain carbonic acids that can metabolize bone, leaving imprints on the contact surface of bones or teeth as their surface is dissolved (fig. 4.1). Root imprints can mimic natural morphologies such as the imprints of blood vessels (fig. 2.65) covered in chapter 2. Many times deep rooting marks are confused with the cultural modification practice of etching designs on bones (chapter 7).

Fig. 4.1

Extinct White Shark
Upper Tooth

Carcharocles megalodon
Miocene

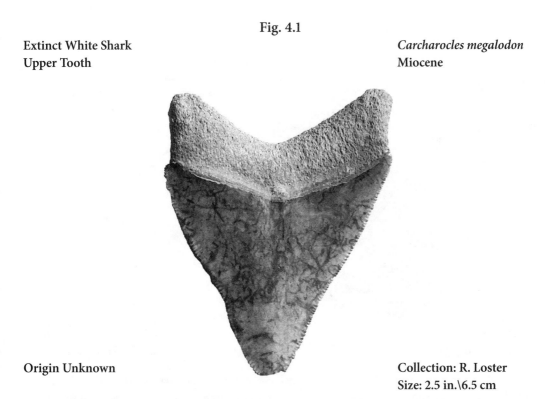

Origin Unknown

Collection: R. Loster
Size: 2.5 in.\6.5 cm

Fig. 4.1. The markings made by plant roots are often mistaken for the imprints of blood vessels or nerves (figs. 2.65–2.66).

Worm Holes, Mollusks, and Insects

Worms, mollusks, and insects will often find newly deposited bones to be an accommodating new home or food source. Worm holes may occur in terrestrial as well as marine deposits (fig. 4.2). They may often mimic nerve holes, pathologies, or holes drilled by early Native Americans. Some bones and teeth are so riddled with holes as to make them obvious non-mimics (fig. 4.3). Some mollusks can bore holes into bone, shell, and rock by emitting phosphoric acid. Other mollusks often attach themselves to bones deposited on the ocean floor, before or after fossilization has occurred (fig. 4.4). If attachment occurs before the bone is fossilized, it will often make a depression on the bone or tooth at the point of attachment. If attachment occurs after a fossilized bone has resurfaced on the ocean floor, a good cleaning will usually remove all traces of mollusk involvement. Mollusk attachments often mimic pathologies, and some erroneously believe them to be scars of giant squid attacks (covered under the topic of pathological shark teeth in chapter 6). Finally, large bones with a high spongy (cancellous) bone content may be subject to dermestid beetle or other insect burrowing (fig. 4.5).

Fig. 4.2

Extinct White Shark   *Carcharocles megalodon*
Lower Tooth   Miocene

Peace River,   Collection: R. Sinibaldi
DeSoto County, FL   Size: 3.25 in.\9 cm

Fig. 4.2. Burrowing clams may have inadvertently drilled into this "meg" tooth as they drilled into the limestone to anchor themselves to the floor of the prehistoric ocean. The teeth were not specifically targeted by the clam, but contained within the limestone formation occupied by the clam.

Fig. 4.3

Extinct White Shark
Upper Tooth

Carcharocles megalodon
Miocene

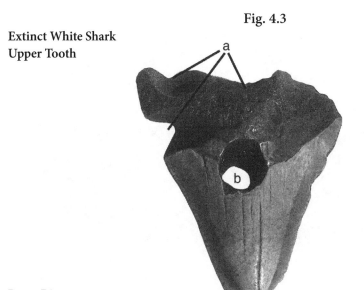

Peace River,
DeSoto County, FL

Collection: A. Kerner
Size: 2 in.\5 cm

Fig. 4.3. The additional holes at (a) enable identification of the hole at (b) as a naturally occurring mimic. See figures 7.101–7.102 to compare this tooth with shark teeth drilled as pendants by early Native Americans.

Fig. 4.4

(a) White-tailed Deer Antler
(b) Dugong Rib

(a) *Odocoileus virginianus*
(b) *Metaxytherium floridanum*
Miocene

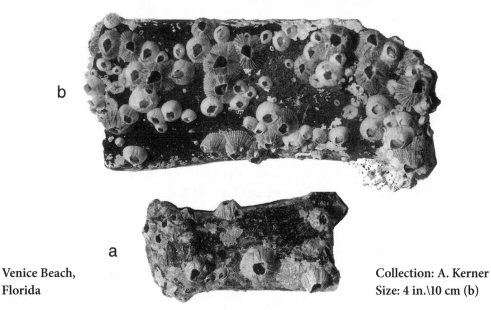

Venice Beach,
Florida

Collection: A. Kerner
Size: 4 in.\10 cm (b)

Fig. 4.4. Any fossilized item that resurface on the ocean floor becomes a convenient surface where barnacles can attach. If the barnacles are removed during preparation of the specimen, distinctive markings will occur on the surface (see fig. 6.38).

Fig. 4.5

Bone Fragment
with Insect Burrowing

Undetermined species
Pleistocene

Peace River,
DeSoto County, FL

Collection: A. Kerner
Size: 3 in.\7.5 cm

Fig. 4.5. This small bone fragment bears the evidence of an insect burrowing before the fossilization process occurred. Possibly ants or termites.

Disarticulation and Trampling

It is rare to come across a fossil skeleton that is still completely articulated (fig. 4.6). In fact, many mounted museum specimens are composites (parts from many individuals of the same species) or include reconstructed bones to complete the mount. Even rarer to find are complete death assemblages, technically termed **thanatocoenoses** (singular, thanatocoenosis). A death assemblage may contain the complete or nearly complete remains of multiple individuals of the same or multiple species. In most instances, however, the bones and teeth have become disarticulated. Disarticulation has many causes, including scavenging by animals after death, weathering, geological forces, and trampling by other animals. An animal's bones may sometimes be disarticulated but still associated, as often happens in river or stream deposits (called fluvial environments in scientific literature), catastrophes such as floods or avalanches, and trampling, or with minor scavenging (fig. 4.7). Trampling effects on bone are very common but generally need a scientific expert to determine (fig. 4.8). All these processes might mimic selective food acquisition or butchering by early Native Americans.

Fig. 4.6

Oreodont

Merycoidodon culbertsoni

Articulated Rear Foot

Oligocene

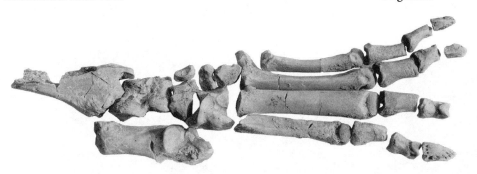

Harrison,

Collection: D. Letasi

Nebraska

Size: 5 in.\12.5 cm

Fig. 4.6. On rare occasions, completely articulated specimens are found. Almost all the bones in the rear foot of this oreodont were found articulated (together) as they would have been during life.

Fig. 4.7

(a), (b) Rhino Skulls

(a), (b) *Chilotherium* sp.

(c), (e) Sheeplike Antelope

(c), (e) *Paleoryx* sp.

(d) Three-toed Horse

(d) *Hipparion* sp.

Miocene

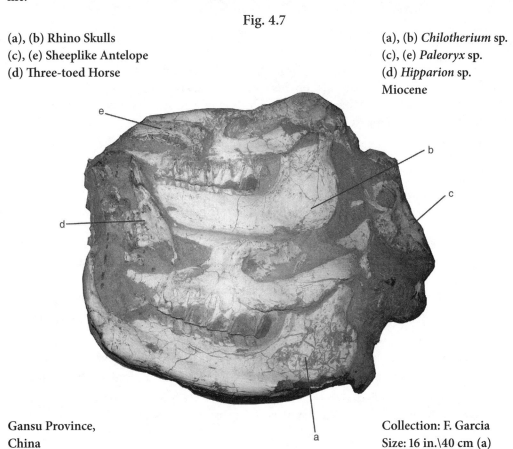

Gansu Province,

Collection: F. Garcia

China

Size: 16 in.\40 cm (a)

Fig. 4.7. This matrix holds the remains of five different animals from three distinct species. (a) and (b) are rhino skulls, (c) and (e) are sheeplike antelope skulls, and (d) is the skull of a three-toed horse. A deposit like this is probably the result of some prehistoric catastrophe.

Fig. 4.8

Trampled Bone

Undetermined species
Pleistocene

La Belle Highway Pit
Hendry County, FL

Collection: FLMNH
Size: 1.5 in.\3.6 cm

Fig. 4.8. Note that the parallel scratches on this bone are unequal in depth and width. It is believed that these marks could have been caused by trampling when this bone was lying on a surface layer of shell. Compare these marks to rodent gnawing marks covered in chapter 5, figures 5.47–5.50.

Geological Alterations

The process of fossilization is in itself a geological/chemical alteration to the bone or tooth, but in addition to the process of fossilization, geological forces may further alter the state of a specimen beyond molecular replacement of organic by inorganic materials. Other geological alterations include, but are not limited to, pressure alterations, **acid alterations**, chemical alterations, and **split line cracking**. Once again, as with biological alterations, geological alterations can mimic pathologies as well as cultural modifications. The original topography of the landscape may also affect bone assemblages. Slopes, gullies, crevices, sinkholes, and other natural anomalies of the ground where an animal died can act as either collecting points or dispersal agents of a bone assemblage.

Pressure

Bones and fossils buried in deep sediments can be exposed to extreme pressure from the weight of the overlying matrix. Geological pressure can alter a fossil in

Fig. 4.9

Freshwater Herring
Complete Skeleton

Diplomystus dentatus
Eocene

Kemmerer,
Wyoming

Collection: R. Sinibaldi
Size: 7 in.\18 cm

Fig. 4.9. The skeleton of this fish has been pressed flat through geological pressure over millions of years.

a variety of ways. Three-dimensional fossils can be pressed into flat two-dimensional impressions (fig. 4.9). This is common for plants, fish, and soft-bodied animals that lack skeletons. Extreme geological pressure can also bend, distort, or flatten fossil bone (fig. 4.10). Pressure that is extreme and prolonged may also cause crystals to form in bone cavities (fig. 4.11). Crystal formation often takes place in bone cavities when percolating ground water, laden with solutes, undergoes a decrease in pressure in the bone cavity itself, causing precipitation and crystal growth. Crystal growth within a bone cavity can eventually obliterate the outer layers of bone, destroying the specimen completely. Obviously, geological pressure can fracture, crush, or destroy fossils completely. Bone that has bent or distorted under extreme pressure may mimic pathological bone. Many bones that are found broken may not fit exactly into place during reconstruction, as some may have been distorted by extreme pressure over time.

Acid Alterations

Bones that end up in rivers, lakes, or ground saturated with acidic water often develop acid alterations.[8] Naturally occurring acids in water, soil, or even an animal's stomach can attack the outer surface layers of bone. Bones or teeth that

Fig. 4.10

Oreodont
Skull

Merycoidodon culbertsoni
Oligocene

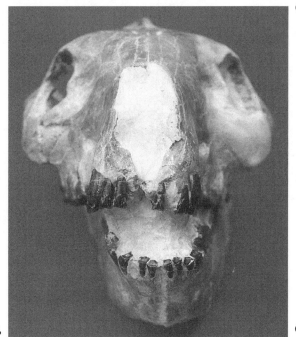

Dawes County,
Nebraska

Collection: R. Sinibaldi
Size: 4.25 in.\11 cm

Fig. 4.10. This oreodont skull has been distorted through the forces of geological pressure.

Fig. 4.11

Oreodont Bone
Crystallized Marrow Cavity

Merycoidodon sp.
Oligocene

Dawes County,
Nebraska

Collection: R. Sinibaldi
Size: 2.5 in.\6 cm

Fig. 4.11. It is not uncommon for the hollow portion of long bones to fill with minerals that crystallize under extreme pressure over long periods of time.

Fig. 4.12

Mammoth   *Mammuthus* sp.
Juvenile Spit Tooth   Pleistocene

Suwannee River,   Collection: A. Kerner
Florida   Size: 3 in.\7.5 cm

Fig. 4.12. This tooth has been exposed to several types of acids. First, the roots of the tooth were exposed to the acids from a gland in the front of the mammoth's mouth to help spit or exfoliate old and worn teeth. Second, this tooth most likely was inadvertently swallowed and therefore exposed to stomach acids (accounting for its shape). Finally, the tooth may have been exposed to ground acids after being deposited.

are swallowed and exposed to stomach acids (fig. 4.12), or specimens that were exposed to other enzymes produced as the body decays, termed autolysis, can cause pitting or other alterations of a fossil. Exposure to diluted acids in water or soil can produce pitted surface marks (fig. 4.13). Prolonged exposure may eventually dissolve most or all of the bone or fossil (fig. 4.14). Acid alterations may occur before, during, or after fossilization. Acid leaching may also accelerate the process of delamination (discussed under atmospheric alterations). Acid alterations may mimic tendon and ligament attachment scars, bone infections, arthritis, or cultural modification. In some rivers the acids are so severe that no bones survive, only the much harder enamel of teeth.

Chemical Alterations

Chemical reactions that occur during the process of fossilization may introduce various colors into the bone or tooth. Many times the fossilized teeth of a specimen will be a different color from the surrounding bone as a result of differing chemical reactions of the enamel and the bone with the infiltrating chemical compounds (fig. 4.15), or because of differences in porosity between bone and teeth. This differential fossilization of teeth is different from the process that

Fig. 4.13

Horse
Astragalus (ankle bone)

Equus sp.
Pleistocene

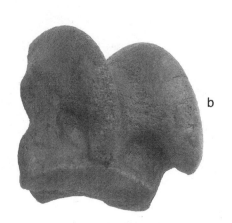

Peace River,
DeSoto County, FL

Collection: R. Sinibaldi
Size: 2.75 in.\7 cm (a)

Fig. 4.13. Compare the surfaces of the horse astragalus exposed to severe acid leaching (a) to a well preserved specimen (b).

Fig. 4.14

Unidentified Bone
Shank

Undetermined species
Pleistocene

Peace River,
DeSoto County, FL

Collection: R. Sinibaldi
Size: 5.5 in.\14 cm

Fig. 4.14. This long bone shank has been exposed to severe acid leaching, rendering it unidentifiable.

Fig. 4.15

Oreodont
Skull/Maxilla

Merycoidodon culbertsoni
Oligocene

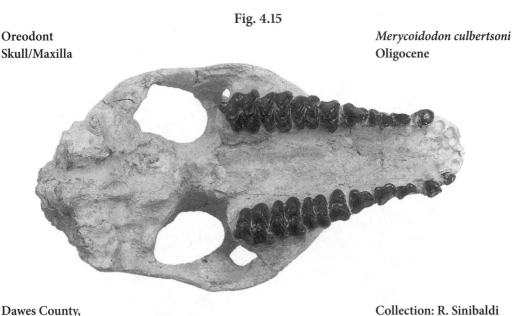

Dawes County,
Nebraska

Collection: R. Sinibaldi
Size: 8.5 in.\21.5 cm

Fig. 4.15. The chemical reactions that took place during the fossilization of this oreodont skull turned the bone into a white opal and the teeth jet black. An example of one matrix having different effects on various parts of the same specimen.

produces two-tone bone that has faded from the sun or weather (discussed under atmospheric alterations). Many specimens of the same species may fossilize in a variety of colors depending on the surrounding matrix composition (fig. 4.16).[9]

Split Line Cracking

Split line cracks may form as expansion occurs in the process of mineralization. Split line cracks may also be caused by wet-dry cycles and freeze-thaw cycles (weathering). These cracks run longitudinally along the length of the bone and are considered the most common type of bone destruction (fig. 4.17). The depths of the cracks may vary (fig. 4.18). It is often difficult or impossible to determine whether a split line crack was caused by mineralization or weathering; however, the results are always the same: cracks along the length of the bone.

During growth, and life in general, bones form to best resist stresses that occur across them. Bone fibers tend to run lengthwise in all long bones to adapt them to resist the stresses they are most likely to encounter during life. After an animal dies, however, these processes shrink and expand bone material. The bone thus forms split line cracks lengthwise in the path of least stress resistance.

Fig. 4.16

Camel
Upper Molars

Paleolama mirifica
Pleistocene

a

b

(a) Suwannee River, FL
(b) Withlacoochee River, FL

Collection: A. Kerner
Size: 1.25 in.\3 cm

Fig. 4.16. Each of these camel teeth mineralized into different colors as the result of a different surrounding matrix.

Fig. 4.17

Capybara
Tibia (distal end)

Hydrochaeris holmesi
Pleistocene

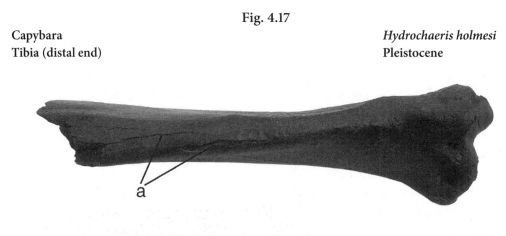

a

Horse Creek,
DeSoto County, FL

Collection: R. Sinibaldi
Size: 7 in.\18 cm

Fig. 4.17. This capybara tibia presents a typical example of split line cracking, a natural occurrence running longitudinally down the shaft of bones.

Fig. 4.18

Manatee
Rib Bone

Trichechus sp.
Pleistocene

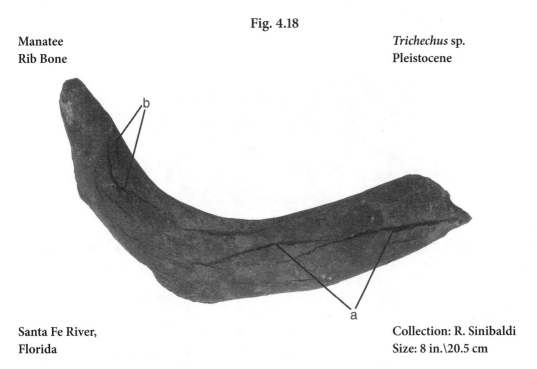

Santa Fe River,
Florida

Collection: R. Sinibaldi
Size: 8 in.\20.5 cm

Fig. 4.18. This manatee rib has some very deep split line cracks (a) and others that are very shallow (b).

Split line cracks may eventually split the bone into long slivers that may mimic trampling and various cultural modifications, including butchering, marrow processing, and tool making. Other forms of bone breakage are described in a discussion of pathological fossils and compression bites in chapter 5, and in the section on hydrological alterations and trampling in this chapter.[10]

Hydrological Alterations

The effects of various forms of water, known as hydrological effects, may alter bone in a variety of ways before, during, and after fossilization. These effects may be caused by ocean surf, river currents, polishing, or dissolution. The effects of ice are covered in the next section, atmospheric alterations. Hydrological effects are also great mimics of pathologies and cultural modification.

Ocean Surf

Fossils exposed in ocean deposits may be subject to currents or wave action that can tumble fossils. The effects of this tumbling can vary. Extreme tumbling may cause a polished effect on very dense bone (fig. 4.19); however, less dense material may shatter or completely deteriorate when exposed to wave or cur-

Fig. 4.19

Toe Bone   Undetermined species
                                                             Miocene

Venice Beach,   Collection: R. Sinibaldi
Florida   Size: 1.37 in.\3.5 cm

Fig. 4.19. This toe bone tumbled in the ocean surf for so long, it was polished smooth and is unidentifiable.

rent action (fig 4.20). Generally, ocean effects on fossils occur after fossilization, as most green (fresh) bone cannot withstand the impacts of surf or currents for very long. Ocean-deposited fossils may also be affected by worms and mollusks (discussed under biological alterations, this chapter).

River Currents/Polishing

Bones deposited in rivers may become polished. Polishing of fossils is common in rivers and may be caused in two ways. A specimen may tumble down a river slowly, for long periods of time and over great distances, eventually acquiring a polished surface. A stationary specimen may also be polished by fine sands and abrasives[11] continually washing over all or part of it (fig. 4.21). It is generally impossible to determine how a specimen came to be polished, by travel or by having abrasives travel over it. A fossil exposed to large items passing over it, or traveling too fast over larger items, may become chipped or fractured (fig. 4.22). Finally, items sitting on the bottom of a river may be stepped on inadvertently by people and animals, or, worse, have an anchor or heavy item tossed onto them. Items that have been tumbled, polished, chipped, or fractured may mimic various cultural modifications. See chapter 7 for specimens that were obviously polished by Paleo-Indians or later Native Americans.

Water Dissolution

Bones or fossils that sit in rivers or lakes may go through **water dissolution**. Water dissolution is similar to acid alterations as solvents in the water dissolve parts of the exposed bone (fig. 4.23). In many cases it is very difficult to tell

Fig. 4.20

Tapir
Partial Jaw

Tapirus veroensis
Pleistocene

Venice Beach,
Florida

Collection: R. Sinibaldi
Size: 4 in.\10.1 cm

Fig. 4.20. After eroding from a fossil layer, this tapir jaw could not withstand the pounding of the ocean surf, losing its front half and all the crowns of its teeth.

Fig. 4.21

Tapir
Upper Molar

Tapirus veronensis
Pleistocene

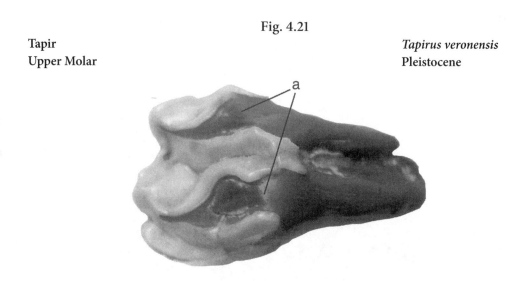

Rainbow River Springs,
Marion County, Florida

Collection: R. Sinibaldi
Size: 1.75 in.\4.5 cm

Fig. 4.21. This tapir tooth was lodged in a lime rock crevice with the river passing over the exposed side, slowly polishing away the enamel (a).

Fig. 4.22

Bone Fragments

Undetermined species
Pleistocene

Peace River,
DeSoto County, FL

Collection: R. Sinibaldi
Size: 5.7 in.\14.5 cm

Fig. 4.22. These bone fragments could not withstand tumbling down a river after eroding from a fossil layer.

Fig. 4.23

Mastodon
Lower Tusk

Mammut americanum
Pleistocene

Leisey Shell Pit,
Hillsborough County, FL

Collection: R. Sinibaldi
Size: 6 in.\15.3 cm

Fig. 4.23. This lower mastodon tusk displays classic water dissolution markings caused by acid in the water.

the difference between a specimen exposed to ground acids and one that went through a process of water dissolution. Water dissolution may mimic acid alterations, pathological infections, or cultural modifications.

Atmospheric Alterations

Atmospheric alterations can occur before a specimen is fossilized or after it is re-exposed. Alterations may include fading, delamination, and various weathering effects. If the remains of an animal are not buried immediately, atmospheric alterations may begin as soon as the bone is defleshed. Atmospheric alterations are not usually mistaken for other processes. Atmospheric alteration is sometimes referred to simply as weathering.

Fading

After a fossil has been subjected to many different processes, the specimen is often re-exposed at the earth's surface to the sun's UV rays, causing fading.[12] A full side of a specimen, or as little as a corner or bony process, may receive direct sunlight for the first time in thousands or millions of years. In a short time, months or maybe a year, the exposed section becomes faded or bleached by the sun. The remaining buried portion retains its original fossilized color. This process causes two-toned specimens (figs. 4.24–4.25). Note that a two-toned specimen should not be confused with a specimen in which the bone is one

Fig. 4.24

Drum Fish   *Pogonias cromis*
Mouth Plate   Pleistocene

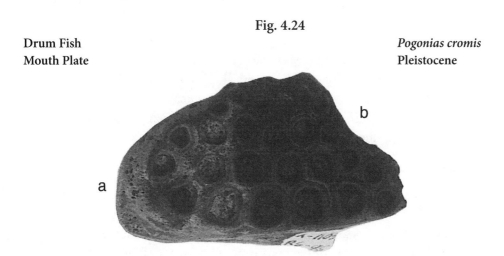

Apollo Beach,   Collection: R. Sinibaldi
Hillsborough County, FL   Size: 2.25 in.\5.7 cm

Fig. 4.24. This drum fish mouth plate at one time was half exposed to the sun (a), and half buried (b), creating a two-toned specimen attributed to fading, not chemical reactions (see figs. 4.15–4.16).

Fig. 4.25

Mammoth
Molar Tooth

Mammuthus species
Pleistocene

a

Peace River,
DeSoto County, FL

Collection: R. Sinibaldi
Size: 8.5 in.\21.5 cm

Fig. 4.25. This mammoth tooth had one corner eroding in a river bottom when the author found it. The exposed corner was still evident after preparation and years of display.

color and teeth are a different color or shade of color. That effect is caused by differential chemical reactions between the compounds in bones and teeth and the surrounding matrix (discussed in chemical alterations, this chapter; figs. 4.15–4.16). In addition, the exposed surfaces of specimens in river or lake bottoms may be infiltrated by tannic acids or other chemical compounds, causing a two-tone effect on the fossil.

Delamination

Delamination is a process that occurs before the specimen fossilizes. The outer layers of bone may peel away or delaminate as the result of exposure to sun, rain, and/or extreme hot and cold temperatures (fig. 4.26). Delamination will often occur only in the part of the bone exposed on the surface. The buried underside of the bone may receive enough protection from the elements to prevent delamination (fig. 4.27). After partial or extreme delamination, a bone may become buried and fossilized, preserving those effects (fig. 4.28). Subfossil or modern bones often immediately begin to delaminate when removed from their deposit site if not treated properly (fig. 4.29).

Fig. 4.26

Black Bear
Mandible

Ursus americanus
Late Pleistocene

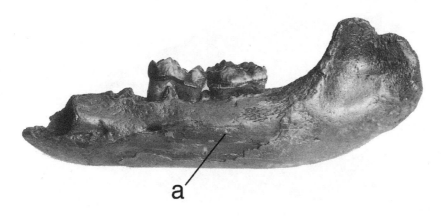

Withlacoochee River,
Florida

Collection: D. Letasi
Size: 5.2 in.\13.3 cm

Fig. 4.26. A large layer of the outer bone delaminated from the surface of this black bear jaw, exposing the surface to the elements (compare with fig. 4.27).

Fig. 4.27

Black Bear
Mandible

Ursus americanus
Late Pleistocene

Withlacoochee River,
Florida

Collection: D. Letasi
Size: 5.2 in.\13.3 cm

Fig. 4.27. This portion of the black bear jaw was probably stuck in the ground or facing down and displays no evidence of delamination (compare with fig. 4.26).

Fig. 4.28

**Bone Fragment
with Delamination**

Undetermined species
Pleistocene

Peace River,
DeSoto County, FL

Collection: R. Sinibaldi
Size: 3.75 in.\9.5 cm

Fig. 4.28. This bone fragment shows signs of severe delamination that occurred before the bone completely fossilized.

Fig. 4.29

**White-tailed Deer
Femur**

Odocoileus virginianus
Recent

Santa Fe River,
Florida

Collection: R. Sinibaldi
Size: 6.75 in.\17.3 cm

Fig. 4.29. This deer femur was not fully fossilized. Shortly after it was removed from a river deposit, the bone began to delaminate.

Weathering

The effects of freeze-thaw, nocturnal-diurnal, and hot-cold cycles may cause a bone to shatter. If initial exposure to the elements causes split line cracks, those cracks may fill with water. If the water freezes, the bone quickly splits or fragments. Turtle shells from the Badlands of South Dakota and Nebraska are notorious for being affected by this process (fig. 4.30). Weathering may occur before, during, or after fossilization. Any time the bone is exposed or close enough to the surface it may be affected by weather extremes. Teeth still in their jaws are often subject to the effects of freeze-thaw cycles. Teeth contain many natural nooks and crannies into which water can seep and then expand during a freeze. Teeth are composed of different elements that can also expand and contract at different rates, causing splitting and cracking during extreme weather conditions. It is a shame when exposed fossils are not collected before being destroyed by the effects of weathering; however, this is the case with multitudes of specimens in very remote areas.

Fig. 4.30

Tortoise
Shell or Carapace

Stylemys nebrascensis
Oligocene

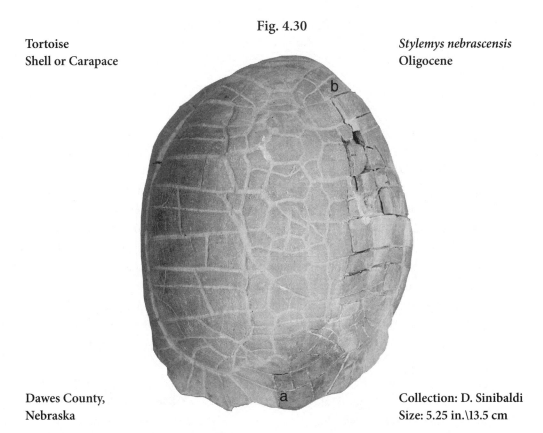

Dawes County,
Nebraska

Collection: D. Sinibaldi
Size: 5.25 in.\13.5 cm

Fig. 4.30. The edge of this tortoise shell from (a) to (b) was eroded by exposure to the weather. Had the carapace been left for another season of erosion and exposure, the entire shell would have fragmented beyond recovery.

CHAPTER 5

Pathologies in Fossil Bones

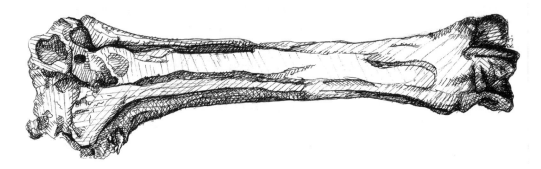

The scientist who pauses to examine every anomaly . . .
will seldom get significant work done.
Thomas S. Kuhn

Introduction

Specializing in the pathologies of fossilized bones (and teeth, covered in chapter 6) is becoming increasingly popular among both amateur and professional paleontologists. This once-overlooked field[1] is now an area of study in its own right.[2] In the past, pathological bones and teeth were treated as curios or oddities by the uninformed. Their scientific value is now fully recognized by all fossil enthusiasts. The study of pathological vertebrate fossils is often best accomplished through collaboration between a paleontologist and a medical scientist specializing in bone disorders.[3]

Pathological changes to the functional or structural morphology of a bone can be produced by disease, injury, stress, attack, or feeding. By definition, disease, injury, and stress can produce true pathological changes to bones. Attack marks that exhibit healing are also pathological. Feeding marks that occur after death, or attack marks that do not exhibit healing, are technically called pseudopathologies. Pseudopathologies are grouped with pathologies in this book; however, pseudopathologies can also be considered a type of biological alteration and could have been grouped with chapter 4 subject material. Pseudopathologies fall under the broader field of taphonomy, the study of death assemblages.

By understanding which marks belong on bones (covered in chapter 2), and which marks were caused by natural alterations (covered in chapter 4), one can begin to recognize markings that are truly unusual. Markings that do not normally appear on bones are generally indicative of a pathological effect (cultural modification of bone can also produce unusual markings and is discussed in chapter 7). By comparing fossil bones to those of modern animals with various known diseases or injuries, scientists have been able to diagnose similar diseases and injuries in prehistoric animals. Although inferential, many conclusions regarding pathological diseases or injuries in the paleontological record can generally be considered accurate when diagnosed by a professional with access to a validated database.

Feeding and attack scenarios, however, are far more speculative in nature. Without a "witness" to the incident, it is often difficult to determine which scavenger or predator made cut or bite marks in a particular bone. In rare instances, matching predator to prey is possible. For example, we know that alligators often attempt to bite and crush turtles. These attacks leave a very distinct tooth pattern on turtle shells; furthermore, if a turtle survives the attack, we know the shell heals in a certain way.

Scientists can also match tooth patterns from bite marks on a fossil bone to the jaw patterns of many possible fossil candidates from the same time period. Through a process of elimination, the possible attacker can often be narrowed down. In some rare instances, exact tooth patterns from a jaw will precisely match holes in a bone. In even rarer instances, a tooth or partial tooth will break off in the bone and fossilize together with the victimized bone. Feeding and attack scenarios all fall in the area of pseudopathology.

The range of pathologies identified in fossil bones is limited in this publication for several reasons: (1) pathological fossils are fairly rare, (2) the infective organisms and soft tissues involved in many pathological lesions do not fossilize, (3) some diseases produce superficially similar-looking lesions on bones, (4) similar-looking lesions often require expensive equipment (e.g., X-rays, CAT scans, a scanning electron microscope [SEM]) to diagnose the exact pathological cause, (5) it sometimes takes a bone histologist (someone who studies the microscopic differences in bones) to identify pathologies at the cellular level, (6) literature on pathological fossils (other than dinosaur material) is extremely rare at the amateur level, and (7) photographically, many bony lesions would appear indistinguishable without extreme magnification or special photographic preparation (microscopic slide pictures, X-ray pictures, etc.) to enhance presentation. Although microscopic pictures, CAT scans, and X-rays would be interesting, these are generally unavailable to non-specialists. Presenting and explaining those procedures here would, therefore, not enlighten most non-specialists on "what their fossils can tell them."

It is the intent of this chapter and chapter 6 to give the reader a broad knowledge of pathological fossils. Knowing and recognizing a pathological feature in general is the first step. As a result of the limited manner in which bone can respond to various stressors, more often than not it takes a professional to determine the exact cause of any specific pathological feature on a bone. Rothschild and Martin (1993) rightfully point out that "the study of paleopathology confirms the basically healthy nature of extinct organisms." Pathological fossils are relatively rare.

Ankylosis and Syndactyly

The unnatural fusion of bones is termed **ankylosis**. Ankylosis can occur between bones and joints for many reasons (fig. 5.1). Fusion can be caused by conditions such as traumatic injuries, infections, or developmental disturbances. **Osteoarthritis** does not lead to fusion or ankylosis. This is a common misconception of many amateurs who label almost all fused bones severe osteoarthritis. Osteoarthritis is discussed on page 163.

Syndactyly is the fusion of toes caused by developmental disturbances (fig. 5.2), contrasted to fusion caused by traumatic injuries (fig. 5.3); However, naturally occurring fusion of foot bones is also an evolutionary response in artiodactyl **cannon** bones. Cannon bones of **artiodactyls** are the fused 3rd and 4th

Fig. 5.1

Horse   *Equus* sp.
Fused Carpal Bones   Pleistocene

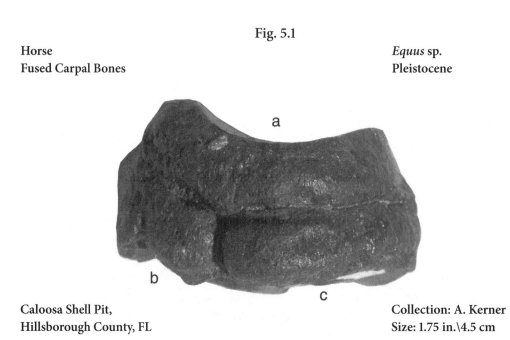

Caloosa Shell Pit,   Collection: A. Kerner
Hillsborough County, FL   Size: 1.75 in.\4.5 cm

Fig. 5.1. These three *Equus* carpal bones have fused together, a condition known as ankylosis. As this is an isolated find, the cause is unknown.

Fig. 5.2

Fused Cat Toe Bones

Undetermined species

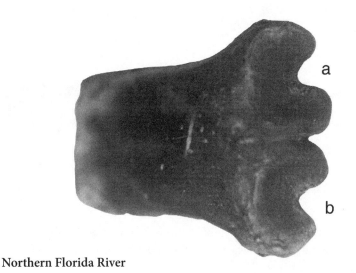

Northern Florida River

Collection: B. Fite
Size: 1.12 in.\2.9 cm

Fig. 5.2. This pair of developmentally fused toe bones is more than likely a congenital anomaly. Compare with figure 5.3, toe bones fused as a result of injury. It is uncertain whether this cat would have had two claws at the end of these fused toes, a single claw, or a set of two fused claws similar to the toe bones.

Fig. 5.3

Giant Armadillo
Fused Hoof Cores

Holmesina floridanus
Pliocene

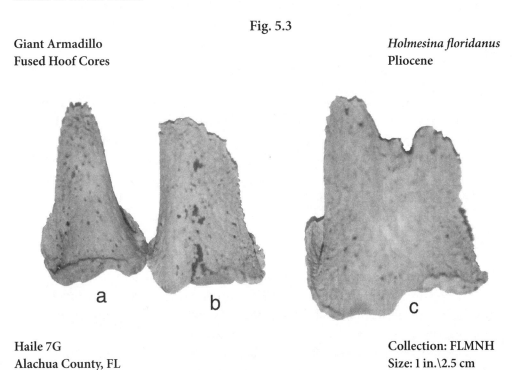

Haile 7G
Alachua County, FL

Collection: FLMNH
Size: 1 in.\2.5 cm

Fig. 5.3. Hoof cores (a) and (b) are typical of a giant armadillo. Hoof core (c) is a fused pair of hoof cores, believed caused by injury. It is unknown whether the adjacent toes were also fused.

Fig. 5.4

White-tailed Deer   *Odocoileus virginianus*
Cannon Bone   Pleistocene

Withlacoochee River,   Collection: R. Sinibaldi
Marion County, FL   Size: 7.5 in.\19 cm

Fig. 5.4. The cannon bones in most artiodactyls (even-hoofed mammals), such as this deer, are the naturally fused 3rd and 4th metatarsals or metacarpals of the foot. This condition is not pathological, but an evolutionary development.

metacarpals (front) or metatarsals (back) of the foot (fig. 5.4). The fusion that creates cannon bones is not a pathological feature. It is an evolutionary response, an adaptation that strengthens and stabilizes that area of the animal's foot.

Necrosis and Sequestrum

Bone **necrosis**, also referred to as bone death, occurs when a bone or area of the bone loses its blood supply. Fractures that disrupt the blood supply in the periosteum (outer layer) may result in dead bone. The healing process consists of removal of dead bone and replacement with new bone tissue once the blood supply is restored. Erosion of dead bone and deposition of new bone occur simultaneously and may result in a large swelling of fibrous new bone that will eventually be remodeled. Large areas of new tissue may resemble a tumor (fig. 5.5).

For necrosis to be evident on a fossilized bone, the animal must have survived the trauma or infection long enough for some healing to have taken place. Bone necrosis can be caused by a variety of injuries or afflictions, including infection (fig. 5.6), dislocation, fracture (fig. 5.7), injury to the surrounding soft tissue, vitamin deficiency, and some forms of carcinoma (cancer).

Sequestrum is a type of necrosis or bone death caused by infection. Islands of dead cortical bone result when pus within the marrow cavities cuts off blood supply. The sequestrum (plural, sequestra) is then surrounded by thickened, hard, vascularized bone (fig. 5.8).

Fig. 5.5

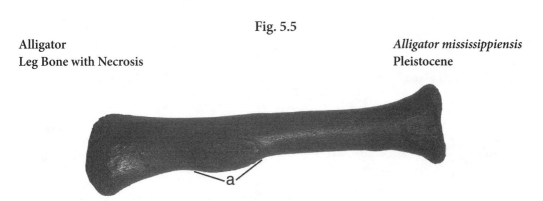

Alligator
Leg Bone with Necrosis

Alligator mississippiensis
Pleistocene

Santa Fe River,
Florida

Collection: J. Tatum
Size: 6.5 in.\16.5 cm

Fig. 5.5. This alligator leg bone has a large area of fibrous new bone (a) that resembles a tumor, probably the result of an infection in the surrounding tissue.

Fig. 5.6

Camel
Pathological Toe Bones

Hemiauchenia macrocephala
Pleistocene

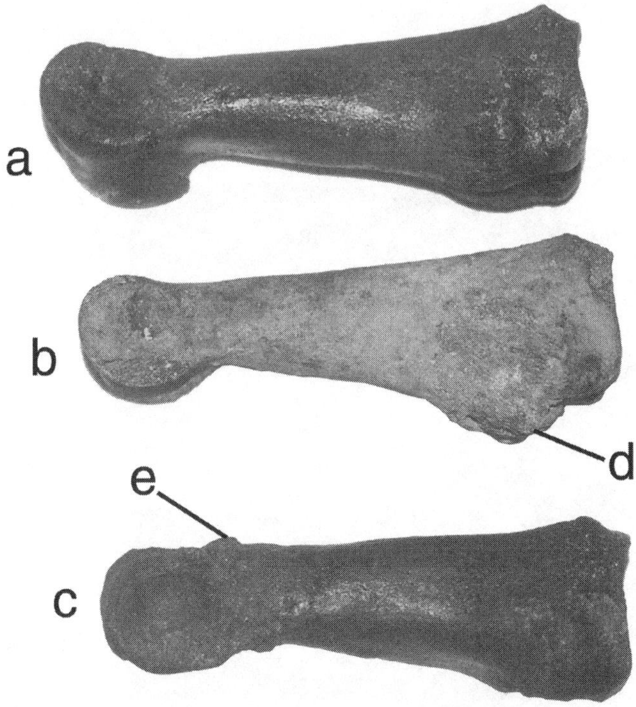

(a), (c) Withlacoochee River, FL
(b) Sarasota County Land Mine, FL

Collection: T. Sellari
Size: 3.75 in.\9.7 cm (a)

Fig. 5.6. Specimen (a) is a normal camel toe bone from the Pleistocene. Toe bone (b) exhibits a fibrous growth at location (d), as does toe bone (c) at location (e). These examples of bone necrosis were probably caused by infection or minor trauma.

Fig. 5.7

(a) Raccoon Leg Bone
with Healed Fracture
(b) Bird Tarsometarsus (foot)
with Healed Fracture

(a) *Procyon lotor*

(b) Undetermined species

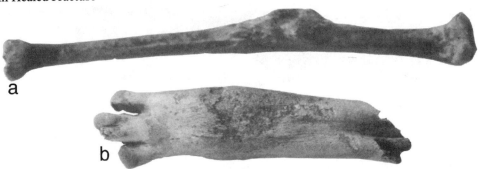

a

b

Charlotte County Shell Pit (b),
Florida

Collection: T. Sellari
Size: 1.62 in.\4 cm

Fig. 5.7. A raccoon leg bone (a) and bird bone (b) both exhibit healed breaks that developed areas of possible necrosis of the bone. It would take X-ray documentation to confirm this diagnosis.

Fig. 5.8

Partial Leg Bone
with Sequestrum

Undetermined species
Pleistocene

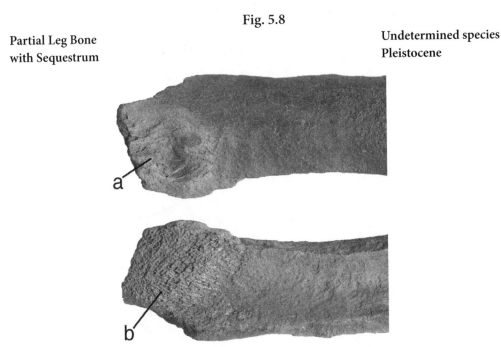

a

b

North Florida River

Collection: A. Welberry
Size: 6 in.\15 cm

Fig. 5.8. The broken shank of this unidentifiable leg bone exhibits an area of possible sequestrum. The inside view (b) displays the highly vascularized bone within the marrow cavity indicative of sequestrum. The outer view (a) also displays traces of the effect.

158

Osteitis

Osteitis is a term referring to inflammation of bone. Although many types of osteitis occur, two types occur most frequently: **osteoperiostitis** and **osteomyelitis**. Both types of osteitis occur as the result of infection or irritation of bone tissue caused by trauma, infection of the blood, or infection of the surrounding tissue. Generally, the causative agent cannot be determined in archaeological or paleontological materials.

Osteomyelitis involves an infection to the medulla area of the bone, the central marrow cavity (fig 5.9). This occurs when pus-producing bacteria enter through the skin of an infected wound adjacent to the bone or via the bloodstream from an infection (usually some type of *Staphylococcus* bacteria) elsewhere in the body. This infection generally destroys spongy bone in the medulla and may lead to cortical bone death (necrosis), sequestrum, and pus cavities, and in extreme cases the entire diaphysis may die. Osteomyelitis can be suspected when the diaphysis is unnaturally or asymmetrically swollen along its length (fig. 5.10). The metaphyseal region may also appear swollen, and external bone may be unnaturally textured, stringy, or layered (fig. 5.11) and show abnormalities (as opposed to a smooth surface in normal cortical bone).

Osteoperiostitis (periostitis in some literature) involves infection and/or inflammation of the surface morphology of cortical bone. Unhealed osteoperiostitis is characterized by lesions of bone that may appear more porous and

Fig. 5.9

Rib Bone
with Osteomyelitis

Undetermined species
Pleistocene

Withlacoochee River
Marion County, FL

Collection: A. Kerner
Size: 7 in.\18 cm

Fig. 5.9. This rib bone displays an infection in the medulla (a) termed osteomyelitis. As no trace appears on the outer bone, the infection may have been carried via the bloodstream.

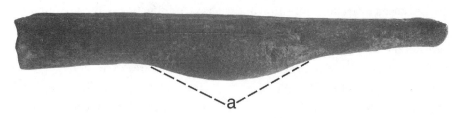

Fig. 5.10

White-tailed Deer Cannon Bone
with Osteomyelitis

Odocoileus virginianus
Pleistocene

Northern Florida River

Collection: A. Welberry
Size: 5.75 in.\14.5 cm

Fig. 5.10. This deer cannon bone exhibits a large area of infection. Osteomyelitis can be diagnosed when the diaphysis is unnaturally swollen along its length. This type of pathology can also represent a hematoma.

Fig. 5.11

Camel Toe Bone
with Osteitis

Hemiauchenia macrocephala
Pleistocene

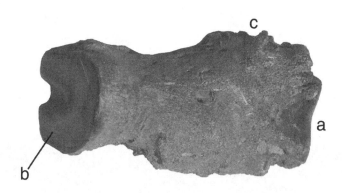

Suwannee River,
Florida

Collection: J. Tatum
Size: 3.25 in.\8.5 cm

Fig. 5.11. Although the articular surfaces at (a) and (b) are unaffected, the cortical bone of this camel toe shows signs of extreme osteomyelitis.

Fig. 5.12

Large Cat Metapodial Bone
with Osteoperiostitis

Undetermined species
Pleistocene

Withlacoochee River,
Florida

Collection: J. Tatum
Size: 3 in.\7.5 cm

Fig. 5.12. This metapodial bone from a large cat exhibits severe osteoperiostitis to the cortical bone at (c), but articular surfaces at (a) and (b) are unaffected. Note the porous nature of the bone at (c).

lamellar than unaffected bone (fig. 5.12). In cases of healed osteoperiostitis, the bone may be denser and less porous, but still retain distinct markings from the surrounding unafflicted bone (fig. 5.13). Osteoperiostitis may occur in conjunction with osteomyelitis and may need an expert diagnosis to determine the complete pathological history of the bone. Furthermore, osteoperiostitis may be primary or secondary. Primary osteoperiostitis affects smaller regions of bone, and the affected area appears to have additional layers adhered to the surface (fig. 5.14). Secondary osteoperiostitis arises in conjunction with other diseases (such as osteomyelitis). It may be extremely difficult in fossil specimens to differentiate between primary and secondary osteoperiostitis.

Bone Discontinuities

Among the first paleopathologies recognized by paleontologists at the turn of the century were bone discontinuities. Bone discontinuity leading to gross repair and deformation is fairly common in the paleontological record. Bone discontinuities occur most frequently as the result of traumatic injury; however, severe diseases and infections may also lead to fracturing and bone discontinuity. As the bone heals, formation of new bone tissue and **resorption** and reorganization of traumatized bone may lead to a noticeable deformation (fig. 5.15).

Fig. 5.13

Horse Cannon Bone
with Osteoperiostitis

Equus sp.
Pleistocene

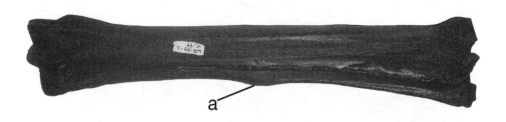

Withlacoochee River
Marion County, FL

Collection: A. Kerner
Size: 11 in.\27.5 cm

Fig. 5.13. This horse cannon bone exhibits a healed area of osteoperiostitis (a). Modern wild horses often display similar afflictions from running in herds and being kicked in the shins. This wound could also represent a hematoma.

Fig. 5.14

Bison Cannon Bone
with Osteoperiostitis

Bison antiquus
Pleistocene

Withlacoochee River,
Florida

Collection: T. Sellari
Size: 12.8 in.\32 cm

Fig. 5.14. The severe osteoperiostitis at surface location (a) on this bison cannon bone is difficult to attribute to primary or secondary osteoperiostitis and might also be attributed to a tumor.

Fig. 5.15

Proboscidean Rib Bone
with Discontinuity

Undetermined species
Pleistocene

La Belle Highway Pit,
Hendry County, FL

Collection: FLMNH
Size: 9 in.\23 cm

Fig. 5.15. The proximal end of this proboscidean rib bone was broken and separated from the remainder of the rib. End (a) would articulate with a vertebra, and site (b) displays traumatized bone in the process of being resorbed and reorganized. Compare with figure 5.16, another view of this specimen.

In the wild, spontaneous repair seldom leaves a smooth healed surface, similar to repairs of human or domesticated animal bones by doctors or veterinarians; further, lack of treatment often leads to infection (fig. 5.16), improper bone placement, and other secondary pathological features (fig. 5.17). Many times, evidence of pathological effects of bone discontinuities and traumatic fractures can lead a paleontologist to form a hypothetical scenario of progression of the pathologies present in a specimen. In the popular literature, a scientist will usually have these scenarios printed in *italics* to signify a hypothetical situation.

Arthritis

Arthritis occurs when the cartilage of a joint cannot repair itself fast enough to keep pace with the rate of deterioration. Many types of arthritis can be found in the paleontological record; however, only a few may be recognized by the nonspecialist.[4] Among these are spondyloarthropathy, spondylosis deformans, **osteoarthritis,** and general erosive types of arthritis. It may be extremely difficult to determine the type of arthritis a fossil is displaying if the specimen is

Fig. 5.16

Proboscidean Rib Bone
with Discontinuity

Undetermined species
Pleistocene

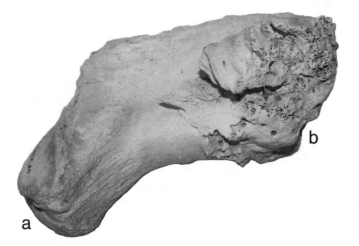

La Belle Highway Pit,
Hendry County, FL

Collection: FLMNH
Size: 9 in.\23 cm

Fig. 5.16. A second view of the pathological rib bone shown in figure 5.15 reveals signs of infection and proliferation of additional bone. Note the lighter color of the specimen; this picture was shot in the museum after the bone had completely dried out. The other end of the rib bone was not recovered but would presumably have a similar pathological feature.

Fig. 5.17

Camel Cannon Bone
with Discontinuity

Hemiauchenia macrocephala
Pleistocene

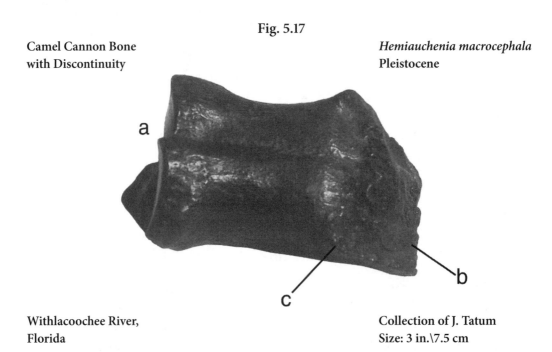

Withlacoochee River,
Florida

Collection of J. Tatum
Size: 3 in.\7.5 cm

Fig. 5.17. This camel cannon bone has an intact proximal articular surface at (a). The bone broke at (b), but the animal survived long enough to wear the bone smooth at (b) and develop some lipping at (c).

Fig. 5.18

Horse Tibia
with Arthritis

Equus sp.
Pleistocene

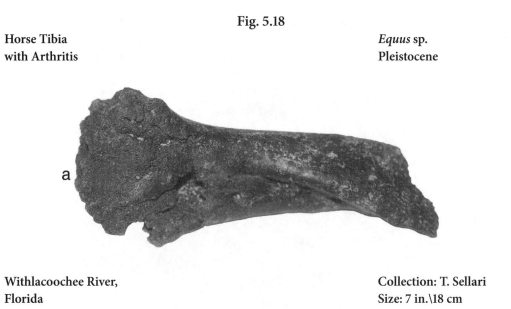

Withlacoochee River,
Florida

Collection: T. Sellari
Size: 7 in.\18 cm

Fig. 5.18. Note the porous surface at the proximal end (a) of this horse tibia. Lack of adjoining bones makes it difficult to attribute this lesion to any particular type of arthritis.

partial or an isolated find. The following section describes some criteria the nonspecialist can use to assist in correctly identifying arthritic pathologies in specimens. Rheumatoid arthritis is not known outside the human record.[5]

Erosive types of arthritis resorb bone. Lesions form at the joint or cartilage margins in erosive types of arthritis (fig. 5.18). Over a long period of time the joint may become porotic, appearing porous on the surface (fig. 5.19). Bone remodeling at the joints may lead to ankylosis or fusing (fig. 5.20). Erosive types of arthritis rarely affect the vertebral column (see spondylosis deformans if a vertebral specimen has osteophytes or lesions, page 171).

Osteoarthritis

Osteoarthritis is generally caused by injury or trauma to the joint cartilage and surrounding bone that has affected normal joint stability and function.[6] Osteoarthritis is usually a type of **pauciarticular arthritis**. Pauciarticular arthritis means that five or fewer joints are affected where joint trauma or destabilization has occurred. Osteoarthritis causes morphological changes in the afflicted joint that may include alteration of the joint surface (fig. 5.21), outgrowths, spicules, or osteophytes at the perimeter of the joint (figs. 5.22–5.23), and polished or grooved surfaces at the joint (eburnation), as may any form of severe arthritis (fig. 5.24). Ankylosis of the joints is *not* a feature of osteoarthritis.

Fig. 5.19

Proboscidean Vertebra
with Arthritis

Undetermined species
Pleistocene

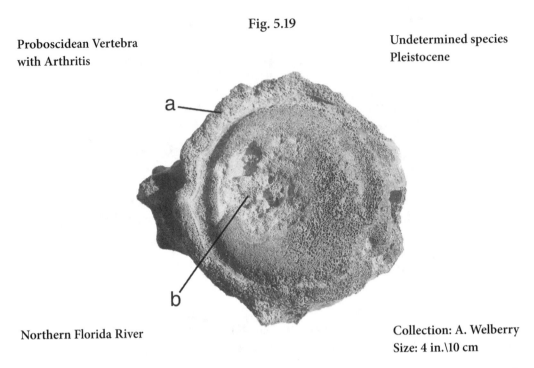

Northern Florida River

Collection: A. Welberry
Size: 4 in.\10 cm

Fig. 5.19. Note the proliferation of bone at the joint margins (a) of this vertebra. The joint surface (b) became porotic as bone was resorbed and redeposited at the margins of the joint. However, this joint surface may be the result of taphonomic processes.

Fig. 5.20

Horse Cannon Bone
with Arthritis and Fused Splint

Equus sp.
Pleistocene

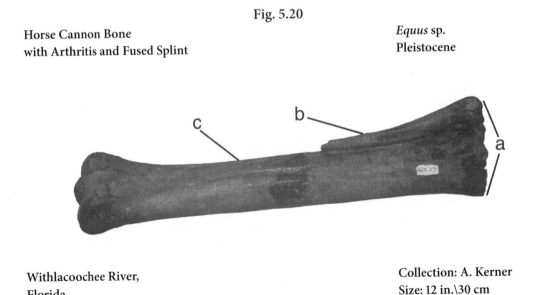

Withlacoochee River,
Florida

Collection: A. Kerner
Size: 12 in.\30 cm

Fig. 5.20. Note the bony lesions forming at the joint surface (a) of this horse cannon bone. The splint (b), usually a separate bone, has fused to the cannon bone (c).

Fig. 5.21

**Bison Cannon Bone
with Arthritis**

Bison sp.
Pleistocene

Missouri River,
Kansas

Collection: T. Sellari
Size: 8.25 in.\21 cm

Fig. 5.21. The joint surfaces (a) of this bison cannon bone have been severely altered as the result of an arthritic condition.

Fig. 5.22

**Horse Cannon Bone
with Arthritis**

Equus sp.
Pleistocene

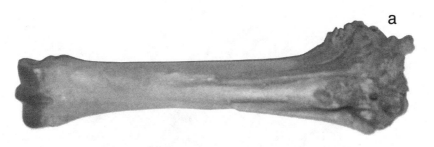

Missouri River,
Kansas

Collection: T. Sellari
Size: 14 in.\35 cm

Fig. 5.22. Note the outgrowths and osteophytes on the proximal end (a) of this horse cannon bone. The distal end exhibits no damage or infliction.

Fig. 5.23

White-tailed Deer Toe Bones
with Osteophytes (b)

Odocoileus virginianus
Pleistocene

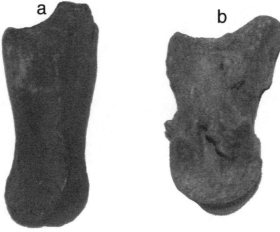

Santa Fe River,
Florida

Collection: T. Sellari
Size: 1.25 in.\3 cm (a)

Fig. 5.23. Compare the deer toe bone from a healthy animal (a) to a toe bone (b) exhibiting spicules on the bone surface.

Fig. 5.24

Bison Tibia
with Grooved Joint Surfaces

Bison sp.
Pleistocene

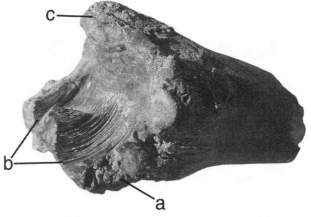

Venice Beach,
Florida

Collection: T. Sellari
Size: 4.5 in.\11.5 cm

Fig. 5.24. The joint margins of the distal end of this bison tibia exhibit some lipping and osteophytes at (a) and (c). The joint surface (b) exhibits extreme grooving or scoring.

Fig. 5.25

Carpal Bone
with Degenerative Arthropathy

Undetermined species
Pleistocene

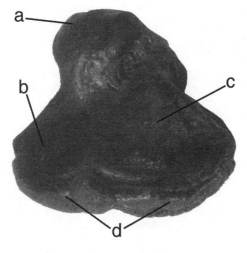

Peace River,
DeSoto County, FL

Collection: R. Sinibaldi
Size: 1.75 in.\4.5 cm

Fig. 5.25. This carpal bone has intact articular surfaces at (a), (b), and (c); however, close inspection of (d) reveals lipping with additional bony proliferation.

Aging in the joints is a rare cause of osteoarthritis and is proportional to the age of the animal. Failure of the cartilage of the joints is the primary condition; however, this condition generally does not fossilize and is rarely found in the paleontological or archaeological records. Secondary changes occur at the next stage and affect the bone tissue. These secondary effects of osteoarthritis are not common fossil finds as far as paleopathologies are concerned.

The result of long-term osteoarthritis is a proliferation of bony tissue around the joint surface that remains smooth as a result of joint wear. This **interarticular** effect may take close inspection to detect (fig. 5.25); however, secondary effects may be very obvious and are commonly referred to as **lipping** (figs. 5.26–5.27). The most common secondary effect is the proliferation of bony lesions, called osteophytes (see next section), at the **periarticular** edges of the joints.

Osteoarthritis is often lumped with other forms of arthritis by amateurs. Osteoarthritis is usually considered age-related "wear and tear" on the bone. Many other types of arthritis occur, some infective in nature (see preceding and following sections).

Fig. 5.26

Camel Vertebra
with Severe Lipping

Paleolama mirifica
Pleistocene

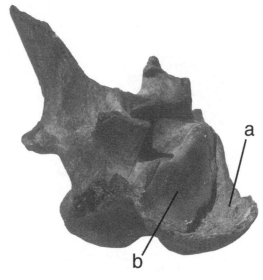

Collection: B. Fite
Size: 3.5 in.\8.5 cm

Fig. 5.26. The lipping (a) from spondyloarthropathy is obvious on this camel vertebra. Note that the vertebral endplate (b) is still smooth.

Fig. 5.27

Sloth Phalanx Joints
Proximal Phalanx (a)
with Degenerative Arthropathy (b)

Megalonyx sp.
Pleistocene

 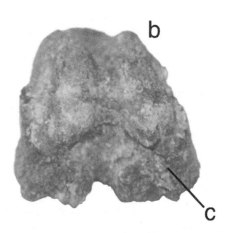

(a) Withlacoochee River, FL
(b) Leisey Shell Pit, FL

Collection: T. Sellari
Size: 2.75 in.\6.5 cm (a)

Fig. 5.27. The lipping of phalanx (b) at site (c) is obvious when compared with a healthy sloth phalanx (a).

Osteophytes, Spondylosis Deformans, Spondyloarthropathy, and Herniated Disks

Osteophytes are often referred to as bone spurs or bone spicules. Any benign bone growths, including osteophytes, projecting outward from a bony surface may also be termed exostoses. They most commonly occur in the vertebrae of aging animals. Osteophytes develop around the perimeter of the outer body of vertebrae. The process of developing osteophytes may be referred to as osteophytosis in the technical literature, or as lipping in layman's terms (fig. 5.28).

Osteophytes may occur on bones other than vertebrae (figs. 5.29–5.30). When they do develop on human vertebrae they are termed **spondylosis deformans**; however, since this affliction has not been definitively diagnosed in other animals, prehistoric animal fossils exhibiting the condition are simply termed pathological anomalies(figs. 5.31–5.33). Osteoarthritis is limited to diarthrodial joints, which the disk spaces of the spine are not. Technically, only if the zygapophyses bear osteophytes can the vertebrae be considered osteoarthritic; if fusion has occurred at these locations of the vertebrae, the specimen can be suspected of having **spondyloarthropathy** (figs. 5.34–5.36). Spondyloarthropathy is an inflammatory form of arthritis characterized by proliferation of reactive

Fig. 5.28

Sloth Vertebra
with Osteophytes

Undetermined species
Pleistocene

Withlacoochee River,
Marion County, FL

Collection: R. Sinibaldi
Size: 2.75 in.\6.5 cm

Fig. 5.28. This sloth vertebra displays osteophytes and lipping at (a), and a large exostosis at (b) on the outer body of the centrum. The specimen is broken at (c) and only partial.

Fig. 5.29

**Large Cat Toe Bone
with Exostosis**

**Undetermined species
Pleistocene**

Withlacoochee River,
Marion County, FL

Collection: T. Sellari
Size: 2.5 in.\6 cm

Fig. 5.29. The underside of this large cat toe bone exhibits a large exostosis. Many amateurs incorrectly refer to these protrusions as osteophytes or "bone spurs."

Fig. 5.30

**Fish Spines
with Exostoses**

**Undetermined species
Late Pleistocene**

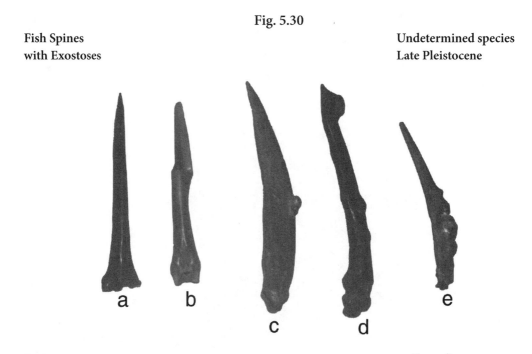

Santa Fe River,
Florida

Collection: A. Kerner
Size: 2.5 in.\6 cm (d)

Fig. 5.30. Fish spine (a) displays no pathological features, while spine (b) exhibits a healed fracture. Spines (c) and (d) exhibit exostoses, and (e), possible infectious lesions.

Fig. 5.31

Mammoth Vertebra
with Osteophytes and Lipping

Mammuthus sp.
Pleistocene

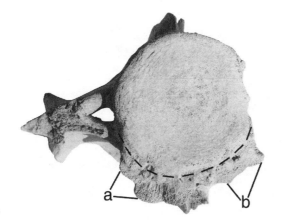

Aucilla River,
Florida

Collection: A. Welberry
Size: 5.5 in.\14 cm

Fig. 5.31. This mammoth vertebra has developed extreme osteophytes on the left side of the centrum at (a) and (b). The dotted line clarifies extra bone material that has proliferated on that side of the vertebral body.

Fig. 5.32

Whale Vertebra
with Osteophytes

Undetermined species
Miocene/early Pliocene

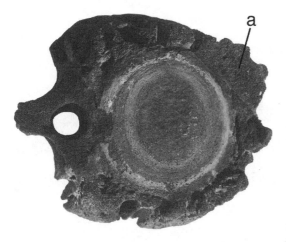

Collection: B. Fite
Size: 6 in.\15 cm

Fig. 5.32. This large whale vertebra has developed severe osteophytes around the entire centrum all the way up to the vertebral spike. A large portion of the extra bone growth has broken off the vertebra at (a).

Fig. 5.33

Camel Vertebra
with Osteophytes and Lipping

Undetermined species
Pleistocene

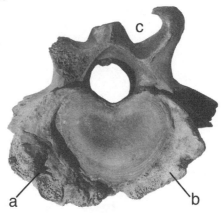

Polk County Phosphate Mine,
Florida

Collection: T. Sellari
Size: 3 in.\7.5 cm

Fig. 5.33. Although the centrum of this vertebra displays extreme osteophytes and lipping at (a) and (b), the zygapophyses (c) exhibit no osteophytes. This condition is considered spondylosis deformans.

Fig. 5.34

Seven Horse Vertebrae
with Spondyloarthropathy

Equus sp.
Pleistocene

Missouri River,
Kansas

Collection: T. Sellari
Size: 16.5 in.\41 cm

Fig. 5.34. These seven horse vertebrae have completely fused, a condition termed spondyloarthropathy. Note that the zygapophyses are almost totally indistinguishable from each other.

Fig. 5.35

Five Vertebrae
with Spondyloarthropathy

Undetermined species
Pleistocene

Collection: T. Sellari
Size: 6 in.\15 cm

Fig. 5.35. These five vertebrae have fused, a condition termed spondyloarthropathy. Note the fusion of the zygapophyses.

Fig. 5.36

Two Fused Deer Vertebrae
with Spondyloarthropathy

Odocoileus virginianus
Pleistocene

Santa Fe River,
Alachua County, FL

Collection: T. Sellari
Size: 3.8 in.\9.5 cm

Fig. 5.36. These two deer vertebrae have completely fused. Little evidence exists of the original morphology of the two bones.

Fig. 5.37

Dolphin Vertebra
with Herniated Disk

Undetermined species
Pliocene–Miocene

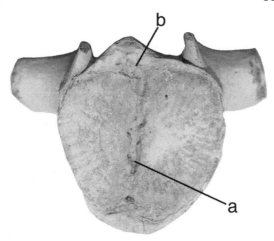

Polk County Phosphate Mine,
Florida

Collection: T. Sellari
Size: 4.25 in.\11 cm

Fig. 5.37. This dolphin vertebra exhibits the scars of a herniated disk at (a). An exit scar (b) is present at the point where the disk protruded from the perimeter of the vertebral body.

bone formation at sites of tendon, ligament, and capsule insertions (Rothschild and Martin 1993).

Vertebrae exhibiting spondylosis deformans may also bear evidence of a herniated disk. The intervertebral disk may **herniate** (extrude) from the perimeter of the vertebral body, leaving an exit scar (fig. 5.37). The cartilage may also herniate directly into the vertebral body, leaving a depression or erosive lesion in the endplate of the vertebral body, usually close to the center (fig. 5.38). These are referred to technically as Schmorl's nodes in the literature.

Pathological Fractures

Unusual stress or trauma to a bone may cause it to fracture. Bones fracture because the force of the stress or trauma is greater than the bone's ability to respond. All bones have evolved in a way to best respond to the most common stresses they will receive in life; however, stresses or trauma are often either too great, or occur at an unusual angle for the bone to cope with the strain. Traumatic injury can produce various types of injuries or fractures. Compression, torsion (twisting), bending, and shearing are the most common types of fractures seen in wild animals. Rothschild and Martin (1993) report that fractures

Fig. 5.38

Giant Ground Sloth Vertebra
with Herniated Disk

Eremotherium sp.
Pleistocene

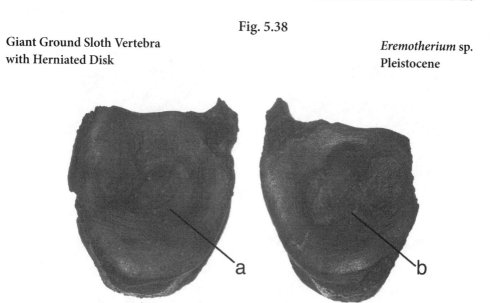

Construction Site,
Pinellas County, FL

Collection: B. Evensen
Size: 5 in.\13 cm

Fig. 5.38. The cartilage of this herniated disk drove directly into the vertebral body, leaving a large depression (a). The disks on both sides of this sloth vertebra were herniated into the centrum (b).

may be caused by force-related factors, including magnitude, direction, loading rate, and duration. The bone's density, fatigue strength, resilience, and elasticity are the factors that determine the bone's susceptibility to fracture (Rothschild and Martin, 1993).

Compression fractures may be caused by a severe blow to the bone, or by a bite by a predator. The assault compresses the bone and creates a depression-type fracture. Many times a bite is severe enough to penetrate the outer bone to the inner bone cavity. The force of the impact will radiate from a central point, leaving a circular scar that may often be larger on the opposite side of the initial impact. Healed bones may leave a large scar opposite the impact and a small depression on the contact side of the bone. Alligator bite marks on turtle shell often exhibit these features (fig. 5.39). Many times, severe bites or blows will be fatal and show no signs of healing. These fatal traumas are technically termed pseudopathologies.

Torsion fractures, also referred to as twisting or spiral fractures, occur when a long bone is twisted or rotated unnaturally along its long axis. Generally, the break will be longer on one side than on the other. A common feature of a spiral fracture is a point formed by the ends of the broken bone. Spiral fracturing of bone is an extremely common occurrence postmortem (after death); therefore,

Fig. 5.39

Turtle Shell Fragment
with Compression Bite

Undetermined species
Pleistocene

Withlacoochee River,
Florida

Collection: J. Tatum
Size: 3.5 in.\8.5 cm

Fig. 5.39. The small depression (a) on the outer surface of this turtle shell is most likely a compression bite mark from an alligator. The compression bite radiated outward, leaving a larger scar on the inner surface of the shell (b). The large scarring and proliferation of bone indicate the turtle survived this attack and healed.

Fig. 5.40

White-tailed Deer Radius
with Spiral Fracture

Odocoileus virginianus
Pleistocene

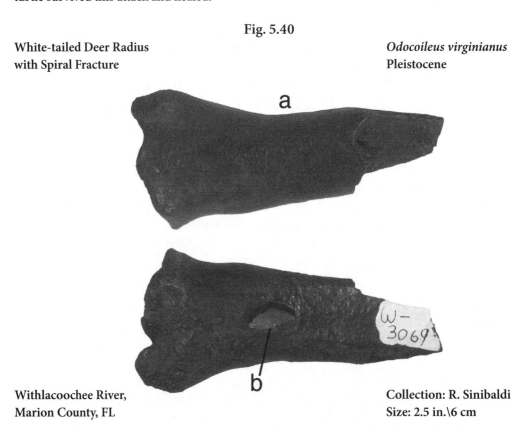

Withlacoochee River,
Marion County, FL

Collection: R. Sinibaldi
Size: 2.5 in.\6 cm

Fig. 5.40. This fractured deer radius, view (a), was caused by a compression bite, view (b), that broke the bone. This specimen is not pathological in that no healing is evident.

Fig. 5.41

White-tailed Deer Radius
with Healed Spiral Fracture

Odocoileus virginianus
Pleistocene

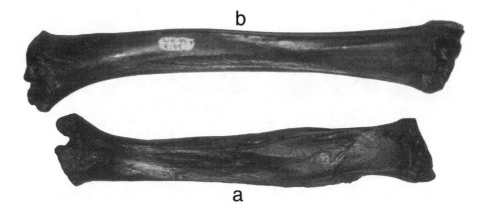

Withlacoochee River,
Florida

Collection: A. Kerner
Size: 6.5 in.\16 cm (b)

Fig. 5.41. Compare specimen (a), a deer radius with a healed fracture, possibly spiral, to the form of specimen (b), from a healthy deer. The bone became misaligned during the healing process.

if no healing scars are present, it is very difficult to determine the time and cause of a spiral fracture (fig. 5.40). In general it takes healing or proliferation of new bone in the form of a callus approximately three weeks to occur. Rothschild and Martin (1993) report that it would be difficult to recognize healing in a fossilized bone if the animal died within three weeks of a bone fracture. A bone may have been broken during an attack, or after death as a result of trampling, human alteration, or an animal's attempt to access the marrow. Animals that survive after sustaining a spiral fracture to a long bone will show some sign of healing, such as bone proliferation and deposition (fig. 5.41). Bone that breaks the skin, termed a compound fracture, may become infected (figs. 5.42–5.44). A displaced fracture may show unusual wear or bone proliferation between the two separated surfaces (figs. 5.45–5.46).

Bending fractures (sometimes referred to as greenstick fractures) often occur when an animal falls from a great distance. In a long bone, the bone under the stress will "give" up to a point, but past that point it will snap. Young animals have flexible bones that may break only partially. In older animals, more rigid bones may pop out a wedge-shaped piece of bone during a bending fracture. Once again, one must be careful to determine whether a fracture occurred postmortem (if no signs of healing or scarring are present), or the animal survived

Fig. 5.42

White-tailed Deer Cannon Bone
with Healed Spiral Fracture
and Compression Bite Marks

Odocoileus virginianus
Pleistocene

Withlacoochee River,
Florida

Collection: A. Welberry
Size: 7 in.\17.5 cm

Fig. 5.42. This deer cannon bone, a foot bone, exhibits a healed fracture at (a). This specimen also displays some postmortem compression bite marks at (b) and (c). The proximal end is missing at (d) and also exhibits compression bite marks.

Fig. 5.43

Camel Toe Bone
with Healed Fracture
and Evidence of Infection

Undetermined species
Pleistocene

Withlacoochee River,
Marion County, FL

Collection: T. Sellari
Size: 3.5 in.\8.5 cm

Fig. 5.43. This camel toe bone displays a healed fracture that may have broken the skin, leading to severe infection in the area. The toe did not heal straight, as evidenced by comparing the angles of the distal end (a) to those of the proximal end (b).

Fig. 5.44

Dire Wolf Metapodial Bone
with Healed Fracture

Canis dirus
Pleistocene

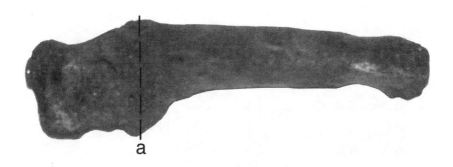

Santa Fe River,
Florida

Collection: T. Sellari
Size: 3.7 in.\9 cm

Fig. 5.44. This dire wolf metapodial may have sustained a compound fracture at site (a). Infection would have led to the additional bone proliferation.

Fig. 5.45

Frog Limb Bone
with Displaced Fracture

Anura, indet.
Pleistocene

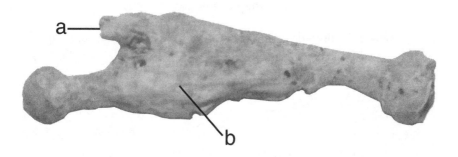

Haile Pit XXB
Alachua County, FL

Collection: FLMNH
Size: 1.25 in.\3 cm

Fig. 5.45. This limb bone broke and healed in a displaced position. End (a) is evident, but end (b) is buried under a proliferation of bone. With the bone healed in this state, the limb would have been considerably shorter than normal.

Fig. 5.46

Alligator
Fused Tibia and Fibula

Alligator mississippiensis
Pleistocene

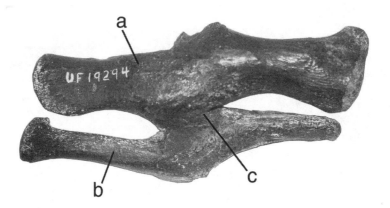

Steinhatchee River,
Dixie County, FL

Collection: FLMNH
Size: 4.5 in.\11 cm

Fig. 5.46. This alligator broke its tibia (a) and its fibula (b). Bone proliferated sufficiently to fuse both bones together at (c) during the healing process.

the trauma. Shearing fractures are caused by opposing forces across a bone; they are, however, indistinguishable from bending fractures in the fossil record.

Pseudopathologies

It is extremely difficult to determine whether marks on a bone were caused by feeding or attack. If an animal survived an attack, some healing will have taken place, leaving distinctive scarring, and marks may be considered pathological. If an animal died in an attack, however, the traces left on the bone may be no different from marks left by scavengers on an already dead carcass; therefore, without an eyewitness to the event, bite marks left on a fossilized bone are referred to as feeding marks. Furthermore, if no healing has taken place, these marks are referred to as pseudopathological (false pathologies).

Several types of feeding marks may be left on bones that fossilize, leaving distinct evidence as a record of their history. In addition to these types of marks, the possibility always exists of cultural modification (covered in chapter 7). The most common types of feeding marks left on fossilized bones are gnawing marks, carnivore and scavenger bite marks, and shark feeding marks.

Gnawing Marks

Rodents are notorious for gnawing on bones and antlers (figs. 5.47–5.48). Bones will often exhibit extensive gnawing, with multiple sets of parallel markings made by front incisors (figs. 5.49–5.50). Rodents gnaw on bones and antlers both for the nutritional value and to keep their incisors sharp and at an appropriate length. Literature also reports that it is not uncommon for larger artiodactyls (e.g., deer, camel, bison) to gnaw on bones;[7] these animals would leave much larger marks and often only single sets of parallel teeth marks (fig. 5.51).

Dogs, cats, bears, and raccoons are also known to leave various types of bite marks on bones for differing reasons (e.g., wolves gnaw on bones, cats eat the flesh off bones, leaving marks). Some larger animals often compress and fracture the bones they bite upon (fig. 5.52); therefore, broken bones with larger gnawing or bite marks may be indicative of larger carnivores or omnivores that both bite/gnaw the bone and break it to get at the nutritious marrow inside.[8] These gnawed, bitten, and broken bones are often great mimics of cultural modification and butchering. It may be noted here that larger bones are often

Fig. 5.47

Bone Fragment
with Rodent Gnaw Marks

Undetermined species
Pleistocene

Peace River,
DeSoto County, FL

Collection: R. Sinibaldi
Size: 2 in.\5 cm

Fig. 5.47. This small bone fragment provides an excellent example of gnaw marks. The gnaw marks overlap so much that their parallel nature has been somewhat obliterated.

Fig. 5.48

White-tailed Deer Cannon Bone
with Rodent Gnaw Marks

Odocoileus virginianus
Late Pleistocene

Rainbow River,
Marion County, FL

Collection: M. & S. Searle
Size: 4 in.\10 cm

Fig. 5.48. This deer cannon bone has been completely gnawed by rodents, rendering it almost unidentifiable.

Fig. 5.49

Opposum Jaw
with Rodent Gnaw Marks

Didelphis virginiana
Pleistocene

Santa Fe River,
Florida

Collection: T. Sellari
Size: 2.75 in.\6.5 cm

Fig. 5.49. Note the parallel sets of gnawing marks on this opposum jaw at (a) and (b). Small, closely set parallel grooves are a telltale sign of rodent gnawing.

Fig. 5.50

Opossum Jaw
with Rodent Gnaw Marks

Didelphis virginiana
Pleistocene

Northern Florida River

Collection: P. Lien
Size: 3.5 in.\8.5 cm

Fig. 5.50. This opossum jaw is covered with rodent gnaw marks. The multiple groupings of double parallel grooves at (a) are excellent examples of the damage inflicted by the two front incisors of a rodent.

Fig. 5.51

Gnawed Horse Limb
From a *Felis concolor* Den

Equus sp.
Holocene

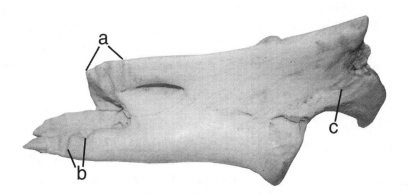

Honduras

Collection: FLMNH
Size: 8.5 in.\21.5 cm

Fig. 5.51. This horse limb bone has been gnawed in half by a cougar. Note the large grooves at (a), (b), and (c), and compare with rodent gnawing marks in figures 5.47–5.50.

Fig. 5.52

Bone Fragment
with Carnivore Gnaw Marks

Undetermined species
Pleistocene

Peace River,
DeSoto County, FL

Collection: R. Sinibaldi
Size: 4.25 in.\11 cm

Fig. 5.52. Note the deep gnawing or bite marks on this unidentified bone fragment. They are relatively large and do not resemble the small parallel gnaw marks of rodents (figs. 5.47–5.50).

found without their articular end processes. The thin articular cortex bone on the end, which is generally softer than the rest of the bone, is often destroyed by animal gnawing, river transport, trampling, or other natural processes. Once the end is destroyed, the underlying soft spongy bone is exposed and quickly destroyed. This leaves one with a long bone missing one or both ends. Generally, the proximal end is larger and softer than the distal end of long bones and is the first to be damaged; therefore, many long bones are missing only their proximal ends.[9]

Compression Bite Marks

Compression bite marks often penetrate the outer layer of the bone (or shell of a turtle) and leave distinct evidence of their occurrence. As with all other components of feeding and attack with no evidence of healing, it is problematic at best to determine whether the bite caused death (attack) or was left postmortem (feeding or scavenging after death) (fig. 5.53). If the bone doesn't fracture from a bite, a small hole on the outside of the cone or shell, and a larger hole on the inside of the bone, will be present in a compression bite (fig. 5.54). The configuration of these holes appears similar to that of a hole caused by a BB going through a piece of glass.

Fig. 5.53

Partial Horse Femur
with Compression Bite Marks

Equus sp.
Pleistocene

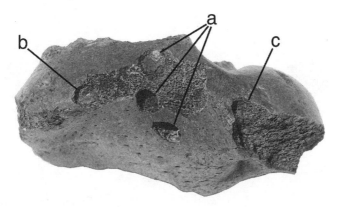

Peace River,
DeSoto County, FL

Collection: R. Sinibaldi
Size: 4.8 in.\9.5 cm

Fig. 5.53. The compression bite marks (a) form a semicircular pattern and probably represent a single bite on the head of this horse femur. Additional compression bites can be seen at (b) and (c). This specimen represents only one half of the femur head.

Fig. 5.54

Turtle Shell
with Compression Bite Marks

Undetermined species
Pleistocene

Withlacoochee River,
Florida

Collection: T. Sellari
Size: 2 in.\5 cm

Fig. 5.54. This turtle shell fragment exhibits two bite marks, a small one at (a), and a larger one at (b). The compression bite at (b) was severe enough to leave a larger scar on the inside of the shell at (c). This shell has fragmented in an unusual pattern, not along the suture lines, which would be typical. Bone proliferation at the bite mark sites possibly strengthened the bone along those sutures.

Fig. 5.55

Camel Toe Bone
with Compression Bite Mark

Hemiauchenia macrocephala
Pleistocene

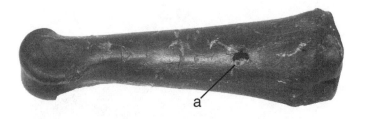

Charlotte County,
Florida

Collection: T. Sellari
Size: 4 in.\10 cm

Fig. 5.55. This camel toe bone exhibits a clear compression bite mark at (a). Additional markings on the toe bone may be from teeth, or from natural alterations during or after deposit (see chapter 4).

Bones of all sizes may exhibit compression bite marks of various sizes (figs. 5.55–5.56). Using current analogues may help to determine which predator or scavenger caused the feeding marks. As an example, turtles are commonly attacked by alligators, and these attacks leave distinctive traces (fig. 5.54). Deer and other herbivores are common prey for various predators. The source of feeding and attack marks can be tentatively identified by attempting to match bite patterns to upper or lower jaws of potential candidates from the same time period (figs. 5.57–5.58); however, one must be careful when developing hypothetical prehistoric scenarios for "unwitnessed" events.

Holes that look like bite marks are sometimes found on fish mouth plates (fig. 5.59); these are believed to be injuries left by stingray stings that occurred when the fish was probing the bottom for food and accidentally ran into a hidden stingray on the ocean floor.

Embedded Teeth

On rare occasions, a tooth or fragment of a tooth from a predator or scavenger may break off and become embedded in a bone (fig. 5.60). Authentic examples of this phenomenon are extremely rare; however, this a common hoax perpetrated by unscrupulous individuals looking to make a quick buck or a name for themselves (fig. 5.61). If one is lucky enough to come across an authentic specimen of this type, it most assuredly would have scientific value. Absolute

Fig. 5.56

Bone Ends
with Compression Bite Marks

Undetermined species
Pleistocene

Santa Fe River,
Florida

Collection: T. Sellari
Size: 2.8 in.\7 cm (left)

Fig. 5.56. Both these bones exhibit compression bite marks. It is typical to find ends of bones with bite marks while the shank has been completely destroyed (also see fig. 5.53).

Fig. 5.57

Mammoth Neck Vertebra
with Compression Bite Marks

Mammuthus sp.
Pleistocene

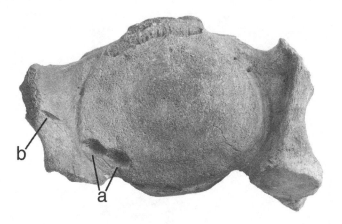

Santa Fe River,
Florida

Collection: D. Letasi
Size: 9 in.\22.5 cm

Fig. 5.57. The bite marks at (a) and (b) align with the dentition of a giant lion that was contemporaneous with this mammoth. Some experts attribute these marks to Paleo-Indians prying apart the vertebrae after a kill.

Fig. 5.58

Saber-toothed Cat (a)
Horse (b)
Predator and Prey

Machairodus giganteus
Hipparion sp.
Pliocene

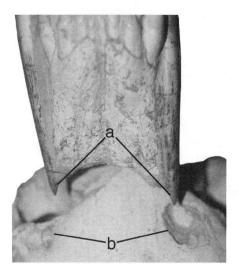

Gansu Province,
China

Collection: F. Garcia
Size: 2.5 in.\6 cm
(between canines)

Fig. 5.58. In an attempt to discover which predator made the compression bite marks (b) on the top of this horse skull, the researcher aligned the sabers (a) from a saber-toothed cat found in the same deposit over them. The match of sabers to bite marks is almost perfect; however, it is possible that other large cats also present at that time could have left this mark.

Fig. 5.59

Porcupine Fish Mouth Plate
with Stingray Injury

Chilomyctems sp.
Pleistocene

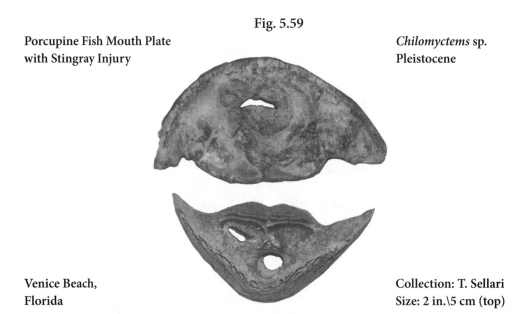

Venice Beach,
Florida

Collection: T. Sellari
Size: 2 in.\5 cm (top)

Fig. 5.59. These mouth plates from porcupine fish display injuries attributed to stingrays. These injuries resemble the holes from compression bites, but they resulted from quite a different cause. Scientists use modern analogues to determine the cause of this type of injury.

Fig. 5.60

Baleen Whale Rostrum
with Embedded Dolphin Teeth

Undetermined Whale species
Undetermined Dolphin species
Miocene

Cargill Phosphate Mine
Polk County, FL

Collection: D. Letasi
Size: 2 in.\5 cm

Fig. 5.60. This bone fragment appears to have two teeth embedded in it at (a) and (b). The possibility exists that these are two compression bite marks that filled with sediment that fossilized, leaving casts of the actual teeth that made the original bite marks.

confirmation of predator and prey in the prehistoric record should be donated to a museum or university.

Shark Feeding Marks

Shark feeding marks on fossilized bone are very common in the paleontological record. Shark feeding marks can often be differentiated from terrestrial carnivores by using a combination of clues. When sharks feed or attack, they tend to use a thrashing motion that can best be described as semicircular; this motion often leaves curved bite marks on the afflicted bone (fig. 5.62). A series of curved bite marks from several teeth in contact with the bone at the same time will be present (fig. 5.63). Finely preserved specimens exhibiting shark feeding marks may even display serration imprints (fig. 5.64). Since sharks are marine animals, they will tend to leave bite marks on marine mammals (e.g., whales, dolphins). Marine mammals tend to have extremely dense bones (see page 36), especially in the rib areas; therefore, shark feeding and attack marks usually occur on very dense bones with little or no marrow cavity (fig. 5.65). Shark feeding marks thus contrast with carnivore feeding and attack marks on

Fig. 5.61

Fake Embedded Tooth   Current Fraud
C. megalodon Tooth in Whale Rostrum   Miocene Materials

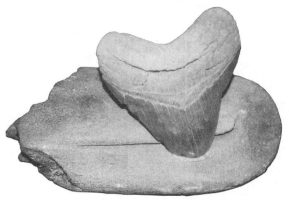

Unknown Location   Collection: Dealer Table
                                                             Size: 5.5 in.\13.7 cm

Fig. 5.61. This large Meg tooth probably had a broken tip and was therefore used in this fake embedded tooth display. Although the dealer did not pretend that the embedded tooth was real, displays like this often change hands many times; somewhere along the line it might be passed off as real to an unsuspecting collector.

Fig. 5.62

Whale Ribs   Undetermined species
with Shark Feeding Marks   Miocene

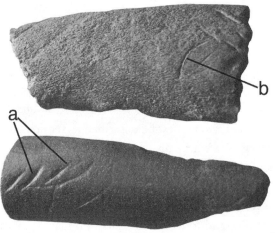

Peace River,   Collection: R. Sinibaldi
DeSoto County, FL   Size: 6.25 in.\15.5 cm (b)

Fig. 5.62. Note the curved bite marks at (a) and (b) on these whale rib bones; they were probably made by a *Carcharocles megalodon*.

Fig. 5.63

Whale Rib Bone
with Shark Feeding Marks

Undetermined species
Miocene

South Carolina River

Collection: V. Bertucci
Size: 4.5 in.\11 cm

Fig. 5.63. This dense whale rib bone has a series of shark feeding marks on its surface.

Fig. 5.64

Whale Rib Bone
with Shark Feeding Marks

Undetermined species
Bite Marks, *C. megalodon*

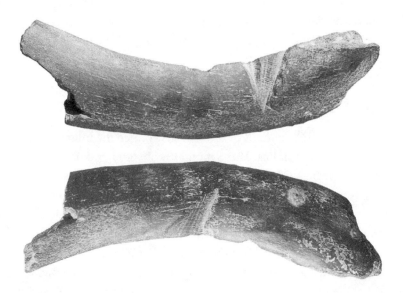

South Carolina River

Collection: V. Bertucci
Size: 8 in.\20 cm

Fig. 5.64. Not only is the bite mark on this whale rib obvious, the serration marks are also exquisitely preserved. Only one shark with serrated teeth ever grew large enough to leave these marks: *Carcharocles megalodon*.

Fig. 5.65

Dugong Rib
with Shark Feeding Marks

Undetermined species
Miocene

Peace River,
DeSoto County, FL

Collection: R. Sinibaldi
Size: 2 in.\5 cm

Fig. 5.65. Two deep shark feeding marks (a) have been left on this dugong rib. Note the dense nature of the ribs of marine mammals (b).

bones usually with larger marrow cavity and less dense bone. In short, curved feeding marks on dense bones are usually attributed to sharks, whereas straight feeding marks on bones with larger marrow cavities are usually attributed to terrestrial animals.

Congenital Anomalies and Problematic Specimens

Deviations that occur as a result of birth defects or genetic mutations are considered **congenital anomalies**. These anomalies are often minor in nature, with no outward effect on the animal's life (fig. 5.66). At other times, a congenital anomaly may be devastating or life threatening. Animals in the wild rarely survive extreme congenital birth defects; therefore, fossilized specimens with severe birth defects are rare. Some congenital anomalies found in the fossil record are identifiable, such as **spina bifida occulta** (fig. 5.67).[10] In the technical literature, anomalies such as **polydactyly** (extra toes), abnormal bone calcifications, cranial asymmetries (misshapen skulls), and a myriad of other problems plaguing the prehistoric fauna are cited. Some anomalies may run through a large portion of a specific population. Scientists with numerous specimens from one locality may be able to identify a recurrent genetic anomaly. It can be pointed out here that life-threatening congenital anomalies are very uncommon in the wild. For humans and domesticated animals, medical treatment is available,

Fig. 5.66

Horse Vertebra
with Congenital Anomaly

Equus sp.
Pleistocene

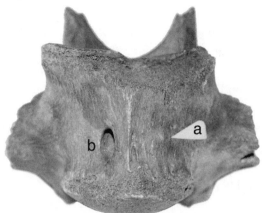

Santa Fe River,
Florida

Collection: T. Sellari
Size: 2.75 in.\6.5 cm

Fig. 5.66. A nerve hole (foramen) is missing at (a) that should resemble the hole at (b). This animal was probably born this way and most likely displayed no ill effects of this anomaly.

Fig. 5.67

Mammoth Vertebra
with Spina Bifida Occulta

Mammuthus sp.
Pleistocene

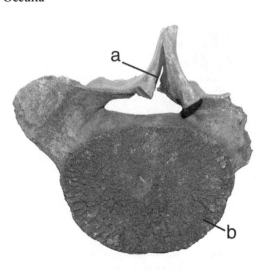

North Sea,
Netherlands

Collection: F. Kocsis
Size: 6.5 in.\16 cm

Fig. 5.67. This mammoth vertebra shows clear signs of spina bifida occulta (a), an incomplete closure or malformation of the bone surrounding the spinal column. Note the lack of fusion of the epiphyseal plate (b); this animal died as a juvenile.

and animals with congenital anomalies have a better chance of surviving, reproducing, and passing on their genetic traits.

Items are many times found that do not fit into any category or diagnosis; their **etiology** is impossible to determine from the current state of the specimen. Anomalies can be congenital, or caused by stresses such as diet or climatic changes. Bone pathologies that cannot be precisely diagnosed are sometimes referred to as nonspecific problematic specimens. The *Journal of Paleopathology* even has a section in each issue for these items called "Problematicals." A few problematic specimens and items of special interest are presented in figures 5.68–5.76. Scientists may invest much time and effort in research of a single problematic specimen; however, a large assemblage of bones with many nonspecific bone infections can be an indicator of the overall health of a population even if the exact problems cannot be determined.

Fig. 5.68

Large Mammal Bone
with Tumor

Undetermined species
Pleistocene?

Origin Unknown

Collection: A. Welberry
Size: 8.5 in.\21.4 cm

Fig. 5.68. The end of this large mammal bone has an anomalous lesion that could be a cancerous tumor, healed fracture, or infection. It would take a specialist with technical equipment to diagnose.

Fig. 5.69

Deer Skull and Antlers
with Antler Anomaly

Odocoileus virginianus
Pleistocene

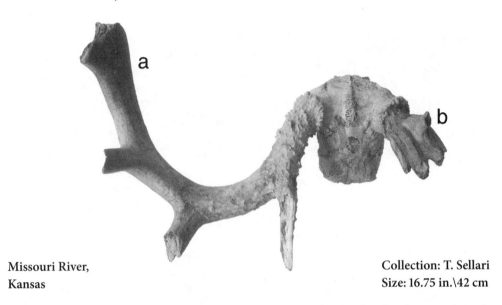

Missouri River,
Kansas

Collection: T. Sellari
Size: 16.75 in.\42 cm

Fig. 5.69. This deer produced a normal antler (a) on one side of its head and a severely malformed antler (b) on the other.

Fig. 5.70

Turtle Shell
with Compression Bite Mark

Undetermined species
Pleistocene

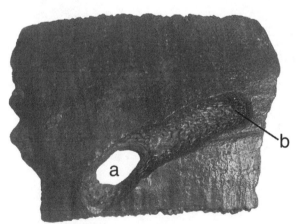

Suwannee River,
Florida

Collection: J. Tatum
Size: 3.75 in.\9.5 cm

Fig. 5.70. This mark may represent an alligator bite that "slipped" (b) before puncturing the shell
(a). There are no signs of healing.

Fig. 5.71

Rib Bone
with Bony Growths

Undetermined species
Pleistocene

Collection: T. Sellari
Size: 3.25 in.\8 cm

Fig. 5.71. This rib bone has many small bony growths of unknown origin; otherwise, the bone as a whole appears quite healthy.

Fig. 5.72

Woolly Rhino Jaw
with Bone Anomaly

Coelodonta antiquitatis
Pleistocene

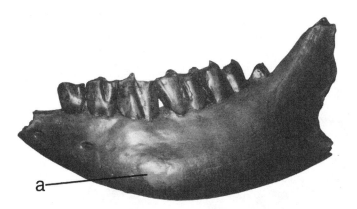

Rhine River,
Germany

Collection: A. Kerner
Size: 13.5 in.\33.5 cm

Fig. 5.72. This woolly rhino jaw has a large section of anomalous bone at (a). The jaw and teeth appear healthy otherwise. The anomaly may be a healed infection or a tumor.

Fig. 5.73

Alligator Toe Bones
with Bone Anomaly

Alligator mississippiensis
Pleistocene

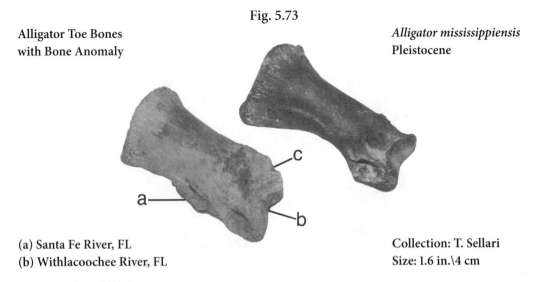

(a) Santa Fe River, FL
(b) Withlacoochee River, FL

Collection: T. Sellari
Size: 1.6 in.\4 cm

Fig. 5.73. Compare the healthy alligator toe bone on the right with the toe bone on the left. A proliferation of bone can be seen at (a), a distorted distal end at (b), and additional profusion of bone at (c). Possible causes include arthritis, infection, and fracture.

Fig. 5.74

Giant Land Tortoise
Carapace Sections

Hesperotestudo sp.
Pliocene

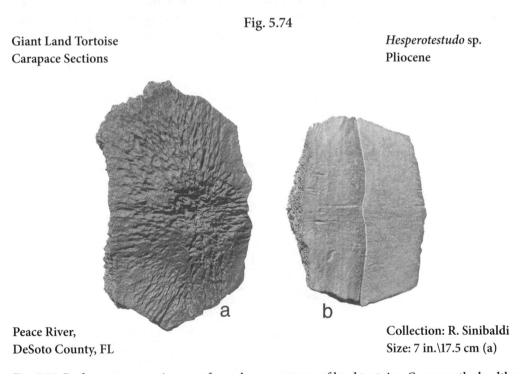

Peace River,
DeSoto County, FL

Collection: R. Sinibaldi
Size: 7 in.\17.5 cm (a)

Fig. 5.74. Both carapace sections are from the same genus of land tortoise. Compare the healthy section (b) with section (a), which exhibits markings that might have been caused by a fungus that infects some turtles between the outer scale and bony portion of shell. This shell fragment remained an anomaly to the author until he showed it to a turtle enthusiast who immediately recognized the markings. Other experts are skeptical of this diagnosis.

Fig. 5.75

Associated Oreodont Bones
with Carnivore Coprolite

Merycoidodon culbertsoni
Oligocene

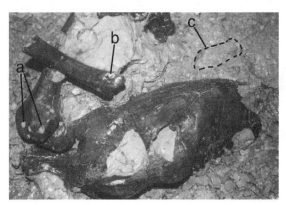

Dawes County,
Nebraska

Collection: F. Garcia
Size: 7.75 in.\19.5 cm
(skull)

Fig. 5.75. The many associated bones of this oreodont skeleton show compression bite marks at (a) and (b). In addition, a carnivore coprolite is seen at (c), just above the skull. Many of today's carnivores demonstrate similar behavior, defecating on or near the remains of their kills to mark their territory and possession of the remains.

Fig. 5.76

Jack Fish
Swollen Spine

Carangidae, indet.
Miocene–Pliocene

Bone Valley Formation,
Polk County, FL

Collection: FLMNH
Size: 2.75 in.\6.5 cm

Fig. 5.76. Swollen dorsal spines of fish are a fairly common find and often baffle the uninitiated as to their identity. In addition, the vertebrae of fish can suffer a similar fate. The phenomenon is technically termed hyperostosis, but the etiology is unknown. The left side is where the spine would articulate with the vertebrae, and the right side is the distal end of the spine. See figure 5.30 for other afflicted fish spines and a healthy comparison.

CHAPTER 6

Pathologies in Fossil Teeth

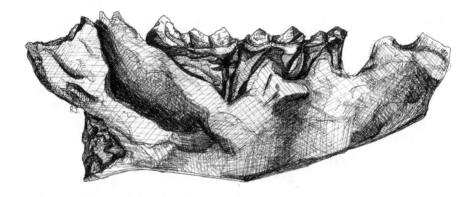

*We all go to the dentist because mammals alone, of living vertebrates,
have permanent teeth.*

Zhe-Xi Luo

Introduction

As with fossilized pathological bones, fossil teeth exhibiting pathologies are
growing in popularity among amateurs and scientists alike. Fossilized teeth
demonstrating some kind of pathological evidence are more prevalent than
fossilized pathological bones for the same reasons that fossil teeth are more
prevalent than fossil bones in general (see chapter 3). The prevalence of fossilized teeth does not mean that pathological anomalies occurred more often in
teeth than in bone in the prehistoric past; just that the pathological teeth had a
better chance of fossilizing because of their hardness. **Dental caries** (cavities),
periodontal disease, abscesses, unusual wear patterns, and feeding breaks are
indicators of some stresses and afflictions that plagued prehistoric animals.

Pathological fossil teeth, as with fossil bones exhibiting pathologies, have
been diagnosed by comparing fossil specimens with modern animals afflicted
with similar diseases or injuries. These diagnoses are considered fairly accurate;
however, determining the causes of unusual wear patterns and feeding breaks
in isolated teeth is often speculative (as discussed in the case of fossil bones in

chapter 5). Sometimes, though, fossil teeth with an extreme wear pattern are still in the jaw, and the jaw may exhibit a healed break, injury, or disease that might have caused a dental misalignment.

Beyond the scope of this book, scientists can do chemical and microscopic analyses of fossilized teeth, usually on large fossil assemblages to determine population dynamics, diet, famine, stress, and other factors. These minute morphological and pathological features are usually not visible to the naked eye and therefore require techniques beyond the capabilities and money constraints of the average amateur, and many poorly funded scientific programs as well.

Dental Caries

When an animal's diet changes from a normal pattern, the pH level[1] of its saliva may be lowered. Lower pH can cause an acidic environment inside the mouth that will begin to demineralize the enamel, cementum, and dentine of the teeth. The acids are produced by the fermentation of carbohydrates, especially foods containing some form of sugar molecule. When this fermentation occurs, a carious lesion (cavity) may form. These lesions may form anywhere on the crown (figs. 6.1–6.2) and, on rare occasions, on the root of the tooth (fig. 6.3). Dental caries are shallow at first, then develop into deeper, more serious lesions. Caries in teeth that have not fossilized will show up as a different color than the enamel or root. In fossilized specimens, care must be taken not to mistake

Fig. 6.1

Mastodon
Lower Molar with Cavity

Mammut americanum
Pleistocene

Wyandotte,
Michigan

Collection: D. Letasi
Size: 5 in.\13 cm

Fig. 6.1. This American mastodon tooth has a small dental cavity (a) just above the gum line (b).

Fig. 6.2

Horse Tooth
Upper Molar with Cavity

Equus sp.
Early Pleistocene

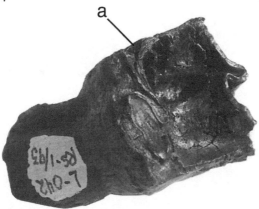

Leisey Shell Pit,
Hillsborough County, FL

Collection: R. Sinibaldi
Size: 1.5 in.\3.5 cm

Fig. 6.2. This well-worn horse upper molar developed a carious lesion (cavity) at (a).

Fig. 6.3

Horse Upper Molar
with Cavity/Abscess

Equus sp.
Pleistocene

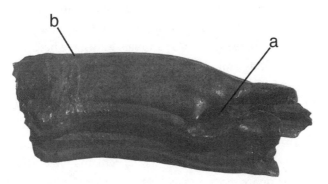

Charlotte County,
Florida

Collection: T. Sellari
Size: 3.25 in.\8 cm

Fig. 6.3. This horse upper molar has developed a carious lesion at site (a), well below the gum line (b). This may have developed into an abscess that infected the upper jaw, but this determination is uncertain without the surrounding jaw/skull material.

Fig. 6.4

Mastodon Tooth
with Missing Enamel

Mammut americanum
Pleistocene

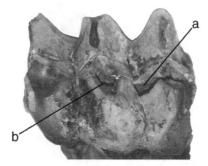

Florida

Collection: FLMNH
Size: 4 in.\10 cm

Fig. 6.4. The occlusal surface of this mastodon tooth was damaged postmortem, probably long after it fossilized. Pieces of the chewing surface are cracked and missing at (a) and (b), giving the appearance of dental caries. True tooth decay is very rare in the fossil record, and teeth exhibiting possible cavities should be inspected carefully.

normal wear patterns that exposed various layers of cementum and dentine, which might have fossilized a different color than the enamel, for dental caries (fig. 6.4). In severe cases of dental caries, a deep pit may form, and an obvious diagnosis is easily made. Let it be noted here that dental caries are extremely rare in the fossil record or in nature in general. Most animals eat what they are supposed to eat and therefore rarely have this problem.[2] Sometimes teeth have weak cementum or dentine that may wear away or erode at a faster rate than the enamel (fig. 6.5). The teeth of some animals may have been inadvertently swallowed and exposed to stomach acids, causing pitting that might resemble a cavity (fig. 6.6).

Determining dental caries in the roots of teeth can be problematic in isolated teeth. The roots of teeth are surrounded by cementum, the softest of the three tooth elements. The roots of fossilized teeth very often show pitting from natural alterations (see chapter 4) while the enamel remains intact (fig 6.7). Teeth that remain in a jaw, or are recovered as a set, allow for comparative analysis of the teeth and their roots (fig. 6.8). If all the roots are pitted, in most cases, exposure to acids in the ground water after death and deposition may be suspected. In some cases large predators such as alligators or crocodiles can swallow whole jaw sections and digest some of the enamel; however, if only one tooth, or one root on one tooth, exhibits pitting, dental caries or some other problem may be suspected (figs. 6.9–6.10).

Fig. 6.5

Horse Molars
Weak Cementum

Equus sp.
Pleistocene

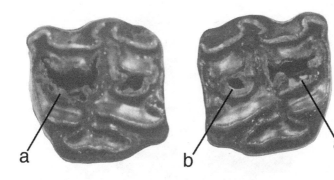

Leisey Shell Pit 1A
Ruskin, FL

Collection: FLMNH
Size: 1 in.\2.5 cm

Fig. 6.5. These horse molars, presumably from the same animal, display an area of weak cementum at (a). Note the normal size of the nerve hole at (b). That hole is surrounded by cementum, folded into the dentine and enamel. Only the cementum is affected in these specimens; whether this condition would have lead to a carious lesion in the enamel over time is uncertain.

Fig. 6.6

Three-toed Horse Jaw
Eroded from Stomach Acids

Nannipus aztecus
Pliocene

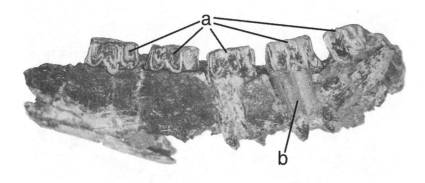

Moss Acres Racetrack
Marion County, FL

Collection: FLMNH
Size: 4.5 in.\11.2 cm

Fig. 6.6. Note the erosion of the enamel (a) on all five teeth present in this three-toed horse jaw. The jaw is believed to have been swallowed by an alligator or crocodile and partially digested by stomach acids. Note that the enamel at (b), a root protected by bone that is now missing, was not eroded by stomach acids.

Fig. 6.7

Camel
Upper Molar

Hemiauchenia macrocephala
Pleistocene

Peace River,
DeSoto County, FL

Collection: R. Sinibaldi
Size: 1.5 in.\3.5 cm (vert.)

Fig. 6.7. The enamel on this camel tooth was much tougher than the roots. Acid leaching has pitted the roots and given the false impression of dental caries.

Fig. 6.8

Artiodactyl
Maxilla with Pitted Roots

Scaphoceras tyrrelli
Pleistocene

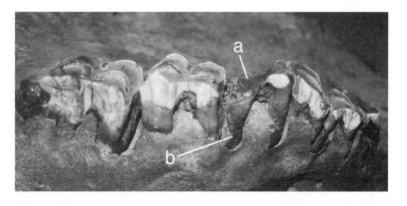

Bonanza Creek
Yukon Territory, Canada

Collection: SI/NMNH
Size: 7 in.\17.5 cm

Fig. 6.8. Note that most of the bone at the gum margin was damaged during fossilization. The third molar (a) is severely worn and appears to have developed some problems, as the root is pitted (b). The other exposed roots appear to have been healthy.

Fig. 6.9

Peccary Jaw
with Pitted Root

Platygonus sp.
Pleistocene

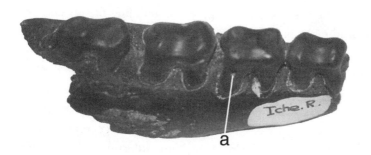

Ichetucknee River
Columbia County, FL

Collection: FLMNH
Size: 2.5 in.\6 cm

Fig.6.9. This peccary jaw is believed to have been swallowed by an alligator and partially digested by stomach acids. In addition, it has a pitted tooth root at (a) that may be the remnants of a carious lesion, the beginnings of an abscess, or further damage from stomach acids. The jaw is too damaged by acids for a certain diagnosis.

Fig. 6.10

Camel Jaw
with Pathological Tooth

Paleolama mirifica
Pleistocene

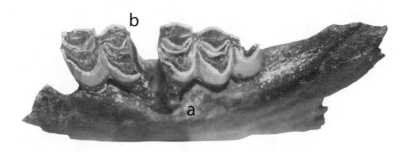

Leisey Shell Pit, 1A
Ruskin, FL

Collection: FLMNH
Size: 3.5 in.\9 cm

Fig. 6.10. This camel jaw displays pitting on the root of the tooth at (a) along with damage to the alveolar socket. In addition, the tooth has wear at (b) unlikely to have been caused by an upper tooth. The tooth could have been damaged by cavity, infection, injury, or some other cause and then continued to be eaten away by an infection.

Dental Abscess

As a dental caries lesion deteriorates, the infection will often proceed into the pulp cavity and tooth root (see fig. 6.3 in previous section). If the infection travels through the root tip and into the surrounding bone, necrosis (death) of the living tissue (nerves, blood supply) surrounding the infection may occur, possibly leading to production of pus. If the infection and pus spread to the surrounding alveolar bone, a pus-filled cavity (dental abscess) will form. Unimpeded infection will continue to increase the size of the pus-filled cavity in the bone until a drainage hole occurs in the alveolar bone surface. In some specimens, if the tooth remains in the jaw, the tip of the root will be visible through the abscess hole in the bone (fig. 6.11). This hole is generally oval to circular in shape, with thinning fragile edges. If the infection continues unimpeded, the hole may enlarge enough to reach the alveolar margin, leaving the tooth with little or no support. A tooth exposed in this fashion is often exfoliated. Therefore, a section of jaw with a missing tooth and a large hole in the alveolar margin may be evidence of an extreme abscess (fig. 6.12).

Fig. 6.11

Bison Maxilla
with Abscessed Tooth

Bison sp.
Late Pleistocene

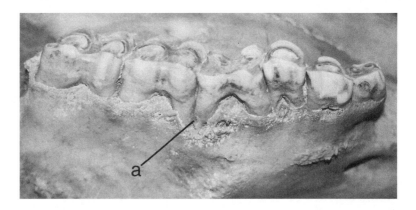

Clark Butte,
Nebraska

Collection: SI/NMNH
Size: 8 in.\20 cm

Fig. 6.11. This bison maxilla has an abscess at the first molar at (a). A small hole can be seen in the tooth root where the bone near the abscess eroded away from the infected area. The remaining teeth appear healthy.

Fig. 6.12

White-tailed Deer
Jaw with Abscessed Teeth

Odocoileus virginianus
Pleistocene

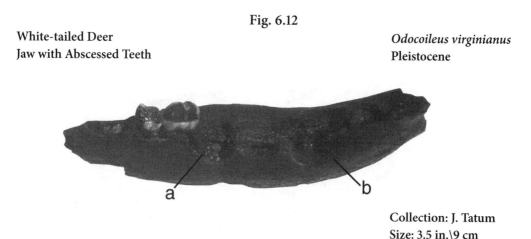

Collection: J. Tatum
Size: 3.5 in.\9 cm

Fig. 6.12. This jaw has a large abscess hole at (a), and another at (b). It has exfoliated several teeth and displays severe bone infection in the jaw.

Dental Hypoplasia

Hypoplasia is a technical term for underdevelopment. Dental hypoplasia is the underdevelopment of teeth and may have several causes, including disease, parasitic infection, and malnutrition (especially lack of vitamin D). During times of infection and disease, the body's immune system is activated at the expense of growth of body tissues, which may result in the slowing of growth in teeth and bones (in bones this condition is referred to as **Harris lines**). Dental hypoplasia can range from very mild to gross. Extremely mild structural abnormalities may be seen only microscopically; gross dental hypoplasia can be seen macroscopically, or with the naked eye. Since hypoplasia is a developmental pathology, it must occur before the enamel of the tooth is fully formed. Short-term disease or illness may cause small malformations, whereas long-term dietary shortages may cause more significant abnormalities. Generally, the malformation appears as a band or bands running parallel to the gum line, because teeth calcify progressively from the occlusal surface to the root. Dental hypoplasia does not include deformations of size or shape, only irregular distribution or partial absence of the enamel surface resulting from deficient calcification. A scientist may be able to determine the animal's age at the time of the malformation by the location of the band on the tooth. Bands closer to the crown occurred when the animal was younger, whereas those near the root occurred when the animal was older (fig. 6.13). These bands may be easily confused with dental calculus that usually occurs at the gum margins. Dental calculus consists of a calcium deposit that can often fossilize on the surface of the tooth. Dental tartar often has ridges and grooves that also run parallel with

Fig. 6.13

Horse Lower Molar
with Dental Hypoplasia

Equus sp.
Pleistocene

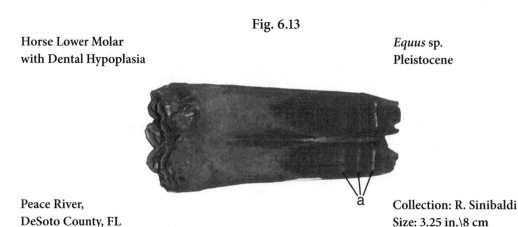

Peace River,
DeSoto County, FL

a

Collection: R. Sinibaldi
Size: 3.25 in.\8 cm

Fig. 6.13. The parallel bands along the bottom of this horse tooth (a) are the telltale signs of dental hypoplasia. These bands are near the tooth root, signifying that this horse went through a stressful dietary period just as the tooth was reaching maturity.

the gum line (fig. 6.14). Dental hypoplasia consists of grooves or bands actually present in the enamel of the tooth. Dental hypoplasia is very prevalent in prehistoric human populations and is most notable on the fronts of the incisors. Dental hypoplasia is a true pathology, whereas dental calculus is not; however, severe dental calculus may lead to periodontal disease, a true pathology, covered in the next section.

Periodontal Disease

Periodontal diseases involve destruction of the alveolar margin as a result of accumulation of dental calculus or plaque. This accumulation causes the gums to swell and the periodontal tissues to become inflamed. Periodontal disease, sometimes referred to as periodontitis, can be diagnosed when the distance between the alveolar margin and the cervix or enamel-dentine junction increases beyond what is typical (greater than 2 mm in humans). This distance will vary between species, and use of a comparative collection may be needed to determine whether damage to the alveolar margin should be suspected (fig. 6.15). In addition to inspecting the distance between the alveolar margin and the enamel-cementum junction, it is important to inspect the contour and definition of the alveolar margin for pathological appearances and bone resorption.

A smaller section or incomplete jaw may show signs of periodontal disease when compared with the rest of the jaw section in a single specimen (fig. 6.16). Furthermore, periodontal disease may be classified in four stages: absent—no resorption, slight—less than one-half of the root exposed, severe—the tooth is exfoliated but the alveolar margin is discernible, and complete—tooth exfoliated and the alveolar margin completely obliterated (figs. 6.17–6.18).

Fig. 6.14

Horse Upper Molar
with Dental Tartar

Equus sp.
Pleistocene

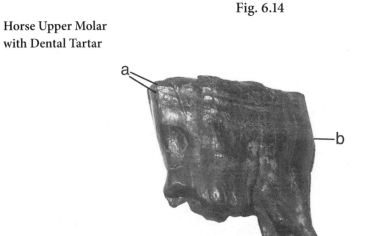

Peace River,
DeSoto County, FL

Collection: R. Sinibaldi
Size: 1.5 in.\3.5 cm

Fig. 6.14. Parallel lines (a) just above the gum line (b) are well-preserved examples of dental tartar (calculus). Close inspection reveals that the lines are on the enamel surface, not embedded in it, as would be the case with dental hypoplasia.

Fig. 6.15

Mammoth Skull Section
Tusk Socket with Periodontal Disease

Mammuthus sp.
Pleistocene

Collection: B. Fite
Size: 22 in.\55 cm

Fig. 6.15. This mammoth skull section has both a normal alveolar tusk socket (a), and a socket exhibiting periodontal disease (b). Compare the blood vessel markings on the healthy socket (a) with the porous, rough nature of the bone on socket (b).

Fig. 6.16

White-tailed Deer Jaw
with Severe Periodontal Disease

Odocoileus virginianus
Pleistocene

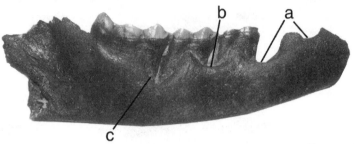

Withlacoochee River,
Marion County, FL

Collection: T. Sellari
Size: 4 in.\10 cm

Fig. 6.16. This deer jaw has exfoliated teeth at (a) and severe damage to the bone at (b) and (c), exposing more than half of the tooth roots. Note that the crowns of the remaining teeth are worn almost to the gum line; this was a very old animal.

Fig. 6.17

Dog Jaw
with Healed Periodontal Disease

Canis familiaris
Holocene

Santa Fe River,
Florida

Collection: T. Sellari
Size: 4.4 in.\11 cm

Fig. 6.17. This Indian dog exfoliated all its teeth at locations (a) and (b), except for the main carnassial (c). The surrounding bone was completely resorbed and the alveolar holes for the roots healed over. This dog apparently survived a very bad bout of periodontal disease. This anomaly might have resulted from severe inbreeding, which was common among the first dogs to appear in North America.

Fig. 6.18

White-tailed Deer Jaw
with Severe Periodontal Disease
and Bone Necrosis

Odocoileus virginianus
Pleistocene

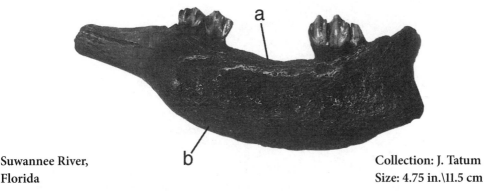

Suwannee River,
Florida

Collection: J. Tatum
Size: 4.75 in.\11.5 cm

Fig. 6.18. This deer lost several teeth at (a) as the result of a severe infection. The bone at (b) displays an enormous infectious lesion. This deer may have sustained a severe jaw injury that developed into a periodontal problem. Note that the roots of the remaining teeth have also been exposed.

Impacted Teeth

In the situation where a tooth does not erupt before the teeth on either side of it, many amateurs use the term "impacted" to describe the condition. Technically, this term is not always correct. Teeth may become impacted for several reasons. Injury to the jaw may cause a misalignment of the teeth, leaving insufficient room for the tooth to reach the surface. A tooth may also be **atavistic**, a "throwback" from an earlier evolutionary stage of development that once again has no room in the "modern" jaw to erupt fully. Finally, a tooth may become impacted for no apparent reason that is discernible from the fossil evidence available (fig. 6.19).

One must use caution when designating a tooth impacted in a jaw. It is possible that an unerupted tooth may be just that, unerupted (but may look impacted in the jaw, fig. 6.20). This situation can occur when the deciduous tooth behind an unerupted tooth has not been shed or exfoliated and the tooth before the unerupted tooth has already been fully replaced (fig. 6.21). The appearance will be that of an impacted tooth between two erupted teeth. This condition can sometimes be revealed by looking for other unerupted teeth beneath the teeth surrounding the one suspected of being impacted. This inspection may require X-ray technology if no gaps exist in the jawbone to visually inspect for an unerupted tooth (fig. 6.22). This situation occurs far more commonly than that of true impacted teeth.

Fig. 6.19

Walrus   Undetermined species
Impacted Tusk   Pleistocene

Alaska   Collection: T. Sellari
                                                               Size: 5.5 in.\14 cm

Fig. 6.19. This walrus tusk became impacted in the bone, apparently with no place to erupt. It grew into a spiral shape (a) within the jaw. Because the overall fossil is incomplete, evidence for the cause of this condition is lacking.

Fig. 6.20

Horse   *Equus* sp.
Jaw with 2 Unerupted Teeth   Late Pleistocene

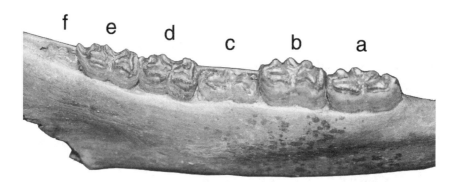

Rhine River,   Collection: A. Kerner
Germany   Size: 8.4 in.\21 cm

Fig. 6.20. Perissodactyls, such as this horse, do not replace their deciduous teeth exactly in order from front to back. Premolars (a) and (b) and molars (d) and (e) have already been replaced by adult teeth. Premolar 4 (c) and molar 3 (f) are just erupting. The resulting pattern makes it appear that premolar 4 (c) is impacted between premolar 3 (b) and molar 1 (d). Note that most *Equus* lack a first premolar.

Fig. 6.21

Tapir Lower Jaw
with Unerupted pm4

Tapirus polkensis
Miocene

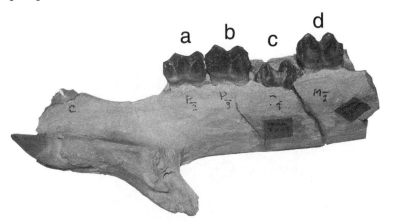

Bone Valley Formation,
Polk County, FL

Collection: FLMNH
Size: 6 in.\15 cm

Fig. 6.21. Premolars 2 and 3, (a) and (b), have fully erupted in this tapir, a perissodactyl. Premolar 4 (c) has not yet fully erupted, yet molar 1 (d) is already fully erupted. This gives the false impression of an impacted tooth; however, this eruption progression is normal for perissodactyls (tapirs, horses, rhinos). Premolar 4 (c) would have eventually moved fully into place. Note that this specimen is labeled as the type specimen for this species of tapir.

Fig. 6.22

White-tailed Deer Lower Jaw
with Adult Tooth under Deciduous Tooth

Odocoileus virginianus
Pleistocene

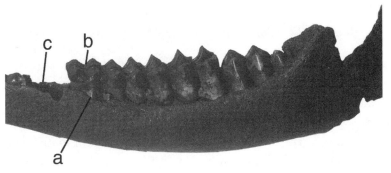

Suwannee River,
Florida

Collection: A. Kerner
Size: 5.4 in.\13.5 cm

Fig. 6.22. This deer jaw provides an example of an adult tooth (a) just beneath a deciduous tooth (b). Tooth (b) would eventually have been replaced by two teeth, tooth (a) and another not yet visible. Enough bone is missing at the gum line to give a view of this progression. Had the animal lived a little longer, tooth (b) would have been exfoliated while tooth (a) remained in the gum line, appearing impacted, as the teeth behind it are fully erupted. The tooth at location (c) was probably lost during fossilization or deposition.

Fig. 6.23

Bear Maxilla
with Missing Canine

Ursus spelaeus
Late Pleistocene

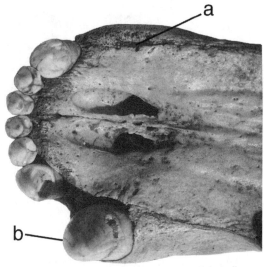

Romania

Collection: B. Fite
Size: 4.5 in.\11.3 cm

Fig. 6.23. This maxilla of a European cave bear exhibits a completely healed alveolar margin (a) where a large canine tooth should be. The opposite canine (b) gives a good example of the size of the missing tooth. While not available, the canine from the lower jaw opposite the missing upper canine may have exhibited an unusual wear pattern or no wear pattern at all. Judging from the bone pattern around tooth (b), the tooth missing at (a) was probably lost very early in life.

Unusual Wear Patterns, Extra Teeth, and Missing Teeth

Some of the most common pathological fossil finds are teeth with unusual wear patterns. The cause of unusual wear to isolated teeth, found separated from the jaw, is often very difficult to diagnose. The majority of unusual wear patterns in teeth have been caused by a traumatic injury to one or both jaws. A broken and improperly healed jaw may cause considerable variation in tooth alignment. Jaws, or sections of jaws, displaying healed fractures may contain pathologically worn, missing, or misaligned teeth (figs. 6.23–6.24). Unusual alignment may also occur as a result of broken or missing teeth (technically termed agenesis or **hypodontia**, fig. 6.25), disease (fig. 6.26), or extreme old age (fig. 6.27). Dental caries may also cause unusual wear patterns (see page 202).

Isolated teeth with unusual wear patterns have caused amateurs and professionals alike to create imaginary scenarios to explain them. While this is not good science, speculation of this kind can be fun; however, there are ways to determine the etiology (study of causes) of unusually worn teeth. Comparative

Fig. 6.24

American Mastodon
Lower Jaw with Crossed Tusks

Mammut americanum
Pleistocene

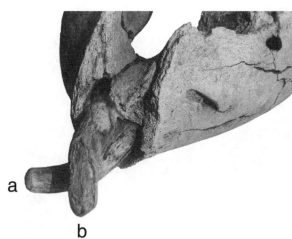

Land site adjacent to
Withlacoochee River, FL

Collection: D. Letasi
Size: 18 in.\45 cm

Fig. 6.24. This mastodon jaw displays a pair of misaligned lower tusks, indicating a congenital anomaly or trauma at a young age. Note the different wear patterns on tusks (a) and (b).

Fig. 6.25

Horse Upper Molar
with Unusual Wear Pattern

Equus sp.
Pleistocene

Peace River,
DeSoto County, FL

Collection: R. Sinibaldi
Size: 1.75 in.\4.3 cm

Fig. 6.25. This isolated *Equus* tooth has an extremely unusual wear pattern. The tooth leaned forward in the jaw and wore down at an approximate 45-degree angle. More than likely, the tooth next to this one was exfoliated, allowing this tooth to lean and grow at an angle. See figures 3.7–3.8 for normal wear patterns on horse teeth.

Fig. 6.26

Saber-toothed Cat
Pathological Jaw and Tooth

Smilodon gracilis
Early Pleistocene

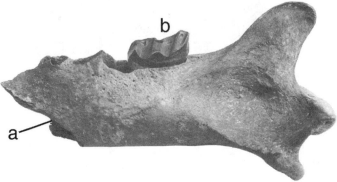

Hillsborough County,
Florida

Collection: D. Letasi
Size: 5.5 in.\13.5 cm

Fig. 6.26. This saber-toothed cat had a severe jaw infection (a) that may have been the cause of, or caused by, an extremely misaligned jaw. The remaining carnassial (b) exhibits an unusual wear pattern. To compare with a normal saber-toothed cat carnassial, see figure 3.22, tooth (d).

Fig. 6.27

American Mastodon Teeth
Extremely Worn

Mammut americanum
Pleistocene

Northern Florida Rivers

Collection: A. Welberry
Size: 3 in.\7.5 cm (left)

Fig. 6.27. These two mastodon teeth are extremely worn, but they are not from an old animal. Mastodons, like mammoths and today's elephants, produced teeth that erupted one at a time and moved down the jaw in conveyer-belt fashion. Each new tooth was progressively larger as the animal grew. See figure 6.1 for a large mastodon tooth without wear and figure 3.58 for a large mastodon tooth with extreme wear from an older animal.

Fig. 6.28

Horse Lower Molar
with Pathology

Equus sp.
Pleistocene

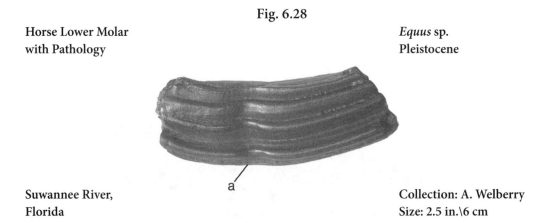

Suwannee River,
Florida

a

Collection: A. Welberry
Size: 2.5 in.\6 cm

Fig. 6.28. This horse lower molar has an anomaly at (a) that might have been produced by an injury to the jaw. For an example of a normal lower *Equus* molar, see figure 3.7.

collections may contain similar teeth of unusual wear still situated in a jaw. Furthermore, current analogous species may give scientists living examples of teeth with unusual wear patterns. Domesticated animals may not provide the best examples of comparative pathological anomalies as they have usually been afforded veterinary intervention and eat very different diets. Domesticated animals may have an entirely different set of pathological assaults to their bones and teeth; therefore, using extant wild animals as analogues for extinct species gives scientists their best chance of developing clues to the formation of pathological fossil bones and teeth.

Teeth from horses (fig. 6.28), dire wolves (fig. 6.29), bison (fig. 6.30), sharks (see next section), camels (fig. 6.31), some sloths (fig. 6.32), and deer (fig. 6.33) all have modern counterparts to use for comparison when determining why a tooth or teeth have a pathological problem. Mammoths and mastodons may be compared to today's elephants (figs. 6.34–6.35); however, some animals may have no current analogue with which to compare teeth. The canines of saber-toothed cats (fig. 6.36), the lower tusks of mastodons (fig. 6.37), and of course the teeth of dinosaurs[3] (not covered in this volume) are well-known examples of specimens with no modern analogues.

Pathological Shark Teeth

No pathological fossil teeth have generated more erroneous speculation as to cause than those of sharks. As discussed on page 113, shark teeth are possibly the most common fossilized teeth of any kind; therefore, fossil enthusiasts will find more pathological shark teeth. Many shark teeth exhibit pseudopathologies, rather than true pathologies. Pseudopathologies, as previously defined,

Fig. 6.29

Dire Wolf Jaw and Tooth
Broken and Worn Carnassial

Canis dirus
Pleistocene

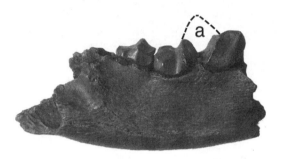
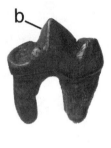

Peace River,
DeSoto County, FL

Collection: R. Sinibaldi
Size: 3.4 in.\8.5 cm (jaw)

Fig. 6.29. Tooth (a) in this dire wolf jaw apparently broke while the animal was alive, as the inside of the break exhibits feeding wear. Compare tooth (b), with a large central cusp, to tooth (a), which is missing the central cusp.

Fig. 6.30

Bison Jaw
Malformed 3rd Premolar

Bison priscus
Pleistocene

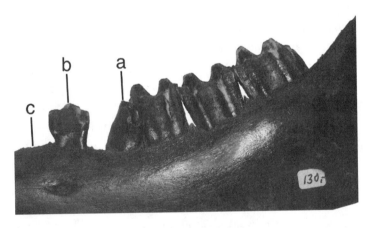

San River,
Przemysl, Poland

Collection: Rotunda Rock
Size: 10.5 in.\26.5 cm

Fig. 6.30. This bison jaw has a severely misaligned tooth, premolar 4 (a). Premolar 3 is present (b), but the second premolar is missing at location (c), probably lost after death. The cause of this anomaly is unknown, but one could speculate that the opposing upper premolars also had significant malformations.

Fig. 6.31

Giraffelike Animal Skull
Exfoliated Lower Molar and
Corresponding Pathological Upper Molar

Undetermined species
Miocene

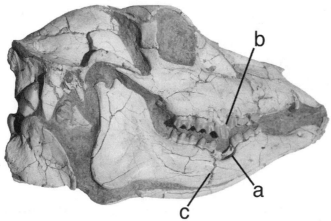

Gansu Province,
China

Collection: B. Fite
Size: 6.5 in.\16 cm

Fig. 6.31. This small giraffelike animal lost a tooth in its lower jaw (a), causing the corresponding upper tooth in the maxilla (b) to have an odd wear pattern in relation to the jaw. The crack at (c) probably occurred during or after fossilization and is unrelated to the missing tooth at that location.

Fig. 6.32

Sloth Jaw
with Abnormal Tooth

Megalonyx wheatleyi
Early Pleistocene

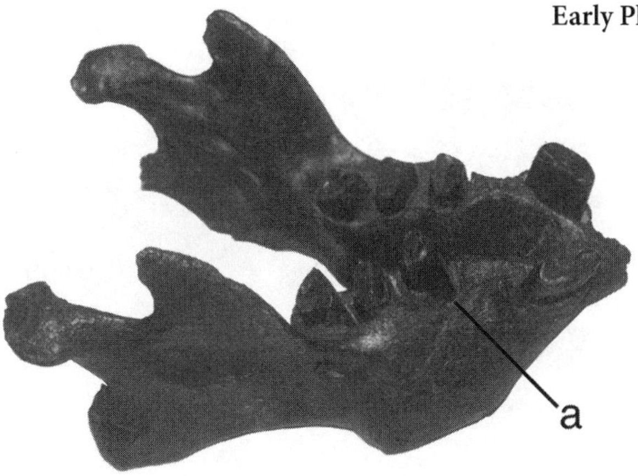

Caloosa Shell Pit,
Hillsborough County, FL

Collection: F. Garcia
Size: 9 in.\22.5 cm

Fig. 6.32. The tooth at location (a) has almost no wear, compared with all the other teeth in the lower jaw of this *Megalonyx* sloth. The corresponding upper tooth at this location was possibly exfoliated. See figure 6.31.

Fig. 6.33

White-tailed Deer Jaw
with Problematic Teeth

Odocoileus virginianus
Pleistocene

Santa Fe River,
Florida

Collection: A. Kerner
Size: 4 in.\10 cm

Fig. 6.33. This deer jaw has a molar with an extra cusp or fold of enamel at (a), and a misaligned tooth at (b) that is pushing into or folding around the adjacent tooth. It is possible that the extra folds in tooth (a) have forced the rest of the teeth forward in the jaw, causing the problem at (b). Several deer jaws from this site have this same anomaly, so it could have been congenital.

Fig. 6.34

Mammoth Tooth
Severely Malformed

Mammuthus sp.
Pleistocene

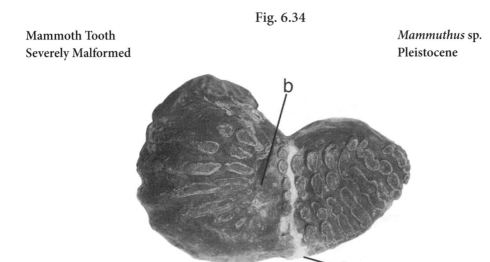

Upper Aucilla River,
Florida

Collection: B. Fite
Size: 9.2 in.\23 cm

Fig. 6.34. This mammoth tooth has a bizarre wear pattern. Although a deposition crack in the tooth was repaired at site (a), the actual curve of the tooth begins at (b). Compare the curved plates in this tooth with the straight plates in normal mammoth teeth in figure 4.25.

222

Fig. 6.35

Partial Mastodon Tooth
with Additional Fused Cusps

Mammut americanum
Early Pleistocene

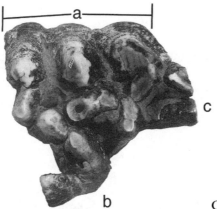

Lower Withlacoochee River,
Florida

Collection: J. Tatum
Size: 5.75 in.\14.3 cm

Fig. 6.35. It is unfortunate that only part of this specimen was found. It apparently represents a situation where two or three teeth fused together in a mastodon's jaw. Side (a) has the appearance of a normal mastodon tooth. Both (b) and (c) may represent portions of other teeth that fused to tooth (a). See figure 6.1 to compare this tooth with a normally developed mastodon tooth.

Fig. 6.36

Saber-toothed Cat
Upper Sabers

Smilodon gracilis
Pleistocene

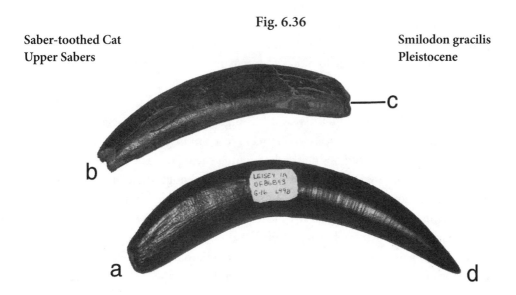

Leisey Shell Pit,
Hillsborough County, FL

Collection: FLMNH
Size: 5.5 in.\13.6 cm
(bottom)

Fig. 6.36. A complete saber (a) from a saber-toothed cat is impressive; however, sabers were often broken during pursuit of prey (b). Note the rounded edges (c), indicating that this big cat probably survived for some time after losing the tip of the saber. The roots of the teeth are at (a) and (b), and the crowns are at (c) and (d).

Fig. 6.37

Mastodon
Broken and Healed Lower Tusk

Mammut americanum
Pleistocene

Withlacoochee River,
Florida

Collection: T. Sellari
Size: 6.2 in.\15.5 cm

Fig. 6.37. When teeth break, they generally do not heal; therefore, this mastodon tusk, a specialized form of tooth, must have broken in the alveolar margin (within the jaw) at an extremely young age. The tusk, contained in the jaw, had time to heal before erupting. See figure 3.37 for normal lower mastodon tusks.

are insults or damage that has occurred during or after the death of the animal, with no signs of healing on the specimen.

Many pseudopathologies have led to wildly imaginative speculations on the part of collectors. The first common misinterpretation of marks on fossilized shark teeth attributes them to attacks by a giant squid,[4] usually on *Carcharocles megalodon*. This assertion may seem comical, but it is believed by some in the amateur world of paleontology. The very large extinct shark was most surely the top predator of its time, and it is highly unlikely that a giant squid would attempt to attack it. The assertion seems even more absurd in that the attack purportedly occurred on the shark's mouth, leaving tentacle marks on the shark's teeth. Thinking of the situation in reverse, although these large sharks may have attacked and eaten giant squid, the momentary encounter between the two animals would hardly leave time for a defending squid's suction cups to leave marks on the extremely hard enamel of the shark's teeth. In reality, these circular marks on teeth (fig. 6.38) are the scars of barnacle or mollusk attachments made after the teeth were shed from the animal and settled on the ocean floor.

Another popular myth about marks on sharks' teeth is that these great predators attacked each other and left bite marks on their adversaries' teeth. Once again, it is highly improbable that the extinct white shark attacked its own species, never mind in a mouth-to-mouth fashion. The serrated markings on the teeth of *Carcharocles megalodon* shown in figure 6.39 were self-inflicted on teeth shed during feeding frenzies. Teeth lost during feeding were possibly

Fig. 6.38

Extinct Giant White Shark
Lower Tooth

Carcharocles megalodon
Miocene

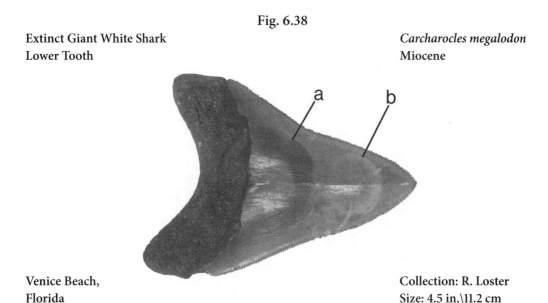

Venice Beach,
Florida

Collection: R. Loster
Size: 4.5 in.\11.2 cm

Fig. 6.38. This megalodon tooth still bears attachment scars, (a) and (b), from a barnacle or mollusk as the tooth lay on the ocean floor after being exfoliated. See figure 4.4 for other specimens with barnacles still attached.

Fig. 6.39

Extinct Giant White Shark
Upper Tooth with Feeding Damage

Carcharocles megalodon
Miocene

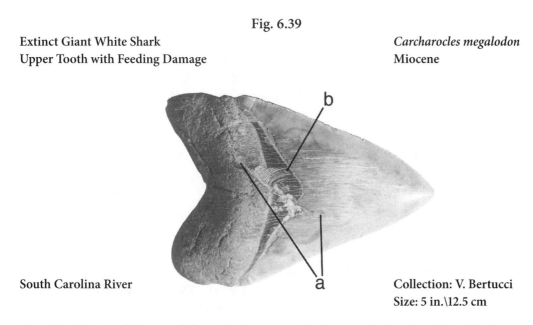

South Carolina River

Collection: V. Bertucci
Size: 5 in.\12.5 cm

Fig. 6.39. This megalodon tooth has a distinct cut mark that runs the length of (a), with clear serration marks at (b). This tooth was probably lost during a feeding frenzy and was accidentally bitten by the original shark or another that was feeding on the same animal.

Fig. 6.40

Extinct Giant White Shark
Upper Teeth with Congenital Anomaly

Carcharocles megalodon
Miocene

Morgan Creek,
South Carolina

Collection: G. Hubbell
Size: 5 in.\12.5 cm (each)

Fig. 6.40. These identical anomalies (a), in teeth from opposite sides of the jaw, would have been expressed only if a congenital birth defect was expressed on opposite sides of the jaw.

caught up with the prey and bitten, and then either swallowed or expelled from the animal's mouth during the melee.

Many fossil shark populations have current modern phylogenetically analogous species for comparison to determine the etiology of fossil shark teeth pathology. If a left and right tooth from a jaw have mirror image anomalies, the pathology can be suspected to be congenital (fig. 6.40). Injuries to the jaws of modern great white sharks have produced teeth exhibiting various types of damage, including severe deformation (figs. 6.41–6.42), partially split teeth (fig. 6.43), fully formed split teeth (fig. 6.44), bent or curved teeth (fig. 6.45), and teeth with wavy edges (figs. 6.46–6.47). Although the exact etiology of each of these occurrences is uncertain even in modern great white sharks, complete jaws exist exhibiting both injury and these anomalies.[5] It is believed that injury to the jaw can affect the germinal tissue of undeveloped teeth, therefore causing a pathological anomaly.

Many extant great white shark teeth display anomalies that would be better categorized as individual differences. Minute side cusps, looking almost like bone spurs, are often described as pathologies when seen on individual fossil teeth (fig. 6.48). Although the occurrence is rare, modern great white jaws have been collected that display this anomaly on every tooth in the mouth.[6] This aberrance may be an atavistic trait. An atavism is the expression of a prehistoric

Fig. 6.41

Extinct Giant White Shark
Pathological Tooth

Carcharocles auriculatus
Middle to Late Eocene

Cooper River,
South Carolina

Collection: G. Hubbell
Size: 3.5 in.\8.7 cm

Fig. 6.41. An injury to the jaw could have produced this severely deformed tooth. Modern great white sharks with jaw injuries have exhibited similar deformities.

Fig. 6.42

Extinct Giant White Shark
Pathological Upper Tooth

Carcharocles megalodon
Miocene

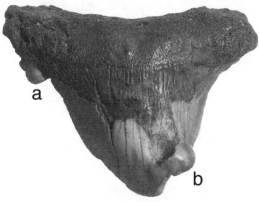

Cooper River,
South Carolina

Collection: G. Hubbell
Size: 2.9 in.\7 cm

Fig. 6.42. A possible injury to the jaw while this tooth forming could have caused the pathological anomalies at (a) and (b), along with the overall malformed shape.

Fig. 6.43

Extinct Giant White Shark
Partially Split Upper Tooth

Carcharocles megalodon
Miocene

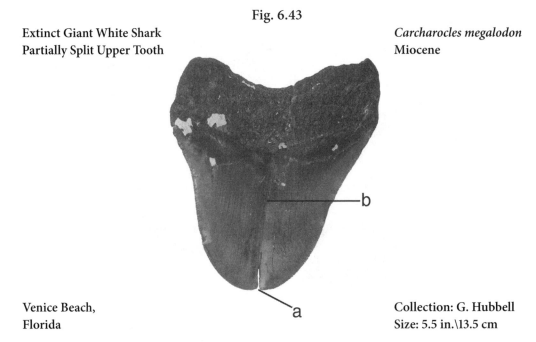

Venice Beach,
Florida

Collection: G. Hubbell
Size: 5.5 in.\13.5 cm

Fig. 6.43. A jaw injury from a stingray barb or billfish spine could cause the effect of partially split teeth. The split is complete at (a) and runs up to (b), where the split does not go all the way through the tooth. Partially split shark teeth are a fairly common pathological find.

Fig. 6.44

Extinct Giant White Shark
Fully Split Upper Tooth
(Composite)

Carcharocles megalodon
Miocene

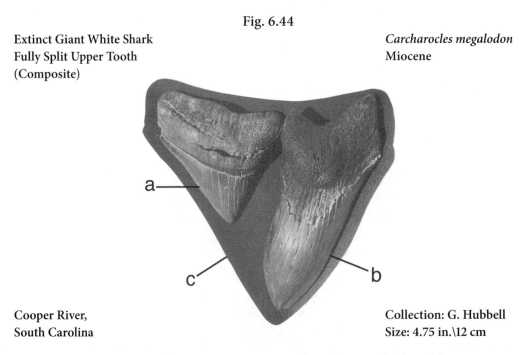

Cooper River,
South Carolina

Collection: G. Hubbell
Size: 4.75 in.\12 cm

Fig. 6.44. A severe injury to the jaw may cause one tooth to split completely and form two pathologically shaped teeth, (a) and (b). Shape (c) shows how the tooth should have looked. The etiology of this pathology was inferred from analogous modern great white jaws with similar injuries. Teeth (a) and (b) were found separately in this case.

Fig. 6.45

Extinct Giant White Shark
Curved Upper Tooth

Carcharocles megalodon
Miocene

Bone Valley Formation,
Polk County, FL

Collection: G. Hubbell
Size: 1.75 in.\4.2 cm

Fig. 6.45. Severely bent or curved shark teeth are a fairly common pathological find. This type of pathology could also be caused by injury to the jaw while the tooth was still forming.

Fig. 6.46

Mako Shark
Pathological Upper Tooth

Isurus hastalis
Miocene

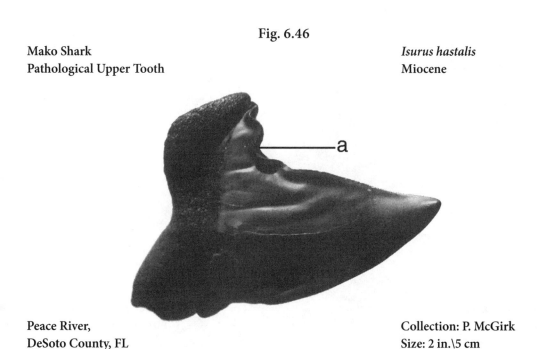

Peace River,
DeSoto County, FL

Collection: P. McGirk
Size: 2 in.\5 cm

Fig. 6.46. Shark teeth with wavy edges, such as at (a), are also a common find. The wavy edges may have been caused by injury to the jaw, infection, or a congenital birth defect.

Fig. 6.47

Extinct Giant White Shark
Pathological Upper Tooth

Carcharocles megalodon
Miocene

Bone Valley Formation,
Polk County, FL

Collection: G. Hubbell
Size: 5.75 in.\14.4 cm

Fig. 6.47. This megalodon tooth exhibits rippled or wavy enameloid surfaces along both sides. This pathological anomaly may occur as the result of injury or infection in the jaw while the tooth is forming (see previous figure).

Fig. 6.48

Extinct Giant White Shark
Upper Tooth with Atavistic Side Cusps

Carcharocles megalodon
Miocene

Venice Beach,
Florida

Collection: R. Loster
Size: 4.5 in.\11.2 cm

Fig. 6.48. The side cusps (a) and (b) on the base of this megalodon tooth may be the expression of an atavistic trait from ancestral sharks that once bore side cusps. On rare occasions, modern great white sharks are found with side cusps on all their teeth.

Fig. 6.49

Extinct Giant White Shark
Pathological Tooth

Carcharocles megalodon
Miocene

Venice Beach,
Florida

Collection: R. Loster
Size: 3.25 in.\8 cm

Fig. 6.49. The etiology of this severely deformed megalodon tooth is problematic. Possible causes could be injury to the jaw during formation, infection during formation, or a congenital birth defect.

trait in a modern animal. The prehistoric ancestors of megalodon sharks had these side cusps on their teeth. Atavisms occur when ancient, silenced DNA is turned on or reactivated accidentally *in utero* and a long-lost trait is again expressed.[7] Finally, many pathological anomalies exist in both the fossil record and the extant record of sharks that would be considered problematic at best; there is no known etiology of their occurrences (figs. 6.49–6.53).

Congenital Anomalies and Problematic Specimens

As with fossilized bones, teeth with anomalies caused by birth defects or genetic mutations are considered congenital. These anomalies may be minor and show few morphological effects, or they may have a considerable effect on tooth morphology. Anomalies in shark teeth were described in the previous section. Specimens of anomalies in the teeth of terrestrial vertebrates, as with those of sharks' teeth, are often prized by amateurs and professionals alike; however, existing pathological sharks' teeth far outnumber those of terrestrial vertebrates.[8] A mammal tooth with a congenital anomaly may be of considerable scientific value and should be offered to the appropriate museum or university to determine its locality of origin. The following plates demonstrate various anomalies, from extra cusps (figs. 6.54 and 6.55), to severely misshapen teeth (fig. 6.55), to misaligned teeth within a jaw (fig. 6.56).

Fig. 6.50

Bull Shark
Tooth with Splitting

Carcharhinus sp.
Miocene

Venice Beach,
Florida

Collection: R. Loster
Size: 0.6 in.\1.2 cm

Fig. 6.50. This problematic bull shark tooth has splits at (a) and (b) that even formed additional serrations. Pathological cause unknown.

Fig. 6.51

Pathological Shark Teeth

Multiple species
Miocene–Holocene

Various Florida Sites

Collection: R. Loster
Size: All teeth approximately 0.5 in.\1.2 cm

Fig. 6.51. Numerous pathological shark teeth from various species are represented here, including a variety of pathological anomalies in the gums, serration, enameloid, and general morphology (shape).

Fig. 6.52

3 Pathological Shark Teeth

Various species
Miocene

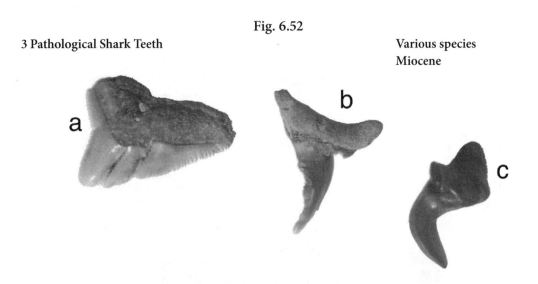

Various Florida sites

Collection: R. Loster
Size: 0.5 in.\1.1 cm (a)

Fig. 6.52. All three of these small shark teeth exhibit some type of pathology. (a) Bull shark tooth with multiple splits; (b) malformed sand tiger shark tooth; (c) severely bent or curved sand tiger shark tooth.

Fig. 6.53

5 Pathological Shark Teeth

Multiple species
Miocene to Pleistocene

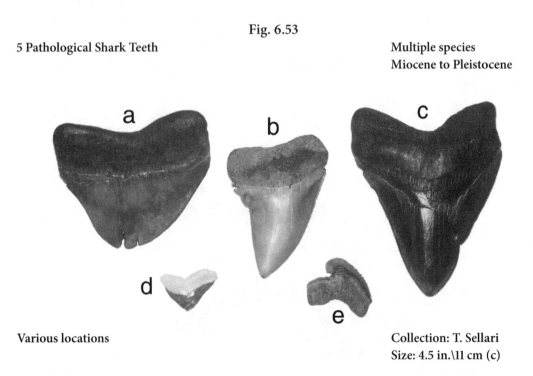

Various locations

Collection: T. Sellari
Size: 4.5 in.\11 cm (c)

Fig. 6.53. (a) A malformed *C. megalodon* tooth with two splits; (b) a mako shark tooth with an enameloid bubble; (c) a *C. megalodon* tooth with a small side split (note extra serration); (d) believed to be a small malformed *C. megalodon* side tooth; (e) tiger shark tooth with a deformity at the gum line.

As with pathological fossil bones, pathological fossil teeth often do not fit any category or description. The specimen is often obviously malformed, but the etiology is impossible to determine. These teeth are considered problematic specimens (figs. 6.57–6.63). As mentioned, scientists may invest much time and effort in researching the case of a single problematic specimen.[9]

Fig. 6.54

Gomphothere
Tooth with Extra Cusp

Gomphotherium sp.
Miocene to Pliocene

Collection: B. Fite
Size: 8.25 in.\20.5 cm

Fig. 6.54. This gomphothere tooth has an anomalous extra cusp attached to the side (a). Note that this tooth exhibits almost no wear pattern, signifying that the animal died with the tooth still in its mouth.

Fig. 6.55

Tapir Tooth
Problematic Morphology

Tapirus veroensis
Pleistocene

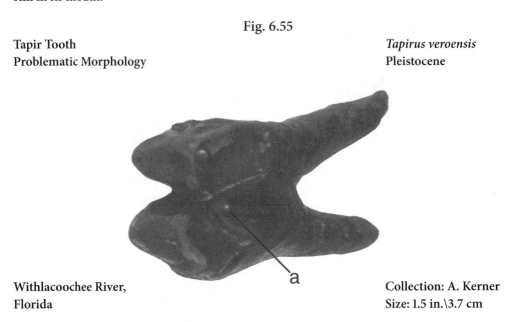

Withlacoochee River,
Florida

Collection: A. Kerner
Size: 1.5 in.\3.7 cm

Fig. 6.55. This tapir tooth has an unusual morphological shape for teeth from that species. It appears to have begun to develop an extra cusp at (a).

Fig. 6.56

Native American Dog Jaw
with Extra Incisor

Canis familiaris
Holocene

Hillsborough County,
Florida

Collection: A. Kerner
Size: 5.25 in.\6 cm

Fig. 6.56. This dog jaw has four incisors on the right side of its jaw instead of the usual three. Early Native American tribes may have become very isolated, and the dogs they owned may have been subjected to excessive inbreeding.

Fig. 6.57

Mastodon Tooth
in Coprolite/Concretion

Mammut americanum
Pleistocene

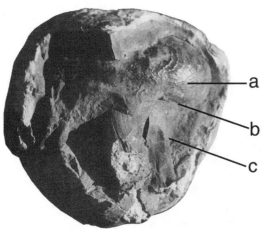

Collection: B. Fite
Size: 1.5 in.\3.5 cm

Fig. 6.57. This baby mastodon tooth is encased in a concretion or coprolite. Proboscideans (mastodons, mammoths) exfoliated smaller teeth as the teeth approached the front of the jaw to make room for the next set of progressively larger teeth. A large carnivore may have inadvertently swallowed this baby tooth while eating the mastodon and it ended up in this coprolite. If a proboscidean swallowed its own exfoliated tooth, it might be pitted with stomach acids (see fig. 4.12). The crown is at (a), the gum line is at (b), and a partial root is at (c).

Fig. 6.58

Camel Tooth
with Fused Extra Cusp

Hemiauchenia macrocephala
Pleistocene

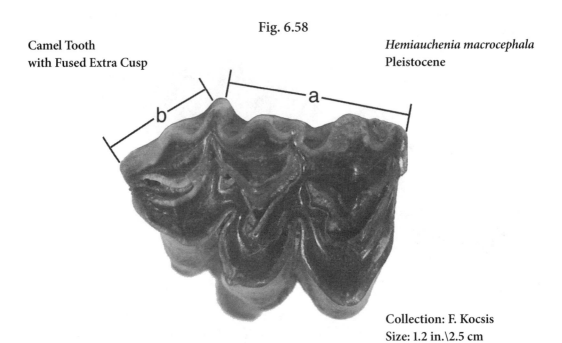

Collection: F. Kocsis
Size: 1.2 in.\2.5 cm

Fig. 6.58. This camel upper molar should have only two sets of selenodont cusps (a); however, a third set of cusps (b) has fused to the tooth.

Fig. 6.59

Pathological Sloth Tooth

Megalonyx wheatleyi
Early Pleistocene

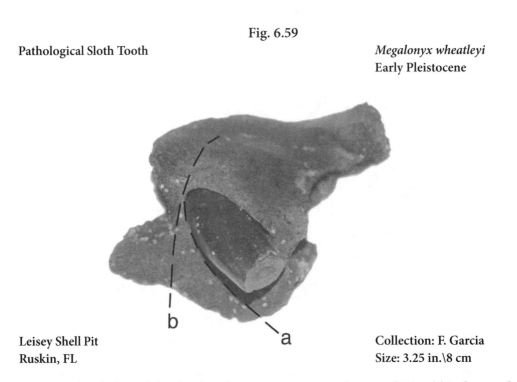

Leisey Shell Pit
Ruskin, FL

Collection: F. Garcia
Size: 3.25 in.\8 cm

Fig. 6.59. This sloth tooth has developed a more severe curve than usual. Line (a) is the actual curve of the tooth, and line (b) the curve it was supposed to take.

Fig. 6.60

Mammoth Jaw
with Misaligned Teeth

Mammuthus columbi
Pleistocene

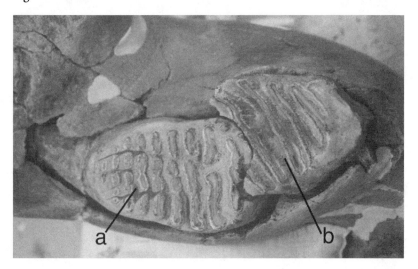

La Belle Highway Pit
Hendry County, FL

Collection: FLMNH
Size: 15 in.\37.5 cm

Fig. 6.60. This mammoth jaw was in the process of replacing tooth (b) with tooth (a), which is pushing it out from behind; however, the teeth are aligned incorrectly and off center. This misalignment caused an unusual wear pattern and shape in both teeth. This pathological problem is not major, but similar to a condition in humans corrected by braces.

Fig. 6.61

Mammoth Maxilla
with Differential Wear

Mammuthus columbi
Pleistocene

La Belle Highway Pit,
Hendry County, FL

Collection: FLMNH
Size: 13 in.\32.5 cm

Fig. 6.61. The two mammoth teeth in this maxilla are noticeably different in size. Some animals chew preferentially on one side of their mouths, causing teeth on that side to wear more quickly. In this example, had the animal lived longer, a thin rim of tooth would have worn off below the dotted line on tooth (b), leaving that tooth very similar in size to tooth (a).

Fig. 6.62

Proboscidean Tusk
Pathological

Undetermined species
Pleistocene

La Belle Highway Pit,
Hendry County, FL

Collection: FLMNH
Size: 5.75 in.\14.8 cm

Fig. 6.62. It is unknown what could have caused such pathological features on this tusk; however, since tusk material is produced in layers from birth, it can be presumed that this pathology began very early in the life of this animal. See figures 3.30–3.37 for comparison with normal tusk material.

Fig. 6.63

Three-toed Horse Teeth
Pathological Upper Molar

Neohipparion eurystyle
Pliocene

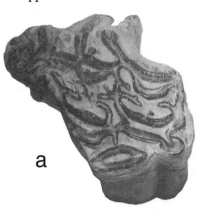

a

b

Gardinier Mine,
Polk County, FL

Collection: FLMNH
Size: 1.5 in.\3 cm (b)

Fig. 6.63. It is uncertain what caused the pathological feature on tooth (a) of this three-toed horse. Compare to tooth (b), a healthy specimen. Both views are of the occlusal surface.

CHAPTER 7

Cultural Modification of Bones, Antlers, and Teeth

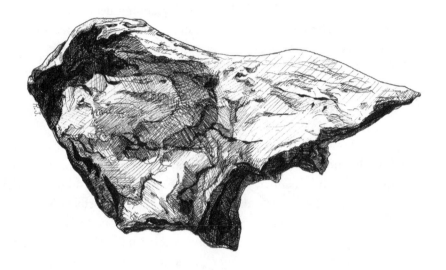

And all our scientific interpretations and theories are simply meaningless.
There are facts, of course . . . but with us as with artists and other impractical people,
here facts are considered as only such as mud and straw unless they can be piled up
into a hypothesis, gaily stuccoed and concealed with theory.

George Gaylord Simpson

Introduction

Cultural modification of bones, antlers, and teeth by Paleo-Indians (the earliest Native Americans), and those Native Americans who followed, truly deserves a book unto itself. It is hoped that what is presented here can give the amateur or beginning paleontologist and archaeologist a reasonable start in recognizing cultural modifications to bones, antlers (a specialized type of bone), and teeth. Any bones, antlers, or teeth that show signs of work by Native Americans can be considered culturally modified. Paleo-Indians and Native Americans worked bones, antlers, and teeth for a variety of reasons. Tools, weapons, instruments, ornaments, and simply butchering of meat from bones are all common examples of cultural modification. It is very likely that these same bone and tooth modifications persisted for thousands of years with little change. Two very different viewpoints determine what can and cannot be considered culturally modified materials. The liberal viewpoint considers many of the markings and breaks found on bones to be the works of Native Americans. The conservative viewpoint attributes very little to cultural modification unless the evidence is extremely strong.[1] This chapter will present both viewpoints on specimens, as well as many specimens on which even professionals cannot agree.

Culturally modified faunal materials (bone, teeth, and antler) provide scientists and amateurs with a major source of information on the lifestyles of early Native Americans. Along with faunal items, stone tools, shells, ceramics, metals, and, on very rare occasions, cultivated plant remains, wood,[2] and other biological materials also provide information about prehistoric cultures. Because they left no written record, these cultures are known mainly from the culturally modified bone, antler, teeth, shell, stone, metal, and other material artifacts found by archaeologists and paleontologists. The classification of culturally modified faunal materials presented in the subsections of this chapter have been artificially imposed by the author to create some order for the reader. Even professional archaeologists have professed that "bone artifacts have long presented problems for archaeologists in terms of functional interpretation" (Walker 1992).

North American occupation by Indians or Native Americans can be broken down into periods or stages.[3] Purdy (1996) notes that archaeologists technically use the term *period* to refer to time, and the term *stage* to refer to a way of life, although many use the terms interchangeably. The **Paleo-Indian period**, approximately 12,000 to 9,000 years ago and of which the **Clovis stage** was the earliest part, was characterized by big game hunting of the megafauna such as mammoths and mastodons; however, consensus on a pre-Clovis period may be emerging with the discovery of new evidence.[4] During the **Archaic period**, 9,000 to 4,000 years ago, Native Americans had to adapt to swiftly changing environments brought about by the end of the last ice age. They lived on deer, fish, shellfish, nuts, berries, and almost anything the land would give them. The **Ceramic period**, 4,000 to about 500 years ago, when first contact was made with Europeans, is noted for development of ceramics, cultivation of plants, and a transition from a nomadic way of life to a lifestyle that included agriculture and culture (mound building and cities). Finally, the period after first contact with Europeans is called the **Historic period**,[5] characterized by trade for glass, iron, horses, metals, guns, and other objects. It is also noted for the almost complete destruction of the Native American way of life and of the people themselves. Archaeologists further divide the Paleo-Indian, Archaic, and Ceramic periods into early, middle, and late.[6]

Laws and ethics governing culturally modified items (artifacts) are generally more stringent than those governing fossils. One should research local and state laws to determine what one can and cannot find and keep. These laws and guidelines differ from state to state, and they differ regarding fossils and artifacts. In general, considerably fewer culturally modified material items exist than fossils. In North America, Paleo-Indians arrived between 10,000 and 12,000 years ago (although new evidence may push these dates back as far as 30,000–40,000 years ago).[7] Therefore, geologically speaking, culturally modified items have been accumulating in North America for only a very short time, compared with the fossil record of more than 3.5 billion years.

Fossil enthusiasts who put enough time into hunting will eventually find culturally modified material even if they are not looking specifically for it. Many amateur and professional archaeologists, by contrast, have fine fossil collections as a byproduct of their hunts for artifacts. Therefore, some knowledge and recognition of culturally modified material is important in both fields. Many fine identification books have been published on stone implements;[8] however, culturally modified bones, teeth, and antler material are not well presented in the popular press for amateurs or undergraduate students.[9]

A cautionary note on culturally modified faunal material is warranted. As a result of the relatively recent nature of many culturally modified items, many may not be fully fossilized, and are thus considered subfossil or modern. These specimens may require special preservative treatment with hardeners developed specifically for this purpose. Before attempting to treat any subfossil specimen, consult an expert. Permanent damage or complete destruction of an item may occur if it is mistreated. As with fossils, this may result in a total loss of information and data on an important specimen that cannot be replaced. In addition, culturally modified bones and teeth are far rarer than other items such as modified shell and stone items. Archaeologist Jerald Milanich reports that at the Hawkshaw site in Florida, more than 15,000 potsherds and 80 chipped stone implements were recovered, whereas only 12 bone artifacts were found. This should give one an idea of the relative importance of modified bone, antler, and teeth for scientific study.[10]

Although the majority of the items presented in this chapter came from Florida,[11] it is believed that the concepts they represent can be applied throughout North America. In addition, many specimens presented are not very old, geologically speaking, and are therefore not fully fossilized; however, it is the writer's opinion that the majority of modifications to the faunal material in the following sections are representative of earlier Native American workmanship from the late Pleistocene.

Unintentional Modifications

Bones, antlers, and teeth are often found with markings that are the byproduct of butchering or use of the materials for other purposes. These markings are unintentional in that they are not planned modifications to the material. Besides marks from butchering, marks or alterations might have been left on discarded materials after the desired portion of the bone was removed. Materials used as percussive devices often have traces of wear on the portion used as a handle as well as on the end used as a hammer or wedge device. In addition, many bones were intentionally split to remove the nutritious marrow or flammable grease from the shank or long part of the bone. Of these types of unintentional modifications, butchering marks are by far the most common cultural modification left in the archaeological or paleontological record.

Butchering and Other Unintentional Alterations

Butchering marks occur on bones, antlers, and teeth generally as a byproduct of removal of meat from the item. These marks are often extremely difficult to differentiate from markings left by gnawing on the bones by various carnivores and scavengers or even marks left on bones passing over rocks or hard river bottoms (fig. 7.1). A scanning electron microscope (SEM) can assist scientists in determining the exact cause of marks left on bones. Marks made by humans on bones by stone implements generally leave sharp V-shaped incised cut marks.[12] Occupation sites, kill sites, and other sites associated with human contact do not provide definitive proof that cut marks found on bones at those sites were made by human hands and tools.[13] These sites have often been visited and scavenged by carnivores after being vacated. In addition, many human occupation sites had some form of domesticated dog that may have chewed on bones at the site. Butchering marks should occur at points on the bone that would be useful for removing meat efficiently (in a correct anatomical position for that bone), and the marks should be of a nature that would be made by the tools available to the associated culture of that site. In this situation, bones with questionable markings found in isolation or in contexts of redeposition are often highly problematic. Markings that cut across tendon and ligament attachment sites are evidence of bone defleshing. Most current literature suggests that cut marks made by humans do not follow the contour of the bone. Cut marks made by humans should be deeper at the portions of bone that are raised and shallower at the portion that is depressed (fig. 7.2). Animal gnawing marks tend to be of

Fig. 7.1

Proboscidean
Butchered or Gnawed Bone

Undetermined species
Late Pleistocene

Peace River,
DeSoto County, FL

Collection: R. Sinibaldi
Size: 3.25 in.\8 cm

Fig. 7.1. The deep cut marks on this bone could have been caused by butchering, but they were more likely caused by the gnawing of a large carnivore.

Fig. 7.2

Camel Cannon Bone
with Butchering Marks

Undetermined species
Late Pleistocene

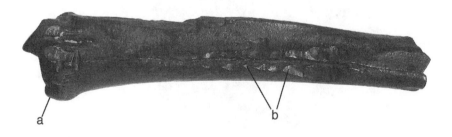

a

b

Suwannee River,
Florida

Collection: J. Tatum
Size: 9.25 in.\23.2 cm

Fig. 7.2. Cut marks at (a) are at a site where tendon and ligaments would need to be cut to detach the bone from adjoining bones. Cut marks at (b) probably resulted from removing meat from the bone. Note that the butchering marks do not follow the contour of the bone.

Fig. 7.3

Horse Tibia
from a Cougar Den

Equus sp.
Felis concolor

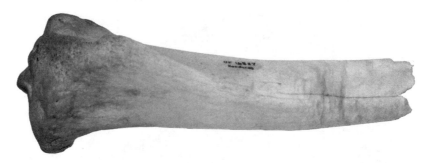

Honduras

Collection: FLMNH
Size: 10 in.\25 cm

Fig. 7.3. Note that the cougar gnawing marks on this horse limb bone follow the curve of the bone at relatively equal depth. Compare these carnivore gnawing marks to the butchering marks in figure 7.2.

Fig. 7.4

Mammoth Tooth
Suspected Modification Marks

Mammuthus sp.
Pleistocene

Santa Fe River,
Florida

Collection: B. Fite
Size: 8.6 in.\21 cm

Fig. 7.4. The marks on the side of this mammoth tooth (a) are far too uniform to be gnaw marks from a carnivore. Had the tooth been found in northern regions, possible glacial scrapings could be suspected. Because it is a Florida specimen, glacial scraping can be ruled out. As for cultural modification, the specimen remains problematic as to what early natives may have been doing (if anything) to this tooth.

Fig. 7.5

Broken Leg Bones
with Spiral Fractures

Various species
Late Pleistocene

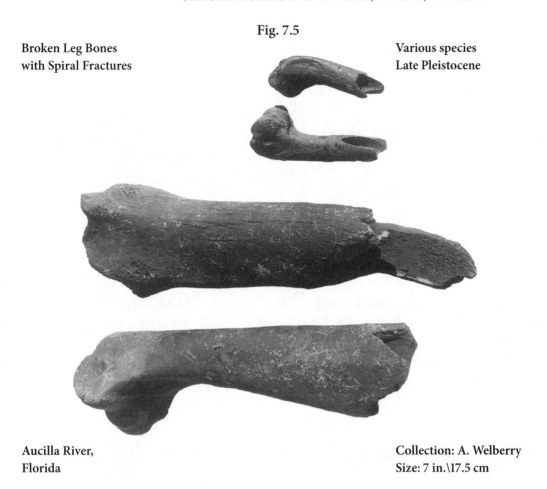

Aucilla River,
Florida

Collection: A. Welberry
Size: 7 in.\17.5 cm

Fig. 7.5. Many long bones break in similar fashion because they developed to resist stresses in specific areas. Finding bones with similar breaking patterns does not automatically mean one can conclude "working" or "butchering" by early natives.

equal depth across the curvature of the bone (fig. 7.3); however, unmistakable markings are sometimes seen on bones, teeth, and antlers in areas that puzzle today's archaeologists (fig. 7.4).

The splitting of bones to obtain marrow for nutrition or flammable grease is a common practice among indigenous cultures. However, distinguishing between splitting of bones by human hands and by the actions of animals is problematic. Most traditional societies remaining today practice some form of this technique. By analogy we can presume with some confidence that early Native Americans also split long bones to obtain the marrow inside; however, research by Lewis Binford suggests that humans rarely split long bones mid-diaphysis. In his opinion the majority of bones reported in the literature as modified by humans represent wishful thinking on the part of researchers (fig. 7.5).[14] In contrast, many other researchers report that it is possible to determine with

Fig. 7.6

Butchered or Modified Deer Jaw   Archaic Period

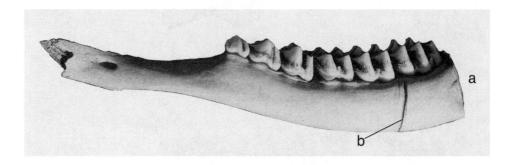

Collection: B. Fite
Size: 6 in.\15 cm

Fig. 7.6. This deer jaw was worked by early Native Americans who cut it completely through at (a) and partially at (b). They may have been in the process of making the jaw into a scraper for removing fish scales or scraping corn off the cob. Historical analogues exist for this type of modification to deer jaws.

Fig. 7.7

Large Bone Fragment (Proboscidean)   Undetermined species
Butchered or Worked   Late Pleistocene

Withlacoochee River,   Collection: J. Tatum
Florida   Size: 5 in.\12.5 cm

Fig. 7.7. This bone was in the process of being modified by early natives. The extremely deep, neat cut at (a) goes far beyond the necessity of butchering.

Fig. 7.8

Horse Ulna
Modified

Equus sp.
Late Pleistocene

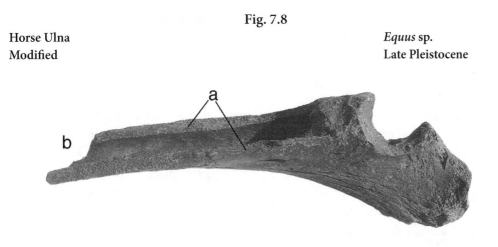

Aucilla River,
Florida

Collection: A. Welberry
Size: 7.5 in.\19 cm

Fig. 7.8. This ulna was probably split to begin processing of the bone, as evidenced by the even split running all the way up (a). The uneven break at (b) probably occurred after the bone was deposited.

confidence when humans have split bones mid-diaphysis.[15] Figures 7.6–7.8 depict butchering and bone splitting. The author has noted items that could not be confidently attributed to human or animal action (for most items shown here, the owner was confident of human alteration).

Finally, bones may be unintentionally altered if used for percussive devices or wedges, or polished from use as a handle. Clear-cut examples of bones and antlers used as handles are discussed under the topic of antler handles and other tools. Bones and antlers used as percussive devices (other than flakers) and wedges are extremely difficult to determine. In analogous modern traditional cultures, a bone or partial bone may be quickly put into use at a butchering site as a wedge to pry apart bones at the joint. These types of tools are referred to as expedient tools in the technical literature. Single-occasion use can alter the bone in a very specific way; however, no long-term wear appears on the portion used as a handle, and the types of damage done to the bone can easily be mimicked by animal action such as scavenging or trampling a carcass after death. Therefore, for the purposes of amateurs, no conclusive evidence (i.e., figures) can be presented of bone modification for use as an expedient tool. Professional archaeologists and paleontologists in a scientific lab usually have access to electron microscopes and other sophisticated devices that can yield clear-cut evidence of bone modification far beyond the capacity of most amateurs. Scientists doing microwear analysis can detect various polish and wear patterns on bone and stone tools that indicate the type of materials that came into contact with the implement, including wood, leather, and bone.

Intentional Modifications

Numerous modifications to bones, teeth, and antlers are fine examples of intentional cultural modification. Items such as fishhooks, bone pins, **atlatl** (spear thrower) components, handles, jewelry, tools, pressure flakers, partially worked bones, and bones with incised designs are all present in the archaeological record. The functions of the majority of these items can be determined with some confidence; however, once again, problematic specimens exist showing clear evidence of cultural modification, although their exact cause or purpose is unknown to the modern observer. The processes of manufacture of many of these items are also often uncertain. Partially worked or unfinished specimens can often give a clue to the intermediate steps in their manufacture but still may fall short of telling the complete story.

Fishhooks and Related Items

A variety of fishing hooks and barbed implements, presumably for use in fishing, exist in the archaeological record.[16] Holding these fragile objects in the hand, one can only marvel that such small items survived in the archaeological record. Furthermore, production of these minute items must have been a remarkable feat of manufacturing and manual dexterity for early peoples. Anyone who has fished with a Shakespeare brand rod and reel and the finest Eagle brand hooks, not to mention monofilament line, and then come home frustrated by the one that got away, will truly appreciate the skill of Native Americans in fishing with these hooks.

The first type of hook (fig. 7.9) features a single small piece of bone, pointed at both ends and usually with a groove etched into the middle for tying to a line. This type of hook is referred to in the literature as a **gorge**, or sometimes a throat gorge. Although not hook shaped, it was baited with the hope that, when a fish swallowed it, it would get lodged in its throat. Once again, one can only speculate on the success rate of such a device. A second type of fishhook, termed a J-shaped fishhook in the literature, is shown in figures 7.10–7.13 and comprises a hook carved from a single piece of bone in the common hook shape we all recognize today. J-shaped fishhooks are usually notched at the head of the hook (near the top of the shank) for tying onto a line. Hooks of this style range from very small to fairly large, from 0.5 to 3 inches or better. It appears that most hooks were carved from a longitudinal section of the diaphysis (shank) of a long bone, which would give a natural hook shape and probably be fairly strong when green. Some of these hooks also had barbs on the point to

Fig. 7.9

Primitive Bone Fishhook   Late Pleistocene
Gorge Style

Withlacoochee River,   Collection: J. Tatum
Marion County, FL   Size: 1.8 in.\4.2 cm

Fig. 7.9. This very primitive "fishhook" was tied to a line at groove (a) and baited. As the fish swallowed the bait, it was hoped the two-ended hook would lodge in the fish's throat.

Fig. 7.10

Bone Fishhook   Late Pleistocene

Santa Fe River,   Collection: D. Letasi
Florida   Size: 2 in.\5 cm

Fig. 7.10. This very traditional-looking fishhook, made of bone, had a line tied below the head at (a).

Fig. 7.11

Bone Fishhook   Late Pleistocene

Santa Fe River,   Collection: J. Tatum
Gilchrist County, FL   Size: 2 in.\5 cm

Fig. 7.11. A very narrow and well-sharpened bone fishhook. Note the groove at the bottom, indicating it was probably made from a deer cannon bone.

Fig. 7.12

Large Bone Fishhook   Late Pleistocene

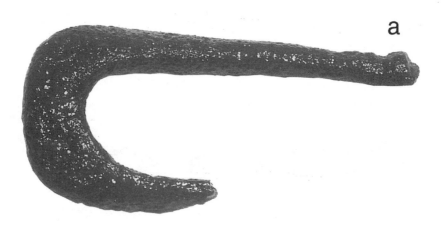

Hillsborough County,   Collection: P. Lien
Florida   Size: 3 in.\7.5 cm

Fig. 7.12. A heavy-duty bone fishhook with traditional head attachment at (a).

Fig. 7.13

Two Small Bone Fishhooks

Late Pleistocene
To Archaic Period

a

b

(a) Santa Fe River, FL

Collection: Ted & Nita Akin

(b) Suwannee River, FL

Size: 0.75 in.\1.5 cm (each)

Fig. 7.13. Although fishhooks made of bone are rare and treasured finds by amateur collectors, this pair of hooks was found on back-to-back trips to the Santa Fe and Suwannee rivers in Florida.

help maintain the fish, once hooked (fig. 7.14).[17] Many more J-shaped fishhooks are found broken than complete (fig. 7.15). It is usually difficult to determine whether the hook was broken while in use, after being discarded, or after fossilization.

A third type of fishhook that appears in the fossil record was manufactured from two separate pieces of bone. These are termed **composite hooks** in the literature. One can only speculate about the advantages of this type of hook. It was probably easier to manufacture in two pieces than to carve a hook from a single piece of bone. In addition, a composite hook may have been stronger than a one-piece hook. In one variation, two small pieces of bone were bound together in a V shape (fig. 7.16). Another style of two-piece hook involved drilling a hole through one small bone and inserting a second bone at an angle to form the hook shape (fig. 7.17). The second bone was often a **baculum**, the penis bone, usually from a raccoon because of its natural curvature.

Finally, included with the fishhooks in this section are barbed harpoon-type fishing tools (figs. 7.18–7.19). These may have been attached to a long wooden shank and used to spear larger fish. In addition, the harpoon may have been attached directly to a line and the long shank pulled back and reloaded with another harpoon point after the first strike was made. Tips of these harpoon

Fig. 7.14

Composite Fishhook
Wood with Bone Barb

Modern Replica

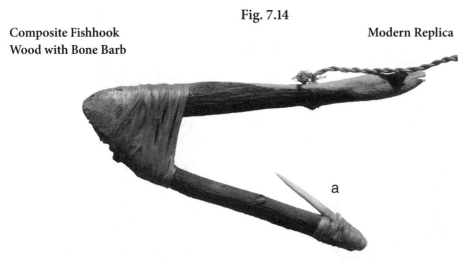

Made by Hermann Trappmann

Collection: H. Trappmann
Size: 5.5 in.\13.5 cm

Fig. 7.14. This modern replica shows one way in which small bone pins were fashioned into the barb portion of a fishhook. Attempting to re-create artifacts with native materials is one way in which modern enthusiasts can test hypotheses. If an experiment does not work, a hypothesis is incorrect; however, if an experiment succeeds, it does not prove conclusively that early Native Americans did things in that way, only that it would have been possible.

Fig. 7.15

Partial Bone Fishhooks

Late Pleistocene

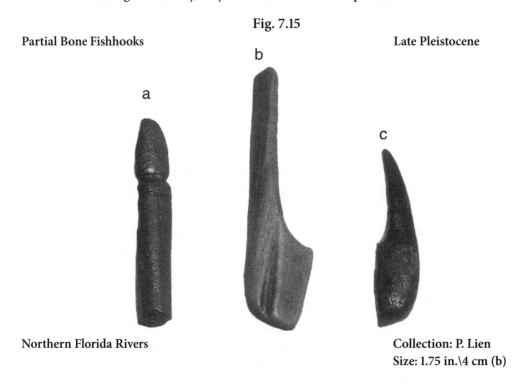

Northern Florida Rivers

Collection: P. Lien
Size: 1.75 in.\4 cm (b)

Fig. 7.15. Broken fishhooks are far more common than complete ones. These partial fishhooks are unmistakable. (a) is a portion of the shank of a fishhook with the groove for line attachment, (b) is the body of a fishhook, and (c) is a fishhook tip.

Fig. 7.16

Composite Bone Fishhook   Late Pleistocene

Withlacoochee River,   Collection: J. Tatum
Florida   Size: 5.5 in.\13.8 cm

Fig. 7.16. It is believed that composite fishhooks were made from a small "barb" of bone (a) attached to a longer shank of bone (b). This combination might then have been attached to a long wooden handle and used as a gig or harpoon.

Fig. 7.17

Composite Bone Fishhook   Late Pleistocene
(a) Deer Antler Tine
(b) Raccoon Penis Bone

Steinhatchee River,   Collection: D. Letasi
Florida   Size: 2 in.\5 cm

Fig. 7.17. This composite fishhook was made by drilling a hole into a deer antler tine (a) and inserting a raccoon penis bone (b).

Fig. 7.18

Bone Barbed Harpoon Tips   Late Pleistocene

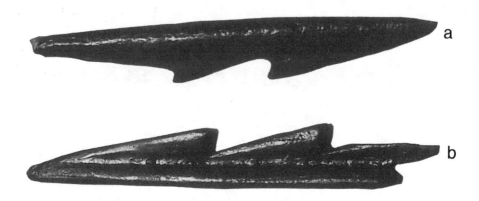

Santa Fe River,   Collection: J. Tatum
Florida   Size: 3.25 in.\8 cm

Fig. 7.18. Tip (a) is believed to be complete. Tip (b) is broken and may have been longer and had an additional barb.

Fig. 7.19

Barbed Harpoon Point   Archaic Period
Deer Antler Tine

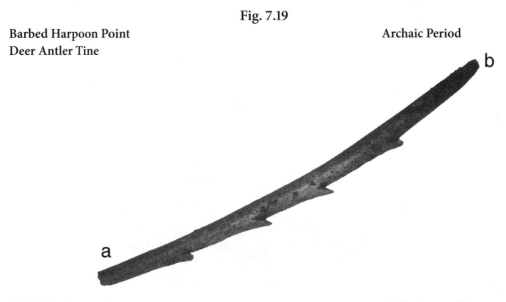

Tick Island,   Collection: A. Kerner
Florida   Size: 5 in.\12.5 cm

Fig. 7.19. The end tip (a) is broken off this almost complete bone harpoon tip. The other end (b) would have been attached to a wooden shaft. In all probability this item was straight when first made. Some scientists believe that bone and ivory have a "memory" and return to their original curvature after years of deposition.

Fig. 7.20

Bone Barbed Harpoon Tips   **Late Pleistocene**

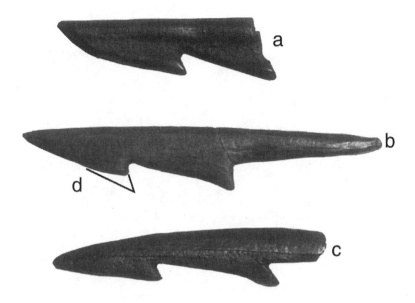

Northern Florida Rivers   Collection of P. Lien
Size: 3 in.\7.5 cm

Fig. 7.20. Three small barbed harpoon tips, probably attached to a long wooden shaft. (a) and (c) are missing part of the shank, and (b) is almost complete, missing only a small portion of a barb at (d).

points are often found broken (fig. 7.20). Another style of harpoon or gigging point was made from a single deer antler tine or bone honed to a very straight point, with an insertion hole at the other end (fig. 7.21). More than 3 inches long, these large points may have been used by Paleo-Indians to harpoon manatees; however, no empirical proof of this use has been found in the archaeological record.

Although fishhooks made of bone are well known in the prehistoric record, finding a fishhook, whole or partial, is always rare and exciting. Upon finding a fishhook, one should take great care in its preservation and treatment; furthermore, the general scarcity of fishhooks may make the find scientifically relevant. Therefore, one should check with the governing archaeological or paleontological organization in the area to see whether it is important in its work. Most organizations will furnish the donor with a cast replica that, when mounted, is virtually indistinguishable from the original.

Fig. 7.21

Harpoon Tip
Deer Antler Tine

Odocoileus virginianus
Archaic Period

Rainbow River,
Marion County, Florida

Collection: R. Sinibaldi
Size: 4.25 in.\10.5 cm

Fig. 7.21. This white-tailed deer antler tine was ground until perfectly straight and pointed. A conical hole was drilled at (a) for attaching to a shaft.

Bone Pins and Related Items

Bone pins are one of the most common artifacts manufactured from bone. The term *bone pin*, sometimes referred to as *bone points*, is a generic term that covers a wide variety of bone modifications with many different functions, some of which are discussed below. Bone pins come in many different sizes, designs, and shapes, and it can be reasonably assumed that this variety corresponded to a variety of functions of bone pins and the cultures that manufactured them. It is believed that the majority of bone pins were made from the metapodials of white-tailed deer; these bone pins often have a troughlike groove running most of their length, derived from the vascular groove inside the bone. Popular materials for the manufacture of bone pins included stingray spines, small mammal ulnae, and other long bones.

The function of some bone pins can be accurately identified through records and drawings of Native Americans kept by later Spanish and French explorers in the New World. According to these records and drawings, some of the larger carved or incised bone pins were used as hairpins. The bounty of bone pins found in many of Florida's rivers may have been lost when Native Americans washed their hair or bathed in the rivers; however, smaller bone pins may have been part of composite fishhooks or other fishing technology items. In addition, many bone pins have been found still inserted into a larger bone or antler handle; therefore, many bone pins were used as piercing tools of some type. Still other bone pins were used as the tips of projectile points. Bone pins may

Fig. 7.22

Bone Pin
in Deer Antler Handle (Composite)

Late Pleistocene

Suwannee River,
Florida

Collection: J. Tatum
Size: 8 in.\20 cm

Fig. 7.22. This finely crafted bone pin was inserted into a deer antler handle and may have been used as an awl. These items were found separately in the river and put together to demonstrate how they were used.

be pointed at one or both ends, inserted into another bone, or engraved; they may be long, short, somewhat thick, or extremely thin, and they may terminate in an end shaped somewhat like the head of a nail, or have a hole in one end.[18] Furthermore, archaeologists believe that as larger bone pins broke they were reworked into smaller pins with a different function from the original.[19] Although the modern-day possessor of a bone pin might tell you its purpose, the functions attributed to the various styles of bone pins are usually purely speculative.

Bone pins found inserted into handles are rare and precious finds. They enable us to state with certainty that bone pins were used as tools for piercing; however, exactly what was being pierced is not certain, and their use as sewing tools, tattooing instruments, awls, or weapons is speculative. Bone pins have been found inserted into deer antler handles (fig. 7.22), small jawbones (fig. 7.23), and larger bone handles (fig. 7.24). In addition, bone pins have been found inserted into clay figurine heads, which can be reasonably attributed to use as ceremonial headgear.

Bone pins that are long and slender may have one pointed end (fig. 7.25), or be pointed at both ends (fig. 7.26). These very plain bone pins may have been used in everyday hair care. There is also a high probability that many bone pins that are found were used as fasteners for "tool kits" in a hide pouch (fig. 7.27). Very often these types of bone pins are found with one end broken off (fig. 7.28).

Fig. 7.23

Bone Pin
in Deer Jaw Handle

Late Pleistocene

Santa Fe River,
Florida

Collection: J. Tatum
Size: 4.5 in.\11.1 cm

Fig. 7.23. A bone pin inserted into this jawbone may have been more ceremonial than utilitarian as the teeth in the jaw would make an uncomfortable handle.

Fig. 7.24

Large Bone Pin
in Camel Bone Handle

Late Pleistocene

Northern Florida River

Collection: P. Lien
Size: 4.5 in.\11.2 cm

Fig. 7.24. A large bone pin was found inserted through a large section of this camel cannon bone. It is uncertain what purpose the tool may have served; however, since camels went extinct at the end of the Pleistocene in North America, it is fairly certain this item is a product of Paleo-Indians.

Fig. 7.25

Large Bone Pin   Archaic Period

Withlacoochee River,   Collection: P. Lien
Florida   Size: 6.5 in.\16.2 cm

Fig. 7.25. This long, slender bone pin was rounded at one end and sharpened to a point at the other.

Fig. 7.26

Bone Pin   Late Pleistocene
Foreshafts

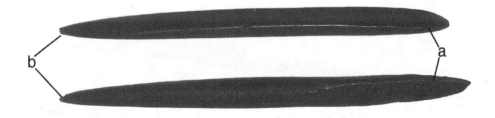

Santa Fe River,   Collection: J. Tatum
Florida   Size: 4.25 in.\10.5 cm

Fig. 7.26. These bone pins with both ends pointed are actually foreshafts for attaching stone points to long wooden spears (see figs. 7.56–7.57). Note the flattened area at (a) for attaching the stone point and the conical end at (b) to insert into a wooden shaft.

Fig. 7.27

Deerskin Carrying Bag
with Bone Pin Fastener

Modern Replica

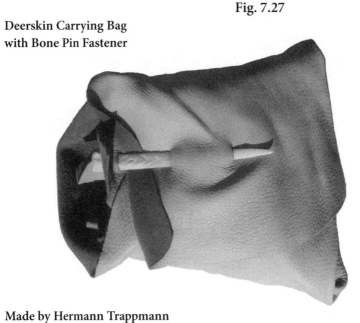

Made by Hermann Trappmann

Collection: H. Trappmann
Size: 10 in.\25 cm

Fig. 7.27. This is a modern replica of a Native American tote bag made of deerskin showing a common example of use of bone pins as fasteners.

Fig. 7.28

Long Bone Pins

Archaic Period

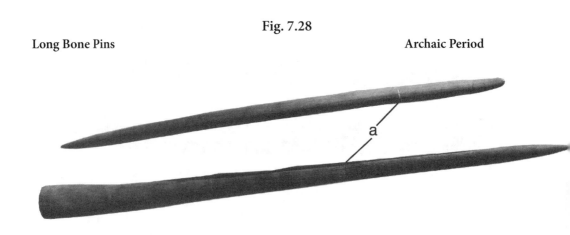

Rainbow River,
Marion County, FL

Collection: M. & S. Searle
Size: 5.25 in.\13 cm

Fig. 7.28. Broken bone pins are a common find. In well-preserved sites, both pieces can be found and reattached. Note repaired break at (a).

Fig. 7.29

Bone Pin Wedges
or Fishhook Barbs

Late Pleistocene

Northern Florida Rivers

Collection: P. Lien
Size: 2 in.\5 cm

Fig. 7.29. These very short bone pins may have been used as wedges for splitting other bones. They may also have been used as the barb portion of a composite fishing hook (see fig. 7.14) or as projectile tips.

It is often difficult to determine whether the break occurred while the bone pin was in use or many millennia later. It is also difficult to determine whether broken bone pins would have had one or two pointed ends. Very short bone pins are often found (fig. 7.29); their use is uncertain, but their length would probably preclude them from certain uses. It has been speculated that short bone pins were used as wedges for splitting other bones or possibly to hold back tissue or meat as animals were being butchered. Long, straight, extremely heavy bone pins may have been **foreshafts** in atlatl components (see page 276). Bone pins with engraving or incising (fig. 7.30) may have been ceremonial hair pins. Bone pins with a hole drilled into one end (figs. 7.31–7.32) evoke the concept of a sewing needle; however, with no direct proof of use as a sewing implement, this style of bone pin may have had other intended uses. Some well-preserved bone pins still bear evidence of **pitch** or other form of adhesive used to attach them to other objects (fig. 7.33).

Bone pins with expanded heads, peg-topped heads, or T-shaped heads (sometimes resembling modern nail heads) carved into the bone (figs. 7.34–7.36), or their original articular end as a head may have been used as **feather holders**. On rare occasions bone pins like these have been found with a ceramic bead that would have been pushed over the pin to hold the feather in place. These expanded heads may appear round or as somewhat long protuberances off to one or both sides (fig. 7.37). As with fishhooks (see previous section), these

Fig. 7.30

Ornamental Bone Pin   Middle Archaic Period
Incised with Geometric Patterns

Withlacoochee River,   Collection: T. Sellari
Marion County, FL   Size: 7.4 in.\18 cm

Fig. 7.30. This long bone pin was completely incised with geometric patterns. It was probably used as an ornamental hairpin. See figures 7.41–7.51 for additional incised items.

Fig. 7.31

Bone Pin Needles   Late Pleistocene

Santa Fe River,   Collection: J. Tatum
Florida   Size: 2 in.\5 cm (top)

Fig. 7.31. These small bone pins with a hole drilled in one end may have been used as sewing needles.

Fig. 7.32

Bone Pin Needle   Late Pleistocene

Santa Fe River,   Collection: J. Tatum
Florida   Size: 6.25 in.\15.5 cm

Fig. 7.32. This long bone pin with a hole drilled in one end may have been used as a sewing
needle.

Fig. 7.33

Bone Pin   Late Pleistocene
with Evidence of Pitch Attachment   To Archaic Period

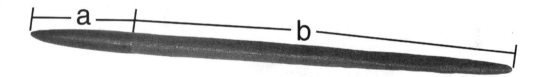

Withlacoochee River,   Collection: A. Kerner
Florida   Size: 6 in.\15 cm

Fig. 7.33. Section (a) of this bone pin still bears evidence of its attachment to or insertion in another object with pitch or resin adhesive. The remainder of the bone pin (b) fossilized differently
than section (a).

Fig. 7.34

Bone Hair Pins

Late Pleistocene
to Archaic Period

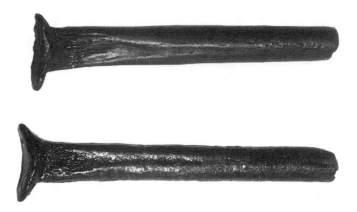

Withlacoochee River,
Florida

Collection: P. Lien
Size: 2 in.\5 cm

Fig. 7.34. These bone pins with an expanded head may have been inserted into another bone or clay ornament for use as feather holder hair pieces.

Fig. 7.35

Bone Hair Pins

Archaic Period

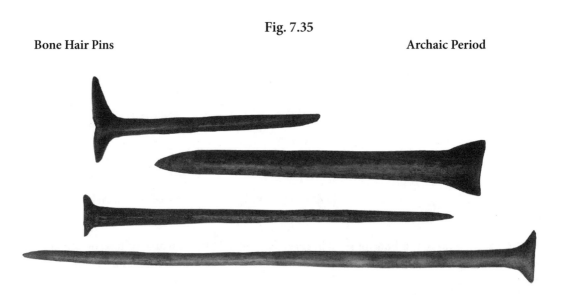

St. Johns River
Lake County, FL

Collection: B. Evensen
Size: 4.4 in.\11 cm (top)

Fig. 7.35. In a well-preserved site, extremely fragile specimens may not only remain intact, but also occur in multiples.

Fig. 7.36

Bone Pin Feather Holder   Protohistoric Period

Chassahowitzka River,   Collection: B. Evensen
Citrus County, FL   Size: 1.8 in.\4.5 cm

Fig. 7.36. Presented here is a variation of a short pin with an expanded "T" head carved from bone. This may have been used as a feather holder.

Fig. 7.37

Bone Hair Pin   Late Pleistocene
                                                           to Archaic Period

Santa Fe River,   Collection: J. Tatum
Florida   Size: 3.25 in.\8 cm

Fig. 7.37. This bone pin with a "push-type" head may have been used to hold feathers when pushed into a bone or clay ornament (compare with figs. 7.33–7.35).

Fig. 7.38

Various Bone Pins

**Late Pleistocene
to Archaic Period**

Florida Rivers

**Collection: T. Sellari
Size: 6.4 in.\16 cm (top)**

Fig. 7.38. Bone pins are a fairly common find in Florida's rivers. They come in a variety of shapes, sizes, and states of preservation.

very fragile bone implements rarely survive in the archaeological record with the expanded head attached and are remarkable reminders of the fine workmanship of Native Americans. The traditional straight bone pin with no extra workmanship is a common find and often found by the dozens at a single site (fig. 7.38).

Finally, as reported by Purdy (1996), some bones and antlers were modified for use with bone pins to be used in the hair. Sometimes engraved, but often plain (fig. 7.39), these items had a hole drilled in them through which a lock of hair could be pulled, then some type of pin inserted to hold it in place. This would make them something like an ancient barrette. An engraved item of similar design (fig. 7.40) was suggested as a possible atlatl counterweight. Note that the hole on this item is of much larger bore and approximately 90 degrees further around the shank of the antler.

Carved and Incised Designs

Designs **carved** or **incised** into bone or antler material can come in a variety of forms. Bones and antlers may have been ornamented to honor and appease the gods, to pay homage to ancestors, to aid the dead in their journey into the next world, to indicate status, to adorn the body, or for utilitarian purposes in ev-

Fig. 7.39

Bone Pin Holder   Archaic Period
Deer Antler

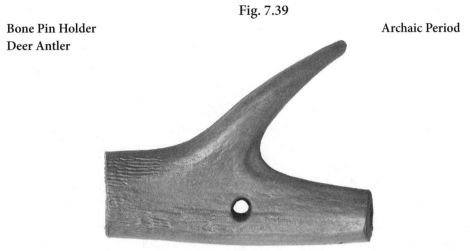

Origin Unknown, Originally   Collection: P. Lien
from the Ben Waller Collection   Size: 3 in.\7.2 cm

Fig. 7.39. This deer antler was drilled and a bone pin (see figs. 7.34–7.37) inserted to hold feathers in the hair.

Fig. 7.40

Atlatl Counterweight   Late Pleistocene

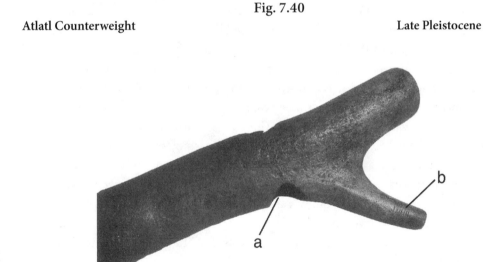

Santa Fe River,   Collection: J. Tatum
Florida   Size: 6 in.\14.8 cm

Fig. 7.40. Compare the size of the hole at (a) in this deer antler, along with its position, to these features in figure 7.39. This object may have been an atlatl counterweight (see fig. 7.45 for the reverse side of this specimen). Note the etchings at (b). If the piece were an atlatl component, could these have been kill tally marks?

eryday survival (Craven in Purdy 1996). R. Dale Guthrie also describes various forms of prehistoric art in terms of a naturalist observer paradigm.[20] It has also been suggested that incising such as tally marks or other symmetrical markings may be forms of **artificial memory systems (AMS)** used by prehistoric cultures to count or keep track of items (Rudgely 1999). When these carved or incised designs do not alter the utilitarian function of an object, the enhancements may be considered early Native American art. A bone pin, atlatl component, or bone handle would function just as well without ornamentation; therefore, the incising or carving can be considered art, whereas the actual manufacture of the item can be considered craft. It is interesting to note that many of the early, large, complex, and finely crafted stone points that required almost incomprehensible skill to make would not be considered art but items made by early Native American craftsmen; however, a piece of bone, stone, or pottery with the simplest zigzag line scratched into it is often considered art and its creator an early Native American artisan.

The subject of Native American cultures and artwork is complex and cannot be completely covered in this book. It is hoped that the brief section presented here will give the reader a glimpse into the possibilities of carving and incising on bone or antler. The Windover site in Florida, an underwater site dated to 7,000–8,000 years ago, demonstrates conclusively that bone was being carved and incised by that time. Each Native American culture had its own trademark designs, styles, and religious themes. For the Southeast alone, motifs and art forms listed by Purdy (1996) include the sun and the moon, the cardinal points, gods of the underworld (fish, frogs), gods of the sky (eagles, falcons), the forked eye, the long-nosed god mask, and the hand-and-eye symbol. Add to these symbols the varied recurring symmetrical patterns that have also been found, and the sheer variety of art styles and subjects is enormous. Items incised in stone have the best opportunity of surviving, followed by shell and then bone. Wood etchings and carvings were probably the most common, as wood is easily worked compared with other media and is readily available; however, wooden items rarely survive for long unless cared for and preserved with modern techniques. Bone items have survived a little better than wooden items in the archaeological record, but compared with the vast quantity of stone items, their presence is meager.

The most common patterns on bone and antler surfaces are symmetrical. They occur on a variety of items, including bone pins (figs. 7.41–7.44), atlatl components (fig. 7.45), bone handles (fig. 7.46), and bone tools (fig. 7.47). Some bone items may be clearly incised while their purported use may remain a mystery (figs. 7.48–7.50). Recall that symmetrical tally marks may also be a form of AMS whose purpose has long been obscured through time. It is also conceivable that some parallel symmetrical etchings on bone may have been primitive

Fig. 7.41

Incised Bone Pin   Archaic Period

Rainbow River,   Collection: P. Lien
Marion County, FL   Size: 4.8 in.\12 cm

Fig. 7.41. This bone pin has faintly incised symmetrical designs spiraling around it.

Fig. 7.42

Incised Bone Pin   Archaic Period

Tick Island   Collection: B. Evensen
Volusia County, FL   Size: 4 in.\10 cm

Fig. 7.42. This is a beautiful example of a completely incised bone pin from the famous Tick Island site in Florida.

Fig. 7.43

Incised Bone Hair Pins   Archaic Period

Tick Island,   Collection: B. Evensen
Volusia County, FL   Size: 4.75 in.\11.8 cm (bottom)

Fig. 7.43. These incised bone pins were probably used as hair pins or feather holders. The amount of ornamentation suggests either ceremonial or decorative use. These were probably more than utilitarian bone pins used as wedges or fasteners.

Fig. 7.44

Incised Bone Feather Holder   Archaic Period

Chassahowitzka River,   Collection: B. Evensen
Citrus County, FL   Size: 4.5 in.\11.1 cm

Fig. 7.44. A series of symmetrical repeating patterns are evident on this incised bone pin, broken off at (a). The pin may also have been used in the hair as a feather holder.

Fig. 7.45

Incised Atlatl Counterweight
Deer Antler

Late Pleistocene

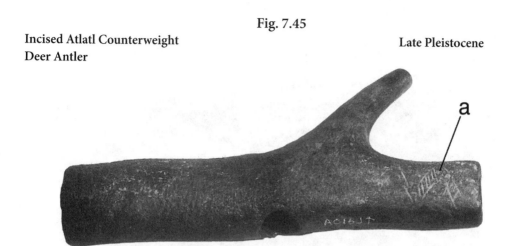

a

Santa Fe River,
Florida

Collection: J. Tatum
Size: 6 in.\14.8 cm

Fig. 7.45. This incised deer antler is believed to be an atlatl counterweight. Note the incised pattern at (a) that suggests a teepee. See figure 7.40 for incising on the reverse side of this specimen.

Fig. 7.46

Incised Bone Handle

Archaic Period

Originally from the
Ben Waller Collection

Collection: P. Lien
Size: 2.5 in.\6 cm

Fig. 7.46. This small bone handle is fully covered with symmetrical incising.

Fig. 7.47

Incised Bone Awl   Archaic Period

Tick Island,   Collection: B. Evensen
Volusia County, FL   Size: 2.6 in.\6.5 cm

Fig. 7.47. This bone awl or point was carved from a deer cannon bone and incised with a symmetrical design. As no wear patterns or scratches are evident, it was probably used ceremonially.

Fig. 7.48

Incised, Carved, and Drilled   Archaic Period
Deer Antler Tine

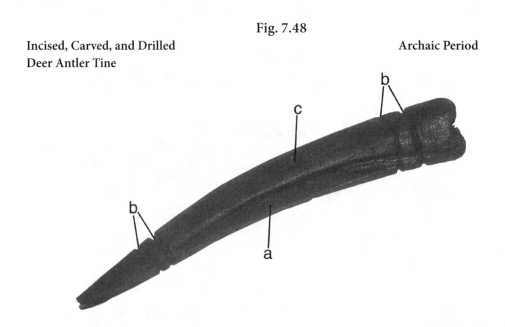

Oklawaha River,   Collection: T. Perez
Marion County, FL   Size: 3.6 in.\9 cm

Fig. 7.48. This deer antler tine has been carved at (a), incised at (b), and drilled at (c). Its intended use is unknown.

Fig. 7.49

Incised Bone   Archaic Period

Tick Island,   Collection: B. Evensen
Volusia County, FL   Size: 5.4 in.\13.5 cm

Fig. 7.49. This bone is completely incised and has holes drilled in several places. Its intended purpose would be complete conjecture.

Fig. 7.50

Incised Bone   Archaic Period

Tick Island,   Collection: B. Evensen
Volusia County, FL   Size: 2.7 in.\7 cm

Fig. 7.50. Views of both sides of this small piece of incised bone show that the crafter took the time to incise exact mirror image designs on both sides.

Fig. 7.51

Incised Deer Jaw   Late Pleistocene

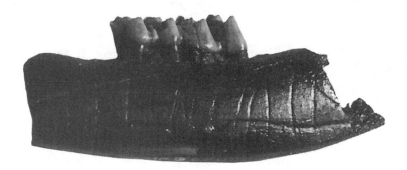

Withlacoochee River,   Collection: J. Tatum
Florida   Size: 3 in.\7.5 cm

Fig. 7.51. This incised deer jaw may have been used as a ceremonial handle (see fig. 7.23).

forms of a rasp, a musical instrument played by rubbing a stick or other implement along the symmetrical etchings.

Random designs or patterns are also common finds on various bone and antler objects (fig. 7.51). Bone modification that conforms to no pattern of design, depth, or placement on the bone may be the work of animal gnawing (fig. 7.52) or trampling. Deep carving or etching on bone is sometimes found that far exceeds the results of butchering (fig. 7.53). It is obvious the bone was worked with a purpose, but that purpose now eludes the modern viewer.

In proposing a neuropsychological model for geometric designs on artifacts, David Lewis-Williams (2002), in his book *The Mind in the Cave*, reports that dots, grids, zigzags, nested curves, and meandering lines are all wired into the human nervous system. No matter what their cultural background, all people have the potential to experience them. These geometric designs can be visualized when individuals experience altered states, whether through trance, psychotropic drugs, illness, or eye pressure. They can be experienced with the eyes closed or open, when the images can be projected onto objects. Lewis-Williams reports that an incising, carving, or painting is usually rendered after an individual exits an altered state. It would be difficult to execute such perfect incising or carving while in an altered state of consciousness; however, memories from the altered state could easily be recalled at a later time and expressed in art.[21] On rare occasions, incised pottery has been found with red or white pigments rubbed into the incisions; additionally, at the Key Marco site in Florida, many wooden items were found that were both carved or incised and painted. Incised

Fig. 7.52

Deer Antler Tine   Archaic Period

Rainbow River,   Collection: M. & S. Searle
Marion County, FL   Size: 7 in.\17.5 cm

Fig. 7.52. This deer antler tine may have been gnawed by an animal or was placed behind something an early native cut into, leaving unintentional marks. It does not resemble typical rodent gnawing (see figs. 5.48–5.51).

Fig. 7.53

Carved Bone   Late Pleistocene

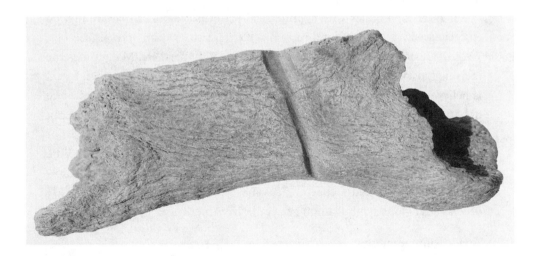

Aucilla River,   Collection: A. Welberry
Florida   Size: 8 in.\20 cm

Fig. 7.53. The groove carved into this large bone exceeds that needed for butchering. The bone's intended design and use are unknown.

Fig. 7.54

Incised Sun Motif

Late Pleistocene
to Archaic Period

Aucilla River,
Florida

Collection: A. Welberry
Size: 6 in.\15 cm

Fig. 7.54. The shank of this disarticulated long bone has been carved with an unmistakable sun motif.

bone items perhaps also had pigments rubbed into their incising to enhance their appearance.

Far rarer than bones with symmetrical patterns are bones that are incised or carved with the image of a recognizable item such as an animal (see figs. 7.124–7.125 at the end of this chapter), object, body part, etc. Many times the incising must be closely inspected and scrutinized to be recognized. Figure 7.54 is believed to be an incising of the sun on the shank of an unidentified piece of bone. The circle and rays possibly depicting the sun are faintly seen and can easily be missed. One can only speculate on the intent of the original artist or owner, as the piece was collected in the mid-1960s in a Florida river with little or no documentation of the circumstances of collection; however, we do know from well-documented archaeological sites that the sun motif was regularly used as a religious symbol among early Native Americans.

Atlatl Components

The atlatl was a form of spear thrower used as an extension of the arm to increase the velocity of the spear.[22] The atlatl could be made entirely of wood; however, many components of the atlatl were often improved with components manufactured from bone, teeth, or ivory and sometimes stone. A projectile point (spearhead) was generally hafted to a foreshaft. The foreshaft was a short

Fig. 7.55

Atlatl and Spear   Modern Replica
(Spear Thrower and Spear Components)

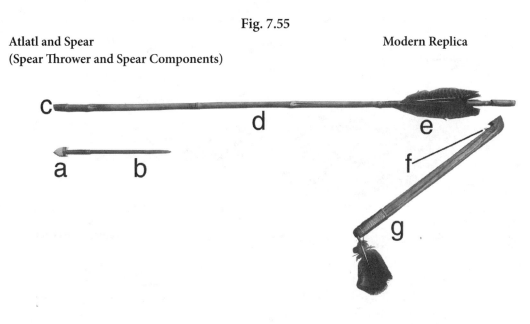

Replica Made By   Collection: R. Sinibaldi
Mike Werner   Size: 50 in.\125 cm

Fig. 7.55. This is a modern replica of an atlatl, or Native American spear thrower. The point is at (a) and was hafted to a foreshaft (b). The foreshaft inserts at (c) into the long shaft (d). Feathers are fletched onto the long shaft at (e). The end of the long shaft inserts into the atlatl throwing arm at (f). The grip of the throwing arm is at (g). The purpose of an atlatl is to extend the length of the arm of the spear thrower and therefore the spear's velocity. Use this modern analogue for comparison with the bone, ivory, and antler items presented in the next few figures.

dowel-like item inserted into a longer spear shaft often several feet long. The shaft may have had feathers fletched to its end or not. The projectile point, the foreshaft, and the long shaft composed the spear. The atlatl was a long wooden implement with a handle at one end, a long shaft (up to several feet in length), and a notched end called the **nock** into which the feathered end of the spear shaft was fit. A replica of an entire atlatl and projectile spear is shown in figure 7.55. The projectile points were almost certainly made of knapped stone and could be up to 6 or 7 inches long during the time of the Paleo-Indians.[23] These points appear to have become progressively shorter over time as the size of game diminished with the extinction of the **megafauna** (large animals) of the late Pleistocene epoch. Atlatl power and accuracy are recorded in several early Spanish accounts of encounters with early Indians in what are now Florida and the Deep South. According to one account, a spear went directly through a horse and killed the Spaniard hiding behind it. In another account, a spear was able to penetrate the metal armor of a mounted Spanish soldier. Unfortunately

Fig. 7.56

Bone Foreshaft   Late Pleistocene
with Simpson Point

Suwannee River,   Collection: A. Kerner
Florida   Size: 5.6 in.\14 cm

Fig. 7.56. It is suspected that Paleo points such as this Simpson were attached to a bone or ivory foreshaft. They were then inserted into a long wooden shaft and launched with the use of an atlatl.

for the Native Americans, the atlatl and spear were no match for the guns, disease, and deceit of Europeans mounted on horses.

Foreshafts could be made of wood, bone (fig. 7.56), or ivory (fig. 7.57). The foreshaft freed the user from carrying more than one or two long spear shanks. A spear shaft was equipped with a projectile point hafted to a foreshaft and "fired" at a target. If the target was struck, the point and foreshaft would remain in the animal. The long shaft would, however, dislodge as the animal ran away, to be recovered and reloaded. This enabled the hunter to carry a small sack with a supply of points hafted onto foreshafts instead of many unwieldy long spears, a likely strategy for traveling light. In addition, the process of manufacturing long shafts that were true and straight was probably not easy; therefore, reducing the number of long shafts needed for hunting might have been important. There is still much speculation as to the use of foreshafts and the method of attaching points. In fact, some still debate whether the foreshaft was truly that; some now believe the implements once designated foreshafts were actually the points. The roughened end attached to a wooden spear shaft and the pointed end speared the prey animal.[24]

At the distal (far) end of the atlatl was a notch or spur where the long shaft was inserted. This notch may have been made of wood, bone (fig. 7.58), or possibly even a tooth (fig. 7.59). The end of the long shaft may have had a reciprocal groove or depression for insertion into the notch. In this way the atlatl could maintain contact with the long shaft while in motion. Bone products would have added strength and flexibility to this component of the atlatl. Bone has a

Fig. 7.57

Ivory Foreshaft   Late Pleistocene

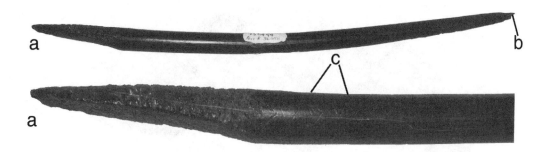

Aucilla River,   Collection: FLMNH
Florida   Size: 12 in.\30 cm

Fig. 7.57. It was once proposed that foreshafts made of ivory, such as this one, were used to attach points to atlatl shafts. The rough area at (a) would have had a point hafted to it, and the pointed end at (b) would be inserted into a long wooden shaft. Note the incising at (c) in the insert. It is now conjectured that end (a) was attached to the long wooden shaft and end (b) used as the actual weapon point.

Fig. 7.58

Bone Nock   Archaic Period
Atlatl Component

Originally from the   Collection: P. Lien
Ben Waller Collection   Size: 1.25 in.\3 cm

Fig. 7.58. This wedge or nock would be used to catch the nock of the shaft of the projectile when an atlatl was used. See figure 7.55 for the location of this component.

Fig. 7.59

Bear Canine Atlatl Nock   Late Pleistocene

Originally from the   Collection: P. Lien
Ben Waller Collection   Size: 2 in.\5 cm

Fig. 7.59. This worked bear canine is believed to have been a wedge used to catch the nock of an atlatl projectile shaft. Note that the root of the tooth is ground completely flat at (a).

greater flexibility and strength than wood and would be far less likely to snap under the pressure of being tossed as part of a large spear. Larger, notched stone or bone counterweights (fig. 7.60), sometimes referred to as **bannerstones**,[25] may have been attached to the distal end of the atlatl. It is believed that these bone additions would have acted as both a notch and a counterweight that would have added even more impetus to the throwing velocity. In addition to this method, it is believed that counterweights with a large hole were also developed and loaded initially near the throwing hand (fig. 7.61). During the motion of throwing the spear, the counterweight would slide up the shank of the atlatl toward the distal end, once again giving additional impetus or snap to the throwing velocity.

Antler Handles, Pressure Flakers, and Knapping Batons

Differences in the properties of deer antler, a very specialized type of bone, from those of most bones in general were significant enough to make deer antler the material of choice for many tools. Deer antler is relatively easily worked if it is soaked for a period of time to give it greater elasticity. Native Americans exploited these properties in many useful ways. In addition to the property advantages of antler material, it was quite abundant. Whether the deer had been killed and butchered or the antler recently shed, Native Americans had great access to this resource. Therefore, use of antler material is quite common in the archaeological record; however, just as with other culturally modified materials,

Fig. 7.60

Bone Atlatl Component   Late Pleistocene

Santa Fe River,   Collection: P. Lien
Florida   Size: 2.8 in.\7 cm

Fig. 7.60. This atlatl component is believed to have formed the base of an atlatl, providing both a counterweight and a nock for the projectile shaft.

Fig. 7.61

Bone Atlatl Counterweights   Late Pleistocene
                                                         to Archaic Period

(a) Withlacoochee River, FL   (a) Collection: P. Lien
(b) Santa Fe River, FL   (b) Collection: J. Tatum
                                                         Size: 3 in.\7.5 cm (b)

Fig. 7.61. Various forms of atlatl counterweights have been found (see figs. 7.40, 7.45). It is believed they were inserted near the bottom part of the throwing mechanism, above the handle. The counterweight would slide down the shaft of the throwing mechanism, adding weight and thus additional velocity to the projectile.

Fig. 7.62

Pressure Flakers
Deer Antler Tines

Late Pleistocene
to Archaic Period

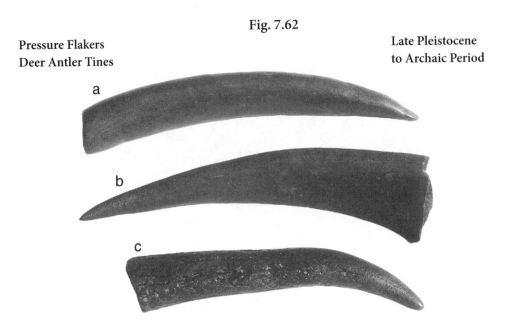

Northern Florida Rivers

Collection: A. Welberry
Size: 3.6 in.\9 cm (a)

Fig. 7.62. Presented are three deer antler tines or tips. Tine (a) has been used as a pressure flaker and is worn smooth at the large end. Tine (b) is a deer antler tine that has broken off its base and exhibits no signs of modification. Tine (c) has a well worn tip and signs of wear at the base, it could be a mimic, or a true pressure flaker.

one must be careful not to attribute every broken or worn antler to use by Native Americans. Mimics, items that look like worked antler as a result of wear or breakage, are often mistakenly designated worked material (fig. 7.62). The effects of trampling, surf, river action, or other natural causes (chapter 4) could have produced a mimic.

The base of the deer antler was often used to manufacture handles for various objects. Both bone pins and stone implements have been **hafted** to antler handles. This is a practice that continued to the Historical period in the West and is one of the better-documented uses of culturally modified materials. Antler handles may have been hollowed out to allow an implement to be inserted (fig. 7.63), or had a groove carved into them to allow attachment as a handle (fig. 7.64). These handles are often extremely worn on the surface from constant gripping (fig. 7.65). It is possible that water action could cause extreme tumbling and polishing; however, it is highly unlikely that it could perfectly carve or hollow out the inner portion of an antler base.[26] On rare occasions an antler base is recovered with the knife blade or bone implement still inserted;

Fig. 7.63

Deer Antler Handle

Late Pleistocene

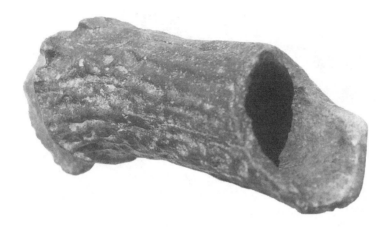

Aucilla River,
Florida

Collection: A. Welberry
Size: 3.75 in.\9.3 cm

Fig. 7.63. This deer antler handle has been extensively worked and is hollowed smooth for the insertion of some type of tool.

Fig. 7.64

Deer Antler Handle

Late Pleistocene

Originally from the
Ben Waller Collection

Collection: P. Lien
Size: 4 in.\10 cm

Fig. 7.64. Two views of this modified deer antler handle show a series of connected holes. Its purpose is undetermined.

Fig. 7.65

Deer Antler Handle   Late Pleistocene

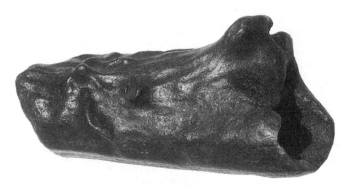

Santa Fe River,   Collection: P. Lien
Florida   Size: 3.5 in.\8.5 cm

Fig. 7.65. The surface of this antler handle has been worn smooth from constant use.

however, this situation is extremely rare. Figure 7.66 is a modern replica of a stone blade equipped with a handle made from deer antler.

Deer antler tines, the tips of the antlers, were often used as **pressure flakers** and **knapping batons** in flint knapping work (fig. 7.67). The knapping batons may have been used to work the initial core material[27] and the pressure flakers to add the last touches to a projectile point, knife blade, or scraper. The elastic property of the antler tine allowed pressure to be applied without causing the flaker to chip. Bone, when green, does not have these properties; wood would be too soft and stone too hard. The almost complete stone implement was held in the hand while the pressure flaker was pressed against the edge of the stone, causing a minute flake to chip off. In this way, knappers (individuals who practice the craft of chipping flakes from stones to make sharpened tools) could put extremely fine edges on their implements. This process also enabled them to work the stone into extremely thin blades if desired. Furthermore, with the use of a pressure flaker, the Native Americans could also rework or retouch damaged blades and points as well as items found from previous generations or cultures, or fashion **pre-forms** (a point or blade with no detail until the user decides exactly how the item will be used) on the spot for different uses. Pressure flakers often exhibit a wear pattern on the contact end and wear on the handle portion of the flaker (fig. 7.68). Flakers are found in a variety of forms, but generally were made from near the tip of an antler tine (fig. 7.69).

It may be added at this point that using a pressure flaker is more of an art than a craft. One small slip, and hours of work are destroyed. A great deal of

Fig. 7.66

Deer Antler Handle
Chert Blade

Modern Replica

Replica made by
Mark Condron

Collection: Mark Condron
Size: 8.75 in.\22 cm

Fig. 7.66. This is a modern replica of a stone blade hafted to a deer antler handle.

Fig. 7.67

Knapping Baton
Made of Deer Antler Tine

Archaic Period

Orange Springs,
Florida

Collection: J. Tatum
Size: 3.25 in.\8 cm

Fig. 7.67. This antler tine was modified into a knapping baton, sometimes referred to as a percussion baton, to strike initial flakes from a stone core in the production of stone implements. Final touches were put on with a pressure flaker (see fig. 7.69).

Fig. 7.68

Knapping Baton or
Atlatl Unfinished Hook

Archaic Period

a

Orange Springs,
Florida

Collection: J. Tatum
Size: 4 in.\10 cm

Fig. 7.68. The rounded end (a) would have been used to press on the edge of a stone implement to flake off extremely small or fine pieces, in order to sharpen the implement. It is also possible that this item is an unfinished atlatl hook.

Fig. 7.69

Pressure Flaker
Deer Antler Tine

AD 1300
Pre-Columbian

Sherman County,
Nebraska

Collection: J. Tatum
Size: 3.5 in.\8.6 cm

Fig. 7.69. This pressure flaker was made from the very end of a deer antler tine. It would have been used to remove extremely small, thin flakes to create a finished stone implement (see fig. 7.70).

Fig. 7.70

Newnan Point
Chert

Archaic Period

a

b

Rainbow River Springs,
Marion County, FL

Collection: R. Sinibaldi
Size: 4 in.\10 cm

Fig. 7.70. A pressure flaker would surely have been used in the fine craftsmanship on this Newnan point (a); (b) is a side view.

experience and knowledge of the properties of different types of stone is required to produce a functional stone implement with a pressure flaker. Modern-day knappers may cheat during the process of making imitation points by using other tools to rough out their pre-forms; however, almost all will resort to a pressure flaker made of antler tine for their finishing touches. Figure 7.70 shows two views of a Newnan point found by the author. This Archaic point, approximately 5,000 years old, was surely produced using some type of pressure flaker. The side view demonstrates the extreme thinness of this point.[28] Although points are not technically considered works of art, anyone who has held a finely crafted large point will realize that the maker was a true artisan.

Tools

Native Americans had many ingenious solutions to the problems of survival, including making a living and accomplishing everyday chores. These solutions often involved the use of modified bones as tools, utensils, and even weapons. With their origins in a variety of cultures spanning a period of at least 10,000 years and a large geographical area, bone implements can be found in signifi-

Fig. 7.71

Fleshing Tool   Protohistoric Period
Bison Cannon Bone

Genoa City,   Collection: J. Tatum
Nance County, NE   Size: 7 in.\17.5 cm

Fig. 7.71. This flesher, used to remove meat from hide, is from the Protohistoric period. Similar fleshers used in the Historic period provide evidence of its intended use, in turn shedding light on earlier forms of fleshers, such as the one in figure 7.72. The serration at (a) may be a fairly recent development. Several carpal bones are still connected at (b).

cant numbers and in many different styles and types, depending on area. In areas such as Florida with few types of stone available, early Native Americans may have made items from bone or fossilized bone similar to stone items in other geographical areas. Once again, as with other topics covered in this chapter, an entire book could be devoted to the bone implements manufactured by Native Americans. Many items described in this section are in various stages of fossilization, from fully fossilized to barely subfossilized. All are believed to be **pre-Columbian** (dating from before contact with Europeans).

Today's archaeologists can often determine the use of an ancient tool by comparing it with a modern analogous item still in use or in use in the recent past. Figures 7.71–7.72 show examples of a **flesher**, a handheld item used to remove any remaining meat from a piece of hide. The specimen from Nebraska is relatively recent, whereas the Florida specimen is fully fossilized. Items like these continued to be used even after European contact. Although Native American women may have chewed on small pieces of hide to soften them for special purposes, it is most likely that the majority of hides, especially large ones, were fleshed out using a tool similar to these.

Arrow shaft wrenches (figs. 7.73–7.74) are a fairly common find, and their use is well established. Shaft wrenches, sometimes referred to as arrow straight-

Fig. 7.72

Fleshing Tool

Late Pleistocene to
Archaic Period

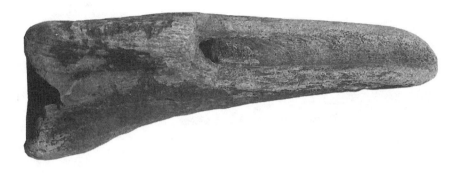

Santa Fe River,
Florida

Collection: J. Tatum
Size: 7 in.\17.5 cm

Fig. 7.72. Compare this very early fleshing tool with that in figure 7.71. Except for the serrated edge shown in figure 7.71, the tools are almost identical.

eners, were used to straighten the shafts of arrows and spears to give them a straight, true flight. The ability to straighten the shaft of an arrow or spear must have been crucial to the success of hunting with a bow and arrow or atlatl. To-day's archers use a compound bow with graphite arrows and a complex sighting device. All their equipment is machined to precision using computerized meth-ods. The shaft wrench was the only known tool and technology used by Native Americans to achieve a quality arrow shaft, upon which their lives depended. Arrow shaft wrenches date back to Old World Paleolithic sites in Europe, and the way they actually work is rather clever.[29]

Bow bearings, a part of a bow drill (figs. 7.75–7.76), were another ingenious solution to a very important problem: making fire and drilling into stone, bone, shell, and wood. It is believed that bow bearings made of either bone or antler were greased with animal fat and the pointed end inserted into a handheld piece of wood or bone. The larger hollow end was fitted with a stick or piece of wood. A string or sinew was wrapped once around the wood and attached at both ends to a bow. The bow may have been made of either wood or a rib bone. By moving the bow in a sawing motion, the user could make the stick revolve extremely fast, causing a great deal of friction and heat. A modern reconstruc-tion of the use of this tool is presented in figure 7.77. This is far more efficient than rubbing two sticks together or trying to rotate a stick in the palms of the hands. A larger and heavier bow bearing would have been employed when drilling objects. The terminal end of the shaft would have been fitted with a

Fig. 7.73

Arrow Shaft Wrench   Protohistoric Period
Bone

Nance County,   Collection: J. Tatum
Nebraska   Size: 6 in.\15 cm

Fig. 7.73. Arrow shaft wrenches were used to straighten wooden shafts of arrows and spears during production. This multiple shaft wrench is unusual. A single wrench is shown in figure 7.74.

Fig. 7.74

Arrow Shaft Wrench   AD 1300
Deer Radius   Pre-Columbian

Sherman County,   Collection: J. Tatum
Nebraska   Size: 4.75 in.\11.6 cm

Fig. 7.74. An arrow shaft wrench produced from a deer radius. Note the fine beveling around the hole.

Fig. 7.75

Bow Bearings
Deer Antler

Late Pleistocene

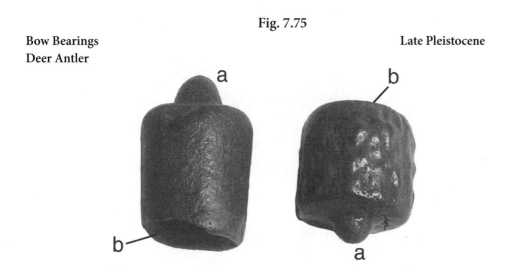

(*left*) Withlacoochee River, FL

Collection: J. Tatum

(*right*) Santa Fe River, FL

Size: 1 in.\2.5 cm (each)

Fig. 7.75. To use a bow bearing, it is believed that the pointed end (a) was placed into a small round board or secondary bone that may have been greased with animal fat (see fig. 7.77). A stick was then placed into the hollow end (b), and that stick wrapped with a bow string. The bow would then be moved back and forth at a fast pace to produce friction and then fire.

Fig. 7.76

Bow Bearing
Deer Antler

Late Pleistocene

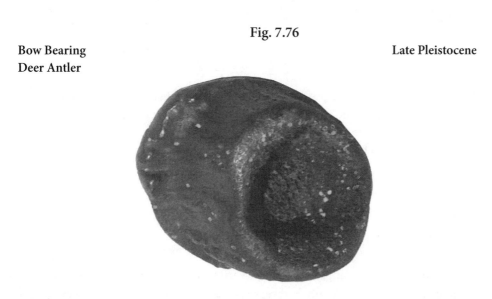

Santa Fe River,
Florida

Collection: P. Lien

Size: 1 in.\2.5 cm

Fig. 7.76. A top view of a small section of deer antler hollowed out for use as a bow bearing. (See figs. 7.75 and 7.77 for a working description.)

Fig. 7.77

Bow Fire Starter   **Modern Replica**

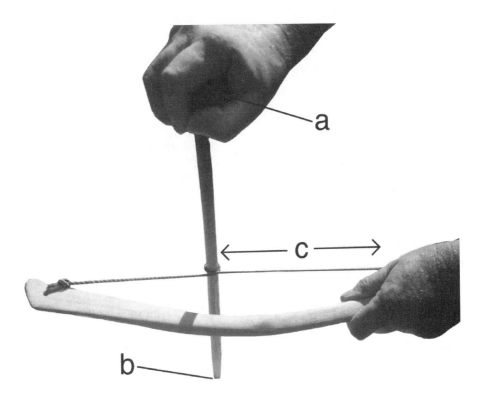

Made by Hermann Trappmann   Collection: H. Trappmann
                                               Size: 10 in.\25 cm (bow)

Fig. 7.77. This modern replica demonstrates how a bow bearing (a), held in the hand on top of a long stick, assists in making fire. The pointed end of the stick (b) is inserted into a piece of hard wood near the ground, and the bow is sawed back and forth, as in motion (c). This creates great friction, and therefore enough heat to quickly start a fire. Note that if a stone tip is added at point (b), a drill is created.

stone drill point; however, the mechanical principle of making fire or drilling a hole was the same.

The largest quantity of items that can be roughly classified together are awls. Awls produced from a range of bones of various animals are so different in style and size that they certainly had very different functions, including working hides and wood, planting seeds, and possibly even tattooing. Some awls are so generalized in shape and size (fig. 7.78) that any statement about their usage would be pure speculation. Awls made from deer antler tines (fig. 7.79) can be detected by wear patterns on the tip from repeated use and are often

Fig. 7.78

Bone Awl

AD 1300
Pre-Columbian

Sherman County,
Nebraska

Collection: J. Tatum
Size: 6.25 in.\15.5 cm

Fig. 7.78. This awl-shaped tool made from bone has a rounded tip. It may have been used for planting seed; it is not sharp enough for punching holes in hides.

Fig. 7.79

Antler Tine Awl

Archaic Period

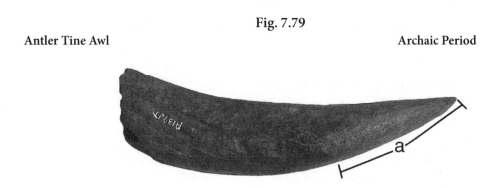

Santa Fe River,
Florida

Collection: J. Tatum
Size: 5.5 in.\13.75 cm

Fig. 7.79. The tip of this deer antler tine has been ground to a sharp point, possibly for use as an awl.

Fig. 7.80

Bird Bone Awl   Archaic Period

Originally from the   Collection: P. Lien
Ben Waller Collection   Size: 2.6 in.\6.5 cm

Fig. 7.80. This bird leg was carved into an awl. The distal articulating surfaces (a) were left as a handle, while the proximal end (b) was removed and sharpened.

sharpened to an extreme point. Many awls were produced by grinding one end of a bone to a point and leaving the natural articular surface on the other end (figs. 7.80–7.82). This process probably maintained much of the bone's original strength and gave the user a comfortable, relatively smooth surface to press upon when using. Figures 7.83–7.84 give two views of an awl produced from a deer cannon bone. Its shape and workmanship definitely give it away as an awl, but its specific use is uncertain. The awls pictured in figures 7.85–7.86 were made from deer ulnae. In the area where they were found, it was a common practice for the indigenous people to tattoo themselves. Some believe that the tips of these awls were dipped into some type of pigment that was then applied by piercing the skin.

It is certain that Native Americans often found bone that was already fossilized. The properties of well-fossilized bone could fill the need for stone in areas where stone materials were scarce. The following two items are believed to have been produced from extremely well-fossilized bone, possibly Miocene in age. Figure 7.87 shows a large piece of bone marrow from an undetermined animal. A groove was ground into this item and the reverse side left flat for resting on a surface. It is believed to have been used in the production of bone pins. Once the bone was worked to approximately the correct diameter and length, finishing touches could be applied by running the pin through the groove on this tool. Fossilized bone was chosen because green or fresh bone would have had no abrasive properties. Figure 7.88 is a dead ringer for some type of hammering head. It appears to have been manufactured from the centrum (center) of

Fig. 7.81

Deer Cannon Bone Awl   Protohistoric Period

Withlacoochee River,   Collection: P. Lien
Florida   Size: 5.8 in.\14.5 cm

Fig. 7.81. As with figure 7.80, the distal end of this deer bone was left as a handle, while the proximal end was removed and sharpened into an awl.

Fig. 7.82

Bone Awls   Archaic Period
Deer Cannon Bone Distal Ends

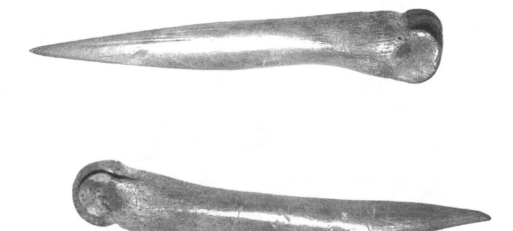

Orange County,   Collection: T. Perez
Florida   Size: 2.25 in.\5.4 cm

Fig. 7.82. The distal tips of a single deer cannon bone were split and modeled into a pair of awls.

Fig. 7.83

Deer Cannon Bone Awl   Archaic to Historic Period

Originally from the   Collection: P. Lien
Ben Waller Collection   Size: 3 in.\7.5 cm

Fig. 7.83. Both ends of a deer cannon bone were removed before making this awl. Compare with figure 7.81, where only one end is processed. The reverse side of this awl is shown in figure 7.84.

Fig. 7.84

Deer Cannon Bone Awl   Archaic to Historic Period

Originally from the   Collection: P. Lien
Ben Waller Collection   Size: 2.75 in.\6.6 cm

Fig. 7.84. The reverse side of figure 7.83.

Fig. 7.85

Tattooing Awl   Archaic Period
Deer Ulna

Rainbow River,   Collection: M. & S. Searle
Marion County, FL   Size: 3 in.\7.4 cm

Fig. 7.85. Many tribes in the Florida area where this awl-shaped tool was found were known to tattoo themselves. It has been speculated that they would have used a tool such as this modified deer ulna.

Fig. 7.86

Deer Ulna Awls   Late Archaic Period

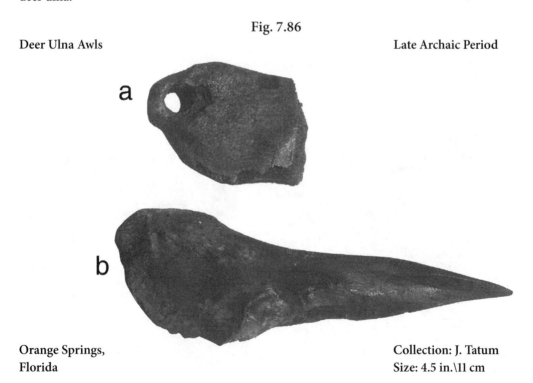

Orange Springs,   Collection: J. Tatum
Florida   Size: 4.5 in.\ll cm

Fig. 7.86. (a) is believed to be a broken version of (b), an awl made from a deer ulna. These have been speculated to be tattooing tools.

Fig. 7.87

Bone Pin Straightener   Late Pleistocene
Large Spongy Bone Section

Steinhatchee River,   a   Collection: P. Lien
Florida   Size: 4.25 in.\10.5 cm

Fig. 7.87. This large piece of spongy (cancellous) bone, probably from a proboscidean, has a
groove cut through it (a) for possible use in producing or straightening bone pins.

Fig. 7.88

Bone Mallet Head   Late Pleistocene
Vertebral Centrum

Aucilla River,   Collection: A. Welberry
Florida   Size: 5 in.\12.5 cm (left)

Fig. 7.88. This large mallet-style head was produced from the vertebral centrum of a large animal, probably a whale.

Fig. 7.89

Bone Agricultural Hoe
Bison Scapula

Historic Period

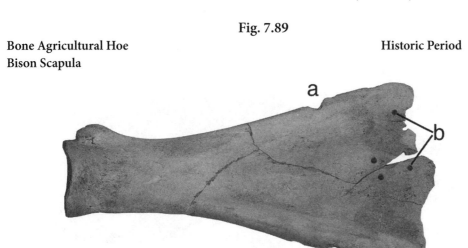

Sherman County,
Nebraska

Collection: J. Tatum
Size: 12.5 in.\31 cm

Fig. 7.89. This bison scapula was notched at (a) to attach to a handle for use as a hoe. The holes at (b) represent repair work done after the hoe was damaged.

a Miocene whale vertebra. It is extremely dense, durable, and heavy. This item may have been used to hammer tent stakes, poles, or other wooden items. Once again, fresh bone would not have provided the properties needed for use as a hammer head.

In western North America, items produced from bison bones are quite common. Figure 7.89 is a bison **scapula** modified for use as a hoe. It is interesting to note that this item was repaired after being broken, as evidenced by the holes drilled into it for binding back together. Each side has a notch for hafting or attachment to a wooden handle. With the abundance of bison, and the ease of notching the sides, one can only speculate as to why an individual would take the time to finely drill and repair broken items such as this one.[30] Repair appears to have been a fairly common practice as many other repaired specimens exist in the archaeological record. Similar repairs have been found on cracked pottery vessels throughout North America.

The next series of plates display various tools whose utility has not been determined with certainty. Figure 7.90 is believed to be a knife blade produced from a scapula of a large animal. With the abundance of fine stone blades, it is hard to speculate what advantage a blade made of bone would have had. Figure 7.91 is a small worked bone that may have been used as a wedge. Wedges were used for a variety of purposes, but mainly to separate joints when butchering

Fig. 7.90

Bone Blade
Large Animal Scapula

Protohistoric Period

Nance County,
Nebraska

Collection: J. Tatum
Size: 7.5 in.\18.7 cm

Fig. 7.90. Thin blades could be made from the scapulae of large animals such as bison, horse, and elk.

animals. Figure 7.92 is a view of a bone handle set on edge to display the broken insertion of another bone. The inserted bone is far larger than a bone pin, and it is uncertain how this item was used. A finely crafted deer ulna (fig. 7.93), with both a large hole and a small hole in the handle, is another problematic tool. The small hole was probably used to tie the tool onto something, but the large hole is a mystery. The last item in this series is a conical point that could have been used as the end of a gig for large fish, a spear point, or an awl attached to a wooden handle (fig. 7.94).

Handheld weapons produced from bone are somewhat rare, and their use is often speculative in nature. Figure 7.95 is a large dagger produced from an alligator jaw. Few of these daggers are known to exist, and they are considered rare and precious items. The one pictured here has had some repair work done to the tip, as indicated in the caption. Whether these daggers were used in everyday activities or were ceremonial in nature is uncertain. Smaller daggers made of deer cannon bones are a little more common, and some speculate that they may have been used as tent stakes.

In some instances, a specimen is found and its use is relatively unknown, especially in the amateur community. This was the case with the modified deer jaw shown in figure 7.96. It takes only the right person to see it and recognize it for what it is, in this case a fish scraper. Once again, cultures that survived into historical times used the sharp, selenodont teeth of deer jaws as fish scrapers,

Fig. 7.91

Bone Wedge
Deer Cannon Bone

Late Pleistocene to
Archaic Period

Withlacoochee River,
Florida

Collection: P. Lien
Size: 3.25 in.\8 cm

Fig. 7.91. This small bone wedge may have been used to separate the joints of animals during butchering.

Fig. 7.92

Broken Antler Atlatl Weight

Late Pleistocene

Santa Fe River,
Florida

Collection: J. Tatum
Size: 1 in.\2.5 cm

Fig. 7.92. A large bone was broken off at its insertion point in this deer antler handle. It is possibly an atlatl weight or the handle of a broken tool.

Fig. 7.93

Deer Ulna Tool

Late Pleistocene to
Archaic Period

Orange Springs,
Florida

Collection: J. Tatum
Size: 6.5 in.\16.3 cm

Fig. 7.93. Large and small holes were crafted for unknown reasons in this modified deer ulna tool.

Fig. 7.94

Bone Point

Late Pleistocene to
Archaic Period

Ichetucknee River,
Florida

Collection: P. Lien
Size: 3 in.\7.5 cm

Fig. 7.94. A perfectly conical point has been fashioned from this piece of bone. It could have been used as a projectile point or a gig for fishing.

Fig. 7.95

Alligator Jaw Dagger

Late Pleistocene to
Archaic Period

Withlacoochee River,
Florida

Collection: P. Lien
Size: 12.5 in.\31 cm

Fig. 7.95. An alligator jaw has been modified into a dagger-type weapon. The tip (a) has been professionally restored. The holes at (b) are naturally occurring tooth sockets; however, the holes at (c) were drilled by early Native Americans, probably to add a hide strap or handle.

Fig. 7.96

Modified Deer Jaw

Archaic Period

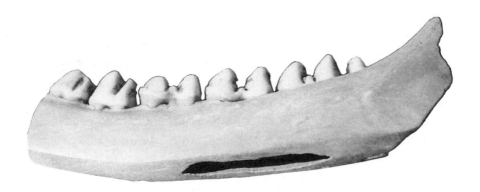

Collection: B. Fite
Size: 2.6 in.\6.5 cm

Fig. 7.96. This deer jaw was modified by cutting through the bottom for an unknown reason. Historical era deer jaws modified into scrapers for fish scales or corn do not have this additional modification.

Fig. 7.97

Bone Bead

Late Pleistocene to
Archaic Period

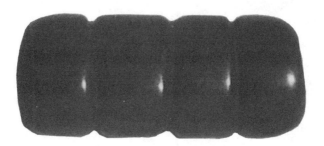

Withlacoochee River,
Florida

Collection: J. Tatum
Size: 2 in.\5 cm

Fig. 7.97. Perfectly formed and decorated beads made of bone are a rare and precious find.

removing scales from small fish before cooking or processing them.[31] Many ways of using bones and teeth survived into historical times in the American Northwest. In the American Southeast, most Native American cultures and ways disappeared before being documented. The author feels that practices of Pacific Coast Native Americans can be applied to artifacts found on the East Coast, especially if done with caution.

Jewelry

The desire to ornament the body with jewelry, specialized clothing, and even tattoos, goes back in the human archaeological record to a time far before the migration of humans to North America. Native Americans used items made from shells, bone, teeth, and, later, ceramics and metals. Among the earliest and most commonly found ornamental artifacts are beads; however, small beads made from bone are a rare and precious find. Finely worked beads come in a variety of shapes, sizes, and ornamental designs (figs. 7.97–7.98). It is presumed that the majority of beads were worn around the neck; however, some may have been worn in the hair or attached to clothing. Some bead-shaped items may have been made for insertion of a bone pin to hold feathers (see section on bone pins).

Pendants, items generally hung from a necklace that may have comprised many beads, may have been very simple (fig. 7.99) or involved much craftsmanship. Pendants were apparently worn to ornament the body, honor the gods, or protect against harm, or for other reasons grounded in superstition. Pendants,

Fig. 7.98

Fig. 7.98

Bone Beads

Late Pleistocene to
Archaic Period

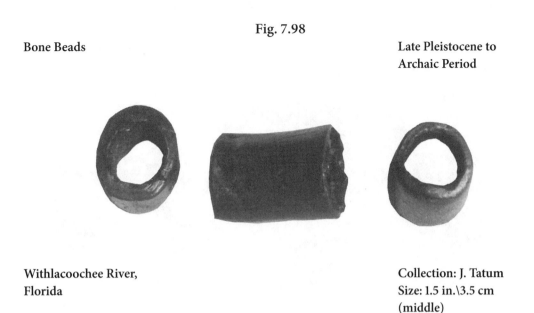

Withlacoochee River,
Florida

Collection: J. Tatum
Size: 1.5 in.\3.5 cm
(middle)

Fig. 7.98. This series of small, undecorated bone beads demonstrate exceptional craftsmanship.

Fig. 7.99

Pendant

Late Pleistocene to
Archaic Period

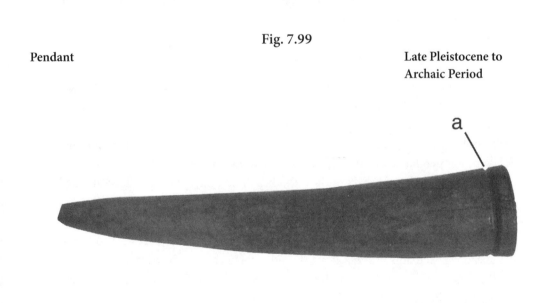

a

Orange Springs,
Florida

Collection: J. Tatum
Size: 3.5 in.\8.5 cm

Fig. 7.99. This item is believed to be a pendant. A groove at (a) has been carved around the base for tying onto a necklace.

Fig. 7.100

Shark Tooth Pendants
(a), (b), (d) Great White
(c) Tiger Shark

Archaic Period

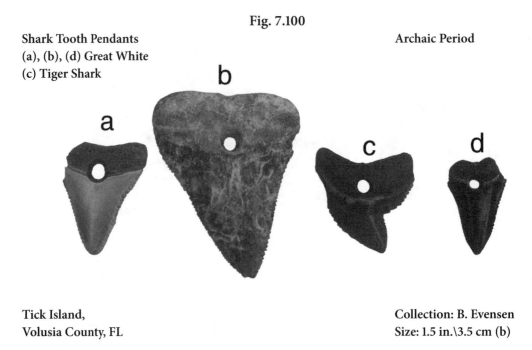

Tick Island,
Volusia County, FL

Collection: B. Evensen
Size: 1.5 in.\3.5 cm (b)

Fig. 7.100. These four drilled shark teeth from the Tick Island site in Florida may have been worn as pendants. Similar teeth were found hafted to a ceremonial war club at the Key Marco site in Florida; therefore, these also may have been part of a tool or weapon. Another possibility is that drilled shark teeth were used to incise bone.

as with most other precious items, were made from many materials. The paucity of pendants produced from bone (compared with use of shell, ceramic, and, later, metals) is probably due to the utilitarian nature of bone compared with other resources esteemed more valuable by Native Americans. Somewhat simple and common pendants found in cultures near oceans or bays are often made from shark teeth, either fresh, found on the beach or taken from a kill, or already fossilized and fortuitously found (figs. 7.100–7.102).[32] These shark teeth may have had a hole drilled into the gum line, or they may have been side notched to be mounted by wrapping. Drilled teeth from a variety of terrestrial animals may have been adornments along the side of a necklace, but were probably not the central pendant. Many shark teeth were found at the Key Marco site that were attached with pitch and strips of raw hide or sinew to war clubs and other ceremonial objects. Furthermore, wear on drilled shark teeth may indicate use as knife blades, drills, engravers (mainly), or other tools. Distributional studies have shown that drilled shark teeth are found more commonly in areas where stone is virtually nonexistent. Archaeologists claim that this finding is circumstantial evidence of their use in tools for doing work normally done with stone implements.[33]

Fig. 7.101

Fig. 7.101

Giant White Shark Tooth Pendant
Carcharocles megalodon

Worked: Archaic Period
Tooth: Miocene

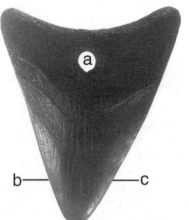

DeSoto County Creek,
Florida

Collection: M. Renz
Size: 3.5 in.\8.5 cm

Fig. 7.101. This isolated find, a worked Miocene *C. megalodon* tooth, was found at the Peace River in Florida. Not only has a hole been perfectly drilled in the center of the root (a) possibly for use as a pendant, but the serrations have also been filed or ground off the edges (b). The lack of serration may be due to wear, indicating this tooth was used as a tool of some type. This specimen is also important because it shows unequivocally that Native Americans used fossilized bones and teeth.

Fig. 7.102

Great White Shark Tooth Pendant
Carcharodon carcharias

Archaic Period

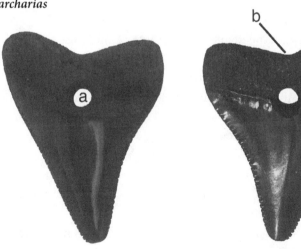

Chassahowitzka River,
Citrus County, FL

Collection: W. Keenan
Size: 1.25 in.\3 cm

Fig. 7.102. This great white shark tooth was drilled at (a), then a shallow groove was filed or worn in at (b), possibly to make the tooth lie flat when hanging from the neck, or to facilitate hafting to a club or tool.

Fig. 7.103

Gorget
Soft-shelled Turtle

Archaic Period

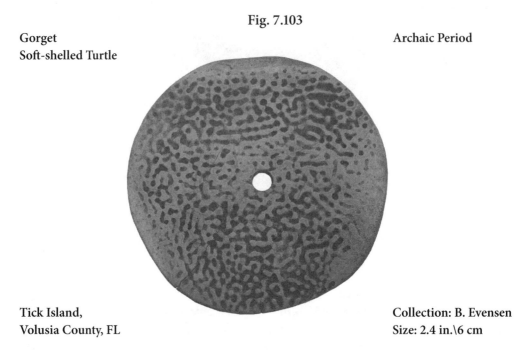

Tick Island,
Volusia County, FL

Collection: B. Evensen
Size: 2.4 in.\6 cm

Fig. 7.103. This Archaic Period gorget from Tick Island, Florida, was carved from a piece of soft shelled turtle plastron. The edges appear to be very worn, which might signify that this item was worn for a long time. Note the natural symmetrical patterns of the shell that are reminiscent of many of the patterns incised in other items.

The terms **gorget**, pendant, and **amulet** are often used interchangeably; however, to the professional they have distinct meanings. A gorget is usually round and worn around the neck or chest as a piece of armor; however, gorgets were often very small and ornamental, and their powers of protection might have been more ceremonial than physical (fig. 7.103). A pendant is any hanging ornamental object, from a necklace (fig. 7.104), ear piece, or clothing. An amulet is an ornament worn anywhere on the body for its reputed powers of protection. For the purpose of this section, displayed items are all classified as pendants because their meaning or purpose has long been lost, and the term is the most general of the three.

Ear spools were inserted into a slit in the earlobe and may have been made from wood, antler (fig. 7.105), or bone. Early Spanish explorers documented the use of ear spools by Native Americans, a practice that may have begun as early as the Archaic period. Feather holders are well documented in the archaeological record from the Archaic period through historic times. Feather holders may have been made of wood, bone (fig. 7.106), or antler. Many feather holders may have been used in conjunction with bone pins. Finally, during the Historic pe-

Fig. 7.104

Shark Tooth Pendant   Archaic Period
Great White Shark

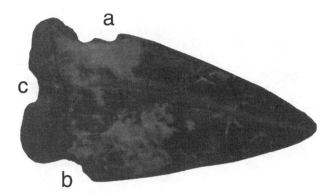

Weedon Island,   Collection: B. Evensen
Pinellas County, FL   Size: 1.5 in.\3.5 cm

Fig. 7.104. This shark tooth pendant was made by notching grooves at (a) and (b), as opposed to drilling a hole at the gum line or in the base as in the specimens pictured in figures 7.101–7.102.

Fig. 7.105

Ear Spool   Archaic Period
Deer Antler

Chassahowitzka River,   Collection: B. Evensen
Florida   Size: 1 in.\2.5 cm

Fig. 7.105. Two views of an "ear spool" made from a deer antler base. Increasingly larger and larger ear spools would have been used after cutting an incision in the earlobe to work up to one of this size.

Fig. 7.106

Bone Feather Holder

Archaic Period

Tick Island,
Volusia County, FL

Collection: B. Evensen
Size: 1.8 in.\4.5 cm

Fig. 7.106. A carved and incised feather holder made of bone. This item would have been used in the hair, along with items such as those pictured in figures 7.34–7.37, 7.43, and 7.44 to hold feathers in the hair.

riod, Native Americans began producing and wearing clothing that would have required buttons that may have been made of wood, bone (fig. 7.107), or shell.

Partially Worked Specimens

An item is often found in the archaeological record that is an example of unfinished work. For some items it is possible to determine what the worker had in mind for the finished object; however, many times it is impossible to tell the worker's intentions for the unfinished object. Figure 7.108 is an unfinished version of the flesher shown in figure 7.71. The only differences between these two items are that the **astragalus** is still fused to the unfinished flesher and the scraping surface has not been completely removed. Both items were made from a bison cannon bone.

Bone pins are one of the more common finds in the archaeological record; therefore, unfinished bone pins are expected (fig. 7.109). Items are often found in the beginning stage of manufacture; although it is not always possible to determine intent, the working cannot be mistaken for accidental modification or a natural mimic. Items that are clearly cut and being processed into something are common (figs. 7.110–7.112); however, in order for a bone, tooth, or antler to be considered in process of modification, the workmanship should appear more than arbitrary, and should not be capable of being imitated by forces of nature (natural fracture, carnivores, climate, etc.)

Fig. 7.107

Bone Buttons

Historic Period

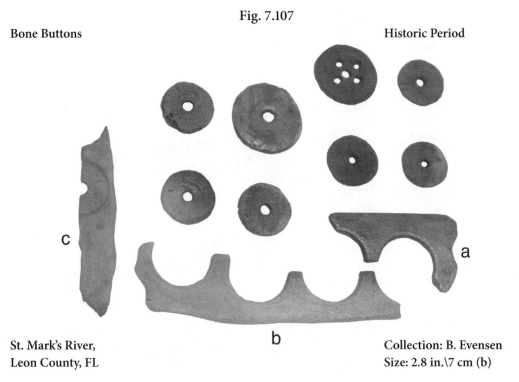

St. Mark's River,
Leon County, FL

Collection: B. Evensen
Size: 2.8 in.\7 cm (b)

Fig. 7.107. After contact with Europeans, Native Americans began incorporating trade items into their clothing and jewelry. Soon after that contact, Native Americans began manufacturing their own similar items, such as these bone buttons used on clothing. (a), (b), and (c) are byproducts of bone buttons.

Fig. 7.108

Unfinished Flesher
Bison Cannon Bone

Protohistoric Period

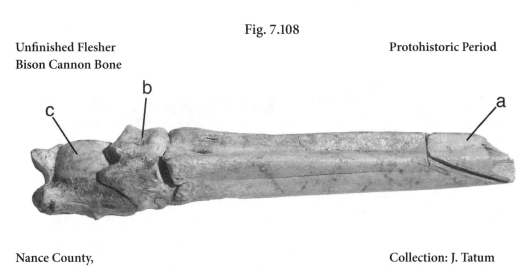

Nance County,
Nebraska

Collection: J. Tatum
Size: 8 in.\20 cm

Fig. 7.108. This is an unfinished flesher. The bone at (a) would eventually be removed. A tarsal bone at (b) and an ankle bone at (c) may also have been removed before use. See figures 7.71–7.72 for complete fleshers and their use.

Fig. 7.109

Partially Worked Bone   Late Pleistocene

Santa Fe River,   Collection: A. Welberry
Florida   Size: 4 in.\10 cm

Fig. 7.109. This bone may have been in the process of being modified into bone pins. Note the additional cut beginning at (a).

Fig. 7.110

Partially Worked Deer Cannon Bone   Late Pleistocene to
                                                         Archaic Period

Withlacoochee River,   Collection: J. Tatum
Florida   Size: 7.25 in.\18.2 cm

Fig. 7.110. This deer cannon bones bears unmistakable evidence of being modified by early Native Americans. Note the perfect crosscut at (a) and the even cuts at (b) running the length of the bone.

Fig. 7.111

Partially Worked Camel Toe Bone   Late Pleistocene

Santa Fe River,   Collection: A. Welberry
Florida   Size: 3 in.\7.5 cm

Fig. 7.111. The fact that this is the toe bone of a camel dates it as late Pleistocene and therefore the workmanship of Paleo-Indians. Its intended use remains a mystery.

Fig. 7.112

Partially Worked Horse Cannon Bone   Late Pleistocene

Aucilla River,   Collection: A. Welberry
Florida   Size: 5.5 in.\13.5 cm

Fig. 7.112. This bone has been split exactly in half. Its intended use is uncertain; however, its identification as fossil horse identifies it as the work of Paleo-Indians.

Problematic Specimens

After all possible uses or purposes have been exhausted, a great number of items still remain that are so out of the ordinary that no modern analogous items exist with which to compare them, even though they were clearly worked by human hands. In this section, figures 7.113–7.122 speak for themselves. Many of these items were presented to the author with speculation by the owners as to the items' uses or what they might have represented. As with partially worked bone, antler, or teeth, any human modification should go beyond what could be considered arbitrary or capable of being created by forces of nature. Objects shaped solely by the forces of nature are called **geofacts** (as opposed to artifacts). If a naturally formed object caught the eye of a prehistoric individual and was carried around or brought to a dwelling, it is termed a **manuport**.[34] Purdy (1991) rightfully points out that "idiosyncratic objects are not significant, no matter how interesting they are, because social scientists cannot determine what they represent to the culture."[35] However, the author cannot stress enough that it is up to a qualified and trained archaeologist to determine whether an

Fig. 7.113

Worked Proboscidean Centrum   Late Pleistocene

Steinhatchee River,   Collection: P. Lien
Florida   Size: 4.25 in.\10.5 cm

Fig. 7.113. Paleo-Indians hollowed out the center of the centrum of a proboscidean (mammoth or mastodon) vertebra. It is possible that animal fat was placed in the center and the item used as a primitive lamp; however, the specimen shows no signs of burning.

Fig. 7.114

Modified Bone   Archaic Period?

Originally from the   Collection: P. Lien
Ben Waller Collection   Size: 2.6 in.\6.5 cm

Fig. 7.114. A Native American spent extensive time carving a serration into this bone. Its possible use is undetermined.

Fig. 7.115

Modified Vertebral Spike   Late Pleistocene
Proboscidean

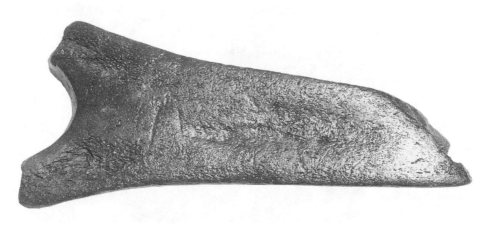

Hillsborough County,   Collection: P. Lien
Florida   Size: 6.75 in.\17 cm

Fig. 7.115. The dorsal spike from the vertebra of a proboscidean has been ground smooth. This must have taken much time. The intent of this bone modification remains problematic.

Fig. 7.116

Questionable Bone Modification   Late Pleistocene

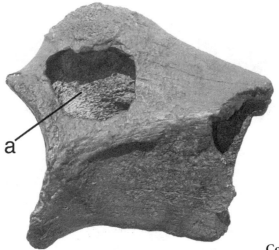

Aucilla River,   Collection: A. Welberry
Florida   Size: 4.5 in.\11 cm

Fig. 7.116. The hole at (a) is the size of a half dollar, too big for a bite mark. In addition, the fragmented breaking does not appear to be a human modification but might be a natural alteration.

Fig. 7.117

Modified Mammoth Carpal Bone   Late Pleistocene

Peace River,   Collection: R. Sinibaldi
DeSoto County, FL   Size: 5.6 in.\14 cm

Fig. 7.117. This mammoth carpal bone has a neatly drilled and beveled hole on one surface. It has obviously been worked, but its intended use remains speculative. The specimen could be a heavy bow bearing handle for a drill.

Fig. 7.118

Drilled Vertebral Centrum

Late Pleistocene to
Archaic Period

Peace River,
DeSoto County, FL

Collection: R. Sinibaldi
Size: 1.2 in.\2.6 cm

Fig. 7.118. The centrum of this unidentified vertebra has a hole drilled directly through the side. This item may have been used as a weight for a fishing net.

Fig. 7.119

Problematic Specimen

Archaic to Historic
Period

Alaska

Collection: P. Lien
Size: 2.6 in.\6.5 cm

Fig. 7.119. This finely crafted bone may have been a weight for fishing, a bead for a necklace, or some other item.

Fig. 7.120

Bison
Humerus

Late Pleistocene

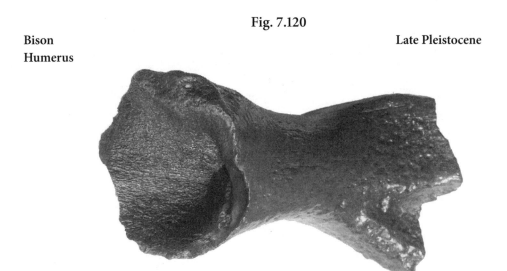

Santa Fe River,
Florida

Collection: A. Welberry
Size: 9 in.\22.5 cm

Fig. 7.120. This bison humerus appears to be polished smooth; however, it is not an artifact. Items, especially heavy bones, that spend a long period of time in a river often gain a polished look (see chapter 4).

Fig. 7.121

Deer
Modified Antler

Late Pleistocene to
Archaic Period

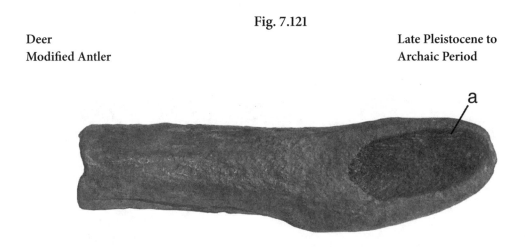

North Florida River

Collection: J. Tatum
Size: 5 in.\12.4 cm

Fig. 7.121. The intended use of this modified deer antler is undetermined. It has been speculated that it was going to be used to make a small lamp like those found in European caves.

Fig. 7.122

Worked Alligator Jaw   Archaic Period

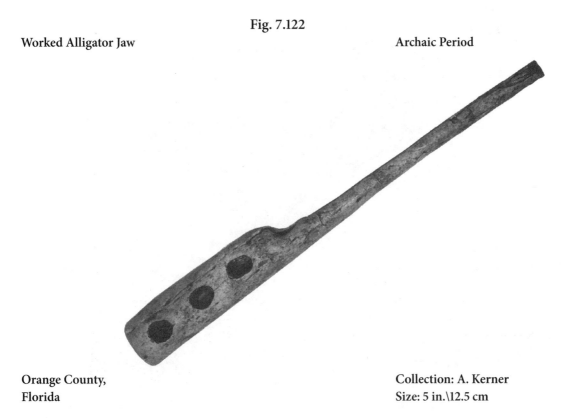

Orange County,   Collection: A. Kerner
Florida   Size: 5 in.\12.5 cm

Fig. 7.122. This finely worked alligator jaw may have been used as a horizontal feather or plume holder, but, again, this is only speculation.

item is significant or important to the scientific community, not amateur collectors who want a nifty curio for their shelves (figs. 7.123–7.125). What I believe Purdy is trying to convey with this statement is that many idiosyncratic specimens, at this time, shed no light on the culture they came from, as we truly do not know the intentions of their makers or owners. In addition, I believe that Purdy would agree that it takes a trained professional to determine whether an item is scientifically significant or not.

There has been much debate over the use of deer toes, and other small bones with holes in them, as whistles. Presented in figure 7.126 are two deer toes and a camel toe with holes in their shank. It is most likely that these items have bite mark punctures; however, if held correctly, all three do produce a low-volume whistling sound when blown upon. It was the initial opinion of the author that most of these specimens were not used as whistles because they do not produce a volume of sound capable of carrying any distance;[36] an avid amateur researcher[37] of Native American culture pointed out that many South American native cultures still make small whistles from bone, ceramics, and other items

Fig. 7.123

Bison Skull
with Projectile Point

Archaic Period

Peace River,
DeSoto County, FL

Private Collection
Size: 13.5 in.\33.5 cm

Fig. 7.123. On extreme rare occasions, the "smoking gun" is found. This bison skull, with an early Archaic stemmed point stuck in it at (a), is direct evidence that a particular culture hunted a specific animal. Items of this nature should reside in museums or research centers. It is hoped that this specimen will find its way there soon.

Fig. 7.124

Incised Atlatl Component
2 Views

Late Pleistocene

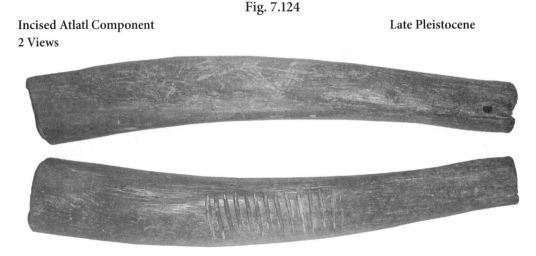

Northern Florida River

Private Collection
Size: 8 in.\20 cm

Fig. 7.124. This bone has been worked into what appears to be an atlatl component. It is also finely incised on both sides. One view shows 14 parallel lines incised in the middle of the bone. There is some speculation that these could be kill tallies; however, an alternative explanation is that another bone or stick was scraped against them to mimic the tapping of a woodpecker or other natural sound. This would be an unobtrusive way to send messages to a fellow hunter without alerting prey. The other side has a drawing etched into it that is explained in the caption to figure 7.125.

Fig. 7.125

Man Hunting Mammoth   Reproduction of Etching

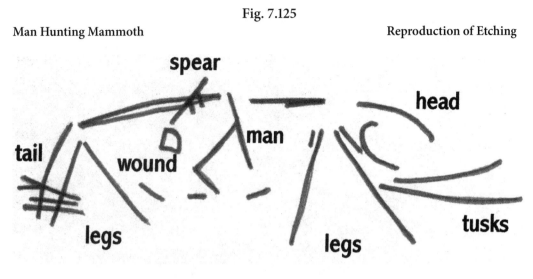

Northern Florida River   Private Collection

Fig. 7.125. This is a reproduction of the etching on the reverse side of the atlatl component shown in figure 7.124. Various parts of the etching are labeled, but the labels are all speculation; however, the etching is a fairly reasonable likeness of a man hunting a mammoth. Items like this should be held in public collections for proper study and displayed for all to see. If it truly represents a Paleo-Indian drawing of a hunting scene, then it would be one of the earliest known in North America.

that produce barely audible sounds. These items are used during prayer to their gods. In other words, the whistles only have to be loud enough to be heard by the owner (and his or her god); they are never meant to be heard by others or used to attract attention. The author has seen specimens of deer toes that were obviously drilled, not bitten, and currently, at least, entertains the possibility that deer toes and other small bones were drilled for use as ceremonial whistles. Finally, it has come to the attention of the author that drilled toe bones may have been used as small bow bearings somewhat like those described previously. In this case, however, the toe bone would be held in the mouth with the drilled hole facing down, the shaft of a drill would be inserted into the hole, and the stone drill bit would be placed on the item to be drilled. Holding the item with one hand and working the bow with the other, the craftsman could then drill small objects without the help of a partner.[38]

It is well documented that Native Americans used sections of turtle shell fashioned into net-mesh gauges to produce fishing nets of standardized size. Sections of fossilized turtle shell often occur in flat rectangular sections that naturally occur where the sutured bone of the turtle separates. To make a net

Fig. 7.126

Toe Bone Whistles
(a), (b) Deer Toe Bones
(c) Camel Toe Bone

Late Pleistocene to
Archaic Period

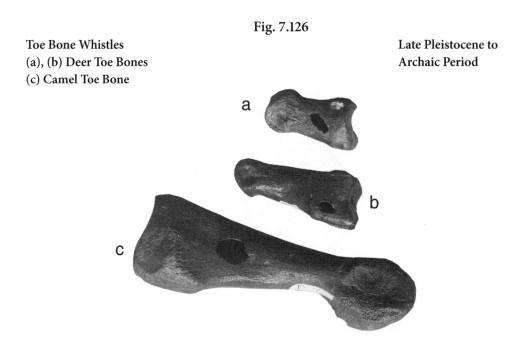

Peace River,
DeSoto County, FL

Collection: R. Sinibaldi
Size: 3.25 in.\8 cm (c)

Fig. 7.126. The use of drilled toe bones as whistles has been long debated. The holes in these three specimens are jagged, asymmetrical, and probably represent bite marks from carnivores or alligators. The items do give a faint whistling sound when blown upon, however.

gauge from turtle shell sections one only had to round off the corners. Well-used net-mesh gauges are generally very worn and smoothed almost to a polish from constant handling and the wear of net cordage. The problem is that, since turtle shell breaks naturally into this pattern, and river and ocean surf wear can produce the same rounding and polish, unless the item comes from a well-documented archaeological site, it is often very difficult to attribute net-mesh gauge use to worn turtle shell with certainty.

Figure 7.127 is the first item believed by the author to be a true culturally modified specimen. It was very dark brown when found in the Peace River in Florida in association with a fossilized camel jaw; however, items can change appearance quickly in tannic waters, and transport from location to location even more quickly. The item was nothing more than a discarded pork chop bone that could have been anywhere from a couple of years to a few score years old. It looks so obvious now, but to a beginner it was very convincing. We all had to start somewhere, and the author humbly began with this "paleo pork chop," as his friends now call it.

Fig. 7.127

"Paleo" Pork Chop   Recent (very)

Peace River,   Collection: R. Sinibaldi
DeSoto County, FL   Size: 2.5 in.\6 cm

Fig. 7.127. When the author first began diving for fossils in Florida's rivers, he was certain this item was a bone modified by early Native Americans. It is almost pitch black and very hard. Upon further inspection the item turned out to be no more than a discarded pork chop bone that had sat at the bottom of the Peace River for only a short time, geologically. The author quickly learned, after some embarrassment, that early cultures did not butcher bones with this precision.

Glossary

A flood of other hypotheses would come to mind, and as he was testing
these, still more came to mind until it became painfully evident that as he
continued testing hypotheses and eliminating them or confirming them their
number did not decrease. It actually increased as he went along.

Robert M. Persig

acid alteration   Markings on a bone or fossil caused by naturally occurring diluted acids in ground water or soil.

adaptation   A change in the structure of an organism that makes it better suited to its environment.

alveolus, pl. **alveoli**   Socket(s) where the teeth are anchored.

amulet   An ornament that may be worn anywhere on the body for its powers of protection according to superstition.

ankylosis   The unnatural fusion of bones; can occur between bones or joints for many different reasons.

ankylose   To fuse.

analogous   Features of organisms that are superficially similar but have evolved through different pathways. The wings of bats and insects are analogous.

analogue   Sometimes referred to as a modern phylogenetic analogue, a related extant species used to infer morphology and/or behavior of an extinct species.

anterior   Facing front.

Archaic period   An archaeological period of Native American culture that ran from 9,000 to 4,000 years ago; characterized by subsistence living on deer, shellfish, fish, nuts, berries, and anything the land would provide.

arrow shaft wrench   A Native American tool used to straighten wooden arrow and spear shafts.

arthritis (infective)   Restricted to the interarticular surfaces of the bone within the joint capsules; infection affects the erosion and proliferation of bone at the articular surface; in extreme cases, bones may become partially fused.

articulation   The portion of a bone where it joins with another bone; often harder and smoother than adjacent bone.

artifact   Any object made by human work.

artificial memory system (AMS)   Any system outside the human brain used to record information, from simple hash marks to the modern computer.

artiodactyl   An order of even-toed hoofed mammals, including deer, bison, camels, pigs, and cattle.

astragalus Ankle bone

atavism The reappearance of a characteristic found in a remote ancestor but not more recent ancestors.

atlatl A spear-throwing implement that enhanced the leverage and force of the throwing arm; could greatly increase the velocity of the spear.

atmospheric alteration Changes to bones and teeth after death that occur as a result of weather conditions, including prolonged exposure to rain or sun, freeze-thaw cycles, hot-cold cycles.

attachment scars Markings left on bones where tendons and ligaments adhered.

atlas First cervical vertebra of the neck; articulates with the skull via the occipital condyles.

auditory bulla Portion of the middle ear that houses the malleus, incus, and stapes.

axis Second cervical vertebra; articulates with the atlas and the third cervical vertebra.

baculum A bone found in the penis of some mammals.

ball-and-socket joint A joint comprising a cuplike socket on one bone into which a round structure at the end of another fits, allows for movement through all planes of motion.

ballast Extra weight used to stabilize an object in water.

bannerstones Counter weights used to add velocity to an atlatl; could be made of bone, antler, or stone.

bilophodont Teeth with two sets of cusps that have fused into ridges

binocular vision The use of both eyes at the same time to look at the same object; gives the animal better depth perception with loss of some peripheral vision.

biological alteration Changes to bones and teeth after death attributable to other living organisms, including worms, tree roots, crustaceans, and insects, and to trampling.

bone pin A variety of small, rather sharply pointed objects carved from bones by early Native Americans.

bone spicules A proliferation of pathological bone around an infected or damaged joint.

bow bearing A primitive bearing made of bone or antler and used to start fire; the bow bearing was greased with animal fat and a wooden shaft was inserted in one end; a bow was then used to rotate the shaft fast enough to start a fire.

brachydont Teeth with low crowns; generally the crowns are shorter than the roots.

brambles Bony armor or plates just below the skin or embedded in the skin.

browser   A herbivore that feeds on leaves, twigs, and the young shoots of shrubs and trees.

buccal view   The side of the teeth facing away from the tongue; the side toward the cheek.

bunodont   Teeth with rounded cusps on the occlusal surface; human, mastodon, and pig molars are examples.

calcify   To change into a hard bony substance.

calvarium, pl. calvaria   The upper domed part of the skull.

cancellous bone   Spongy bone; generally near the proximal and distal ends of long bones, within the centra of vertebrae.

canines   A sharp conical tooth in some mammals typically situated between the last incisor and the first premolar.

caniniform   A tooth shaped like a canine but not a true canine.

cannon bone   In some artiodactyls, the naturally fused third and fourth metapodials that form one bone that bears the weight of the animal. In horses it is the third metapodial alone.

carapace   The hard external protective covering over all or part of certain animals (turtles, armadillos, glyptodonts, trilobites, crustaceans); the shell of certain animals.

carnassial   A specialized form of premolar or molar occurring in upper and lower pairs and typically elongate and notched, used by carnivores for shearing flesh.

carnivores   Animals whose diet consists mainly of meat and bone.

carpal bone   One of a distal series of bones articulating with the metacarpals, in the forelimbs of animals.

cartilage   A firm, flexible connective tissue with many functions, including support and flexibility of joints, growth of bones, and skeletons of cartilaginous fishes such as sharks.

cartilaginous joint   Joints formed of cartilage such as the intervertebral disks of mammals.

carved   Pertaining to bone that has been worked with a knife or other tool and/ or completely or partially reshaped.

caudal   In or near the tail; caudal bones are tail vertebral bones.

cementum   A hard bony material that anchors the roots of teeth into the jaw, found usually on the outside of the root; cementum may be infolded with enamel and dentine in highly specialized teeth.

centrum, pl. centra   The round center portion of a vertebra.

Ceramic Stage   An archaeological stage of Native American culture that occurred 500 to 4,000 years ago; noted for development of ceramics, cultivation of crops, mound building, and transition from a nomadic way of life.

cervical vertebrae   Bony or cartilaginous segments of the neck region.

Clovis Complex Once believed to be the first Paleo-Indians to cross from Asia into North America, between 11,000 and 12,000 years ago.

complex dentition Two or more types of teeth present in an animal's mouth; almost all mammals and some sharks have complex dentitions.

composite fishhook A fishhook comprising more than one piece of material, for example, two pieces of bone, a piece of bone and wood, a piece of bone and antler.

composite specimen A display, mount, cast, or fossil using parts from multiple individuals of the same species to present one complete individual.

compression bite mark A bite mark left as a result of the direct grasp of teeth, as opposed to gnawing; generally leaves a conical hole or crushed bones.

compression fracture A break in a bone caused by a severe blow or a bite of a predator.

condyle A rounded process at the end of a bone; usually articulates with another bone.

congenital anomaly A deformity or malformation either present at birth, or coded for at birth but developing later; can be hereditary or environmental.

coprolite Fossilized fecal matter.

core The bony inner portion of an antler, horn, or claw, generally covered with hair or scale during the animal's life; the bony core is usually the only portion that fossilizes after death.

crepuscular Occurring during dawn or dusk hours.

cultural modification Changes made to bone, antler, teeth, or other items by Native Americans, sometimes for a purpose, including tools, weapons, and ornaments, and sometimes as a byproduct of removing meat or other activities.

deciduous teeth In mammals, temporary teeth, the first to erupt; also called baby or milk teeth.

degenerative arthropathy Joint disease caused by aging; the cartilage between the joints begins to fail, causing a proliferation of bony tissue around the joint surface; the joint surface itself may remain smooth as a result of wear.

delamination A process that peels away successive outer layers of bone (periosteum); caused by sun, rain, or extreme temperature changes; may occur at any time after the bone is defleshed, before, during, or after the fossilization process is complete.

dental abscess A carious lesion that progresses through the pulp cavity into the tooth root, causing infection in the root tip and surrounding bone.

dental battery The entire set of an animal's teeth.

dental calculus A calcium deposit on the surface of teeth; dental tartar; dental calculus sometimes fossilizes on the surface of well-preserved teeth.

dental caries A cavity on the surface of the crown or root of a tooth, caused by an acidic environment in the mouth that begins to demineralize the enamel, dentine, or cementum.

dental hypoplasia An underdevelopment of the teeth caused by disease or malnutrition during the developmental stage; may leave extreme to microscopic abnormalities on the teeth.

dentine A hard, dense, calcareous tissue forming the body of a tooth; usually covered by enamel.

depth perception The ability to judge distances through the use of binocular vision.

dermal denticles Bony armor or plates just below the skin or embedded in the skin.

diaphysis The shaft or long portion of the bone.

dignathic heterodont dentition Teeth in the upper jaw are of a different morphology than teeth in the lower jaw; occurs in some sharks.

diploe Supporting struts of bone found in pneumatized bone.

disarticulated Pertaining to a collection of bones that are separated or not in their correct anatomical order.

distal The end of a bone farthest from the main body of the animal.

diurnal Animals that are primarily active during the daytime; opposite of nocturnal.

ear spool An item that some Native American cultures inserted into an opening cut into the ear lobe.

Eocene A geological epoch that ran from 54 million to 37.5 million years ago.

enamel the hardest external portion of a tooth, consisting of 97% hydroxyapatite mineral (crystallized calcium phosphate).

enameloid The outer surface of shark teeth, very close in nature to the true enamel found in mammalian teeth.

endocast, endocranial cast A cast of the inside of the braincase; forms naturally when the internal brain cavity fills with sediment that hardens into a fossil.

epiphyseal plate The growth plate that attaches the articulating end of a bone (epiphysis) to the shank (diaphysis) until the animal is finished growing.

epiphysis The joint end of a bone; remains unfused until near the end of the growth period of an animal.

etiology The science of causes; the assignment of a cause.

evolution The process by which species change over time; can result in allopatric speciation, which occurs when animals of one species are geographically separated and evolve into two separate species, or sympatric speciation, which occurs without geographic isolation; phyletic evolution occurs when a single species gradually changes over time without splitting into separate species.

exaptation A characteristic that now performs a current function that is subject to selection, but was initially either not shaped by selection at all, or was shaped by selection for a different role.

exfoliate To cast off; a tooth that is lost is exfoliated.

exostosis, pl. **exostoses** Any benign bone growth projecting outward from a bone surface.

extant Still existing on Earth.

extinct Having no living descendant of the same species; no longer existing on Earth.

facet A flat surface on a bone that articulates with the flat surface of another bone, forming a joint at that location.

fading The simple phenomenon whereby exposure to the sun or weathering lightens the color of a specimen.

feather holder A bone, wood, shell, or clay ornament used to hold feathers in the hair or dress of Native Americans.

femur The thighbone in humans; the long bone in the upper rear leg of tetrapod vertebrates; the upper portion articulates with the pelvis and the lower portion articulates with the tibia and fibula of the lower leg.

fibrocartilage A specialized form of cartilage that is stronger and less elastic than other forms of cartilage; found in the intervertebral disks.

file of teeth Comprising all the teeth in the same position in each row of teeth in a shark's jaw. Each tooth in a file is formed exactly the same as the one in front of it.

fleshing tool A primitive tool used to remove excess meat from skin or hides.

foramen, pl. **foramina** A small hole or perforation in bone through which nerves or blood vessels pass.

foreshaft A short dowel-like item used to fasten a projectile point for insertion into a longer spear shaft for use, made from bone, ivory, or wood.

fossil The remains of any plant or animal matter, or traces of their activities; most have gone through a chemical change, replacing organic matter with inorganic matter; some fossils do have organic materials such as original bone or carbon film.

fusion line The union line where two bones have met to form into one.

geofact An object created or altered solely through the forces of nature

geographic variation Small differences within a species from different locations during the same time period; the basis for determining subspecies.

geological alteration Forces within the Earth that alter a bone or tooth from its original state, including the various components of fossilization, pressure, chemical reactions, and geothermal processes.

gliding joint A joint comprising two bones with flat or near flat articular surfaces that allow the bones to slide or glide across one another. Sometimes referred to as plane joints.

gorge (throat gorge) A small bone or wooden fishing hook with two pointed ends and is tied in the middle to a fishing line. When a fish swallows the gorge, it lodges in its throat.

gorget A generally round item worn around the neck as a real or symbolic piece of armor.

gracile Slender, slim.

grazer A herbivore whose diet consists of grasses, sedges, and other ground cover plants.

growth plate A cartilaginous plate (technically called the epiphyseal) between the diaphysis and epiphysis on long bones. It allows for growth until the bone is fully formed.

hafting The primitive process of attaching stone and bone implements to handles or shafts; can involve pitch, sinew, or other natural materials.

Harris lines Distinct lines that form on bones when a young animal goes through extreme stress (e.g., malnutrition, infection) during periods of growth.

herbivore An animal whose diet consists mainly of plant matter.

herniated disk An intervertebral disk that swells and protrudes from between two vertebrae; may leave an exit scar on the bone where the disk protrudes outward.

hinge joint A joint between two bones that allows motion only around a single axis, like the hinge on a door.

Historic period In the New World, a Native American cultural stage after first contact with Europeans; characterized by trading for glass, iron, horses, guns, beads, and other products.

homodont dentition A dental battery comprising morphologically similar teeth.

homologous Pertaining to similar structures of organisms with the same evolutionary origin, for example, the human arm, the flipper of a manatee, and the wing of a bat.

humerus The long bone of the upper arm or foreleg of four-limbed vertebrates. It articulates with the scapula at the shoulder and with the radius and ulna at the distal end.

hydrological alterations Changes to fossils caused by the actions of water, including ocean surf, river flow, tumbling in a river.

hypodontia Missing teeth due to developmental anomalies.

hypoplasia The underdevelopment of teeth or bones as a result of disease, infection, parasites, malnutrition (especially lack of vitamin D).

hypselodont Teeth that continuously grow throughout an animal's life.

hypsodont Teeth with high crowns, as in horses and mammoths; the degree of hypsodonty is measured by the height of the crown above the root. These teeth grow throughout most of an animal's life, finally forming roots at a very late stage.

incised bone Culturally modified bones that have been cut into or engraved with a sharp tool.

incisors Sharp, typically chisel-shaped teeth at the front of the mouth, used by most mammals for biting, and by rodents for gnawing.

insectivore Animals that eat mainly insects.

interarticular Between the articulation of two bones at a joint.

invertebrate An animal that lacks a vertebral column.

isolated find An artifact or fossil that has become displaced from its original context; usually not considered of primary scientific significance because of the loss of contextual information.

keel A bony process that separates two major muscle groups, allowing them to work in opposite directions.

knapping baton A tool used by Native Americans to dislodge flakes of stone while manufacturing an implement or projectile point.

labial view View of the side of teeth that faces the lips.

lateral view Side view of a specimen.

ligaments Tough fibrous bands that attach bones to each other to stabilize a joint.

lingual view View of the side of teeth or jaw that faces the tongue.

lipping A proliferation of pathological bone around an infected or damaged joint; osteophytes; bone spicules.

lophodont Dentition comprising molars and premolars with cusps that have fused into ridges.

lumbar The lower back below the thoracic area.

masseter muscle A large muscle that attaches the jaw to the skull to help produce the chewing motion in mammals.

mandible The lower jaw, consisting of the left and right rami, made of dentary bone in mammals.

manuport A natural object carried or transported by humans away from its original site.

maxilla Upper jaw section of the skull; holds most of the upper teeth.

medial view A view from the midline looking outward.

median sagittal plane An imaginary line dividing the body equally into right and left sides.

medullary cavity Hollow portion of long bones containing bone marrow.

megafauna Large animals weighing more than 100 pounds. The megafauna of the Pleistocene Epoch included woolly mammoths, woolly rhinos, horses, camels, and saber-toothed cats.

metaphysis The end portion of the diaphysis (shank of the bone) closest to the epiphysis (articulating end of the bone).

mimic To have or take on a similar appearance to some other organism for a selective advantage in evolution.

mineralization The most common form of fossilization; the process of replacing or encasing an original substance with minerals present in saturated form in water or surrounding sediment.

Miocene A geological epoch of time that ran from 24.5 million to 5 million years ago.

molar a permanent tooth found in the rear of the jaw of mammals behind the premolars.

molariform A tooth shaped like a molar, but not a true molar; found in the order Xenarthra and other animals.

monocular vision The use of each eye independently of the other, thus seeing differing portions of the landscape simultaneously; most herbivores have eyes on the sides of their head (monocular vision); reduces depth perception but gives better peripheral vision.

monognathic heterodont Dentition in which two or more types of tooth morphology occur in each jaw, changing from front to back; occurs in some sharks, some bony fishes, and most mammals.

morphology A branch of biology that studies the form and structure of plants and animals.

natural alteration (natural modification) Changes that occur in bones after the animal has died as the result of biological, geological, hydrological, or atmospheric forces; processes studied in the discipline of taphonomy.

natural selection A mechanism that drives evolution; random mutations or genetic recombination leading to survival and reproductive success of individuals or groups because the changes make them better adjusted to environmental conditions. Over long periods of time, as genetic qualities best suited to a particular environment are perpetuated, these changes can give rise to new species.

necrosis of bone Death of a section of bone when blood supply is lost in the periosteum (outer layer) as a result of fracture or infection.

neonatal Newborn; during the first month of life after birth.

neural canal The opening within a vertebra through which the spinal cord passes.

neural spike A process of bone attached to the dorsal side of the centrum of a vertebra. A large neural spike indicates strong back muscles.

nock A groove or indentation at the feathered end of an arrow or spear shaft to maintain the shaft on the bow-string or the end of an atlatl.

nocturnal Animals that are active at night time; opposite of diurnal.

occlusal surface The chewing surface of a tooth, where it meets with the tooth or teeth of the opposite jaw.

Oligocene A geological epoch of time that ran from 37.5 million to 24.5 million years ago.

omnivores Animals that eat both plants and meat.

ontogenetic variation Differences occurring during early developmental stages; differences in age.

orthodentine A specialized dentine found in the teeth of xenarthrans: sloths, armadillos, and glyptodonts.

osteitis Inflammation of the bone; may be osteomyelitis (inflammation of the medulla area) or osteoperiostitis (inflammation of the surface morphology).

osteoarthritis Arthritis caused by injury or trauma to joint cartilage or surrounding bone; generally affects only the cartilage and bone where the trauma occurred.

osteodentine A special form of dentine found in the teeth of sharks. The hard outer dentine in the teeth of xenarthrans (armadillos, sloths, glyptodonts).

osteoderms Bones found in the skin of some vertebrates such as alligators, crocodiles, and some sloths; armadillos, glyptodonts, and some turtles have osteoderms also; osteoderms are also called scutes.

osteomyelitis Infection and inflammation of the central marrow cavity of the bone (medulla) caused by a wound or an infection in the bloodstream.

osteoperiostitis Infection and inflammation to the periosteum of bone as a result of injury or in conjunction with osteomyelitis.

osteophyte A small bony outgrowth.

osteosis The formation of bone.

otolith A small bonelike structure composed of calcium carbonate in the inner ear of some fishes.

paleoecology The study of prehistoric environments.

Paleo-Indians The first Native Americans, from approximately 11,500 to 9,000 years ago; characterized as big-game hunters.

pallial dentine A specialized form of dentine found in sharks' teeth.

pathology The study of the essential nature of diseases, especially the structural and functional changes produced by conditions such as injury, disease, attack, and stress.

pauciarticular arthritis Arthritis that affects only a single joint where the trauma or destabilization of that joint occurred.

pendant Any hanging ornamental jewelry object, whether from a necklace, ear piece, or clothing.

periarticular Outer articulating edges of a joint.

periodontal disease Disease that involves the destruction of the alveolar margin as a result of accumulation of dental calculus (tartar) and subsequent infection.

periosteum   An outer membrane that surrounds a bone.

peripheral vision   The area of vision lying just outside the line of direct sight.

petrosal bone   Bone of the inner ear.

phylogenetic analogue   An extant species used to infer behavior of a similar extinct species; modern analogue; modern phylogenetic analogue.

pitch   A black sticky resin produced by evergreen trees and used as an adhesive or waterproofing substance.

Pleistocene   A geological epoch of time that ran from 1.8 million to 10,000 years ago.

pleurapophysis   Vestigial ribs fused to the transverse processes of the lumbar vertebrae of some reptiles.

pneumatized bone   Hollow bone filled with air; characteristic of bird bones, but also found in the skull bones of large animals.

polyarticular   Involving several joints

polydactyly   A condition of extra digits, as in extra toes, claws, or fingers.

postcranial   Occurring below, behind, or after the skull

posterior view   View of the rear or back of the specimen.

pre-Columbian   Archaeological period before significant contact with Europeans.

preform   A stone or bone implement that is not in its final form.

premaxilla   The area of the upper jaw in front of the maxilla; in most mammals the premaxilla typically contains the alveoli for the incisors and canines; in some animals (e.g., artiodactyls) the premaxilla contains no teeth.

problematic specimens   Items that are not easily identified; pathological items whose etiology is unknown; archaeological items whose use is unknown.

proboscidean   Any of the order Proboscidea, animals with tusks and a long flexible trunk or proboscis: elephants, mammoths, mastodons, gomphotheres.

proximal   The end of a bone closest to the head or center of the animal.

pseudopathology   False pathology; specimens with markings not caused by disease or injury that have not shown any level of healing, including feeding marks, compression bites, trampling marks, and rodent gnawing.

pterygoid muscle group   Muscle groups associated with the zygomatic arch (cheek bone).

pulp chamber (pulp cavity)   The interior portion of the tooth containing the blood and nerve supplies.

resorption   The reclaiming of bone matrix by osteoclasts, balanced by the making of new bone by ostoeblasts.

rheumatoid arthritis A type of polyarticular erosive arthritis; affects multiple joints, often bilaterally and symmetrically; known only in humans.

robust Suited for physical strength and stamina.

rugose Ridged, corrugated; full of wrinkles.

sacrum In some animals, a group of fused vertebrae that articulate with the pelvis.

sagittal crest A structure between the right and left parietal bones of the skull; very pronounced in carnivores for attachment of a large temporalis muscle.

Schreger pattern Cross-hatching found in the ivory of proboscidean tusks; angle of pattern can be used to determine the species a tusk came from; the pattern in mammoth tusks measures almost 90 degrees and in those of mastodons, 125 degrees.

scute See osteoderms.

selenodont Teeth with cusps connected by crescent-shaped ridges; typical of artiodactyls such as deer, camel, and oreodonts.

semiaquatic Pertaining to animals that spend part of their time in water.

sequestrum A type of necrosis (bone death) caused by infection.

sexual dimorphism Condition where differences in morphology and/or size exist between males and females of a single species, for example, larger canines and sagittal crests in males than in females of the same species.

silica Silicon dioxide, a hard, glassy mineral found in a variety of forms, including sand, quartz, and opal.

simple dentition Only one type of tooth in both upper and lower jaws; the teeth may be the same size in the entire jaw or progressively smaller toward the back.

Sirenia An order of aquatic mammals that includes sea cows, manatees, and dugongs.

species A subdivision of a genus, usually the fundamental form; a species generally can breed only with members of its own species and shows persistent differences from other species in the genus.

spina bifida A congenital defect of the vertebral column in which the halves of the neural arch of the vertebrae fail to fuse at the midline.

spit tooth Informal term for proboscidean or sirenian teeth that have moved forward through the jaw and been exfoliated after use; spit teeth are usually well worn, have a curved pattern of wear on the rear where the next tooth has pushed them forward, and have roots digested away by a special gland in the animal's mouth.

split line cracks Longitudinal cracks that form on bones as a result of mineralization or weathering cycles of wet-dry or freeze-thaw.

spondyloarthropathy An inflammatory form of arthritis characterized by proliferation of reactive bone formation at sites of tendon, ligament, and capsule insertions.

spondylosis deformans   Bony proliferation on the ventral surface of adjacent vertebrae, producing a bridge (fusion) from one to another.

stereoscopic vision   The use of both eyes at the same time to look at the same object; gives better depth perception at the expense of some peripheral vision.

subcutaneous   Beneath the skin.

subfossil   Specimens that have not completed the various processes of fossilization and retain some portion of their original organic material. Specimens are generally less than 10,000 years old, dating from the late Pleistocene or later. Note that many older items may contain biological materials and still be considered fossils.

suture joint   An immovable fibrous joint in the pelvis and skull that allows for flexibility in the case of live birth (mammals) and quick growth.

syndactyly   The fusion of toe bones resulting from developmental disturbances.

taphonomy   The study of processes that transform shells and bones after death and deposition; the study of death assemblages.

tarsal   One of a distal series of bones articulating with the metatarsals in foot and leg bones in the hind limbs of animals

taxonomic classification   Standardized classification system using binomial nomenclature (genus and species); organisms with shared physical characteristics are members of the same rank.

temporalis muscle   A large muscle that attaches to both the lower jaw and the skull; responsible for up-and-down movements of the jaw and bite strength.

tendons   A dense fibrous cord of connective tissue that attaches muscles to bone.

terrestrial   Pertaining to living on land.

thanatocoenosis, pl. **thanatocoenoses**   A death assemblage containing multiple members of the same species or multiple species. The assemblage is usually representative of a single catastrophe, event, or time period.

thoracic vertebrae   Vertebrae of the upper back, between the cervical vertebrae of the neck and the lumbar vertebrae of the lower back; sometimes exhibit a number of articulating facets for attachment to ribs.

torsion fracture   Break that occurs when a long bone is twisted or rotated unnaturally along its long axis; also referred to as a spiral fracture or twisting fracture.

trampling   Heavy walking by animals that can leave shallow parallel scratches on bones.

unfused bone   Bone that has not completed its growing cycle; articulating ends on long bones may be missing, or sutures on flat bones may not be completely attached; indicative of juvenile animals.

unintentional modification   Markings left on bone, antler, or teeth usually by butchering or other process by humans not intended as ornamentation or for usefulness.

vasodentine   The soft inner dentine in the teeth of xenarthrans (armadillos, sloths, glyptodonts, anteaters).

vertebrate   Animal with a spinal column comprising vertebrae and a brain with coordinated nervous system that travels through the vertebrae.

water dissolution   Process in which diluted acids and solvents in the waters of rivers, lakes, and springs dissolve parts of bones and teeth; similar to acid alterations.

Xenarthra   The magnorder of animals comprising placental mammals, including armadillos, sloths, glyptodonts, and anteaters.

zygomatic arch   A bony arch commonly called the cheekbone.

zygapophysis, pl. **zygapophyses**   A bony protuberance on a vertebra that helps the vertebra articulate with the next vertebra and also prevents dislocation; the prezygapophysis on one vertebra articulates with the postzygapophysis of the next.

Notes

Chapter 1. Introduction

1. In *How to do Archaeology the Right Way*, Purdy (1996) gives an in-depth discussion of the differences between methods in comparative, relative, and absolute dating of an object; furthermore, she breaks absolute dating down into chronometric and calendric. In the abbreviation B.P. (before present), the "present" is 1950, the year radiocarbon analysis was first used.

2. Even with trace fossils such as trackways, burrows, coprolites, etc., it is often difficult to determine with certainty which animal left which trace fossil. In instances when an animal can be linked to a particular trace fossil, that only means a behavior could occur, not that the behavior was typical. Furthermore, even when an extinct animal has a very close extant relative, the behavior and physiology of the two may be markedly different.

3. Rothschild and Martin (1993) stress that the biggest misconception about the fossilization process is the preconception of molecule by molecule replacement of organic molecules with inorganic molecules. They state emphatically that although molds and casts exist and chemical changes may have occurred in the lattice, there is no known case of molecule by molecule replacement in the fossil record. Even very old fossils may possess much of their original materials, with little or no alteration. In many cases the original organic matter becomes encased in the petrifying materials and protected from further decay.

4. For a brief presentation of the various processes of fossilization, see *Simon and Schuster's Guide to Fossils*.

5. Technically, the fossilization process is ongoing. A bone may be only several hundred years old and in a very early stage of fossilization, or several million years old and in a continuing state of fossilization, as additional changes to the specimen may still occur.

6. *Dynamics of Dinosaurs and Other Extinct Giants* by R. McNeill Alexander (1989) and *Dinosaurs, Spitfires, and Dragons* by Christopher McGowan (1983) are two excellent books that cover morphological applications of dinosaur fossils.

7. *Bones: The Utility of Form and Function* by R. McNeill Alexander (1994) presents various aspects of this topic with both extinct and extant examples.

8. The term Paleo-Indians (see comments in preface on the use of this term) is the one most commonly used by amateur and professional archaeologists; however, the term "Indian" itself has fallen out of favor among those seeking politically correct terms and who now prefer the term "Native Americans." The author has begun to see the terms Paleo-Americans, Early Native Americans, Clovis People, and Pre-Clovis People used in place of Paleo-Indians. For a great journey into the feelings of current

Native Americans on the status of the term Indian, and archaeology as a whole, read *Skull Wars: Kennewick Man, Archaeology, and the Battle for Native American Identity*, by David Hurst Thomas (2000).

9. *Florida's First People*, by Robin Brown (1994), explains how Paleo-Indians and later generations of Native Americans may have modified bone, teeth, and antlers as well as shell, stone, wood, and other resources.

10. A scientist may concentrate on a single order, family, or species of animal across topics, as in Bruce J. McFadden's (1992) *Fossil Horses: Systematics, Paleobiology, and Evolution of the Family Equidae*, or scientists may concentrate on a single topic across taxa, as in Peter Ward's (1994) *The End of Evolution* or David M. Raup's (1991) *Extinction: Bad Genes or Bad Luck?* Besides focusing on topics taxonomically, scientists may focus on subjects temporally (within a time period), geographically, or culturally.

11. A growing body of evidence supports the existence of humans in the Americas more than 12,000 years ago.

Chapter 2. The Morphology of Fossil Bones

1. For formulas for strength, speed, size (mass or weight), force, energy costs, and other biomechanical features inferred from bone morphology, see R. McNeill Alexander's (1992) *Exploring Biomechanics; Animals in Motion* and his (1989) *Dynamics of Dinosaurs and Other Extinct Giants*.

2. The collaboration between scientist and artist at the turn of the century, like that between Henry Fairfield Osborne and Charles Knight at the American Museum of Natural History in New York City, produced the first popular murals depicting prehistoric fauna and flora inferred from fossil evidence. Collaborations before this point comprised mostly artists and scientists producing line drawings and plates for scientific papers and presentations. Claudine Cohen also speculates that paleontology may be the only field of science "where art forms an integral part of the scientific work."

3. Gary Hayne's (1991) *Mammoths, Mastodonts, and Elephants* is an excellent example of scientific inquiry on an extant taxa applied to extinct animals, and vice versa.

4. For a full discussion of the contributions of Stephen Jay Gould to concepts of species selection and where they stand today, refer to Lieberman and Vrba's journal article in *Paleobiology* (2005, vol. 31(2), pp. 113–121), "Stephen Jay Gould on Species Selection: 30 Years of Insight."

5. For identifying different types of bones and their articulating joint ends, *Mammalian Osteology*, by Miles Gilbert (1990), and *Avian Osteology*, by Miles Gilbert, Larry Martin, and Howard Savage (1985), are excellent resource books; however, they describe only extant taxa from North America.

6. *Principals of Anatomy and Physiology*, by Tortora and Grabowski (1993), has an introductory section on skeletal anatomy.

7. To this list of joints could also be added the saddle joint, found in the thumb of humans and primates, the condyloid joints between the carpals and radius, and the pivot joint between the atlas and axis (the first two vertebrae in the neck).

8. The vertebral columns of reptiles, amphibians, birds, and fish all have different configurations that would take volumes to describe. The author chose to describe the

general mammalian vertebral column because it is the most familiar to the majority of fossil collectors.

9. An in-depth description and explanation of cartilaginous joints is presented in *Skeleton Keys: An Introduction to Human Skeletal Morphology, Development, and Analysis*, by Jeffrey H. Schwartz (1995). This is an excellent reference book on all phases of human skeletal anatomy.

10. In addition to the restricted island life of the Key Deer, its reduced size may be partially attributable to the principle, known as Bergmann's Rule, that animal body size decreases with latitude; that is, the closer to the equator, the smaller the size of individuals within species. It is believed that larger body size in northern geographic regions enables animals to better conserve body heat in cold temperatures.

11. Many now believe that today's birds are directly descended from dinosaurs. In *The Mistaken Extinction: Dinosaur Evolution and the Origin of Birds*, Dingus and Rowe (1998) completely analyze this theory that has gained much support and evidence.

12. The long bones of amphibians and reptiles develop slightly differently. The ends of their bones are generally encased in a cartilage cap that allows growth to take place much longer; therefore, the maximum size of individuals is not fixed for many reptilian species. The result is that their joint ends are generally less intricate than those of mammals and look looser and less efficient.

13. The stage of development may also affect a bone's ability to survive the processes of fossilization. Bones from very young animals are generally underrepresented in the fossil record because of their relatively fragile nature compared with the robust bones of healthy adult animals.

14. The marine mammal adaptation of extremely dense bones to reduce buoyancy is technically termed pachyostosis. The thickening of marine mammal bones occurs without resorption or remodeling.

15. Ryosuke Motani, in an article titled "Rulers of the Jurassic Seas" (*Scientific American*, December 2000), gives an in-depth look at the body plans and strategies of prehistoric ichthyosaurs.

16. Female birds deposit additional osseous material in the normally hollow shafts of their medullary bone in the weeks just prior to egg laying. It is believed this might be a strategy for storing extra calcium for the requirements of eggshells. Scientists studying fossil bird bones can use this information to determine season of death in a large assemblage of bones.

17. Large sauropod dinosaurs (not covered in this text) had very unique ways of developing strong but light bone to support their enormous bodies. For a complete discussion of this phenomenon, see *Quest for the African Dinosaurs*, by Louis Jacobs (2000).

18. *In the Blink of an Eye*, by Andrew Parker (2003), is an entire book devoted to the importance of the evolution of vision in all types of life on earth. Parker credits the development of vision with the Cambrian explosion of complex life.

19. For additional insights into the workings of the senses (sight, hearing, smell, and touch), see *The Big Cats and Their Fossil Relatives*, pp. 95–103, by Alan Turner (1997). The author also reviews the relation of hearing and sight to the organization of the animal brain.

20. Many animals with true horns that grow throughout their lives and are not shed annually develop rings or check lines that show where growth slowed in the winter. Scientists can use these to determine the age of some animals.

21. The fact that otoliths are often overlooked by fossil collectors is not surprising for more reasons than the simple fact that they are small and nondescript. In *Becoming a Tiger: How Baby Animals Learn to Live in the Wild*, Susan McCarthy (2004) mentions that as late as the 1930s it was generally believed that fish could not hear at all. *What Your Fossils Can Tell You* does not deal with animal behaviors directly; however, those interested in that topic can turn to McCarthy's book, which is an excellent resource for the general audience on animal behaviors, especially learning.

22. Toothed whales and baleen whales have very different hearing systems; toothed whales have evolved the ability to echolocate while hunting, whereas baleen whales have evolved the ability to hear low frequency sounds, enabling them to communicate with each other from long distances.

23. Felidae are distinguished from Nimravidae by the location of their auditory bulla. See *The Big Cats and Their Fossil Relatives* by Alan Turner (1997) for a complete explanation.

24. For a comprehensive look into the evolution of the human brain, see *The Runaway Brain* by Christopher Wills (1993).

25. Most books about human origins contain a chapter or section on the significance of Broca's area, named for Paul Broca, the man who first found and studied it. *The Wisdom of the Bones*, by Alan Walker and Pat Shipman (1996), describes the importance of this lobe impression in *Homo erectus* skulls.

26. For a complete review of the history of craniology and brain to body size ratio see Stephen Jay Gould's (1981) *The Mismeasure of Man*. Focusing primarily on the human brain, this document gives a comprehensive look at the ways in which the braincase has been used (and misused) historically to determine intelligence and human capabilities.

Chapter 3. The Morphology of Fossil Teeth

1. *Fossils, Teeth, and Sex*, by Charles Oxnard (1987), is an entire book devoted to fossil teeth in relation to human evolution. Although the book focuses on hominids and hominoids, Chapter 7 provides in-depth coverage of the problems faced by scientists inferring behavior and traits from fossil teeth—problems that are the same for all paleontologists.

2. The practice of identifying a new species by a single tooth (or bone) was prevalent early in the field of paleontology. In cases where the specimen was legitimately a new species, that fossil is called the type specimen.

3. Carnivores spend much less time feeding (using their teeth) than herbivores; most reptiles and cold-blooded animals spend even less time feeding than carnivorous mammals.

4. This statement holds true for vertebrate fossils only; the biggest "winner" in the overall fossil record for sheer biomass is marine invertebrates. In addition, even with vertebrates, exceptions to the rule occur: dugongs have only 2 teeth per jaw quadrant in use but many, many very dense bones that are common fossil finds.

5. For clarification of taxonomic classification, inferential classification, and the use of Latin, see *Bones and Skulls* by Glenn Searfoss (1995).

6. Large scientific samples used to determine sexual dimorphism may range from several score to several thousand articulated individuals from a single location or stratum. These fossil locations are termed *Lagerstatten*, a German word roughly translated to "mother lode."

7. Geographically defined populations that differ slightly morphologically (and therefore genetically) and that can interbreed at the edges of or in overlapping geographic areas are called clines. Generally, in mammals, size gradually increases as the animal's northern geographic range limits are approached. In extant animals, individuals may still interbreed, and therefore are considered only varieties or races and not separate species; however, in the paleontological record it is not possible to know for sure whether animals with the exact same body plan and differing only in size are different species, different sexes, or just variations of the same species.

8. Technically, the mandible refers to the complete lower jaw (both sides). Only one side of the lower jaw would be referred to as the ramus.

9. A good resource to assist in identifying various fossil teeth (from Miocene to Pleistocene in age) is the series of articles "Whose tooth is this?" by David Thulman, appearing in the *Florida Paleontological Society Newsletter* from 1995 to 1997.

10. *Horses' Teeth: Their Problems, Prevention, Recognition, and Treatment*, by Kai Kreling (2004), is an excellent book for anyone interested in horses' teeth. Although written for today's horse owners and breeders, the majority of the concepts hold true for many species of fossil horses.

11. Ian Lange (2002), in *Ice Age Mammals of North America*, reports that various mammoths would have required between 650 and 770 pounds of food per day, requiring 16 to 18 hours of feeding time.

12. "The Last Decade (More or Less) of Equid Paleobiology" by Richard Hulbert, in *Pony Express* (2004, vol. 13(2)), provides an in-depth discussion of this phenomenon for fossil horses. Hulbert explains in some detail mesowear analysis, which compares the teeth of horses during various evolutionary stages. Visually noticeable, the sharp points on the occlusal surfaces of early horses' teeth slowly disappeared through geological time until we see the flat teeth of today's genus *Equus*.

13. Increasing and decreasing levels of carbon dioxide in the atmosphere affect the growth of plants that use the C3 metabolic pathway. C4 plants are already saturated with carbon dioxide and do not respond to global elevation of carbon dioxide. C3 pathway plants respond to elevated levels of carbon dioxide by increasing photosynthetic activity and therefore growth rate. From this phenomenon, scientists can determine carbon dioxide levels in past environments by examining the ratios of C4 to C3 plants in the teeth of the same species over time.

14. Many artiodactyls such as deer, caribou, elk, and bison have evolutionarily lost their upper incisors and canines and replaced them with a tough bony ridge that assists in cropping vegetation.

15. Determining the subgenera of mastodons by use of tooth morphology is presented in *The Fate of the Mammoth*, by Claudine Cohen (1994), pp. 136–137.

16. For detailed documentation of horse evolution, read Bruce MacFadden's (1992) *Fossil Horses: Systematics, Paleobiology, and Evolution of the Family Equidae*.

17. At least 3 different species, in 2 different genera, of short-faced bears existed during the Pleistocene. Scientists are still trying to figure out whether the Florida short-faced bear, *Tremarctos floridanus*, was a carnivore or an omnivore.

18. The book *Africa's Elephant: A Biography*, by Martin Meredith (2001), gives an excellent historical account of the ivory trade from historical times onward. It is presumed that the ivory from mammoths and mastodons was similarly prized, as many artifacts manufactured from each of them have been discovered in both the Old World and the New World.

19. The principle of using Schreger patterns to differentiate between mastodon and mammoth materials was applied in the Aucilla River Project to determine Paleo-Indian preference for working with ivory (*Aucilla River Times*, vol. 12(1), 1999).

20. Jon R. Luoma's (2000) article in *Audubon*, "The Wild World's Scotland Yard," reports that now, because they can understand Schreger patterns, U.S. Customs agents, using only a magnifying glass and protractor, can seize and prosecute illegal shipments of elephant ivory that have been labeled "mammoth" or "mastodont" in order to be snuck into the country.

21. Dendrochronology, the study of tree rings to determine tree age and growth rate, is very precise and has been used by scientists for a long time. Sclerochronology is the study of periodic features in skeletal parts of organisms with mineralized tissues (bones, teeth, tusks, shells, etc.). "Direct Measurement of Age in Fossil *Gryphaea*: The Solution to a Classic Problem in Heterochrony," by Jones and Gould (1999), presents an excellent example of the study of sclerochronology to solve a paleontological problem.

22. Note also that the 6 cheek teeth in a horse, 3 molars and 3 premolars, are positioned in the horse's jaw in such a way that the first and last tooth press inward, maintaining a tight alignment of all the teeth in the jaw. This configuration prevents food particles from getting between the teeth and creates a stable chewing surface for an animal that spends the majority of its day chewing.

23. It is easier and safer for a veterinarian to inspect a horse's incisors than to look at the surface of its molars far back in the mouth.

24. In horse incisors, on the occlusal surface, are patterns referred to as the cup, star, and mark. The size and location of these three identifying patterns change with the age of the horse as the teeth wear down. A veterinarian or scientist can "read" these patterns to determine a horse's age.

25. The majority of coprolites found are from carnivores, because the high content of bone material in their diets enables their fecal matter to survive long enough to fossilize.

26. The extinct white shark *Carcharodon megalodon* is also referred to in some scientific literature as *Carcharocles megalodon* as there is still much debate amongst experts as to the true genus the specie should belong to. Furthermore, amateurs often refer to the teeth from these sharks as megalodon or Meg teeth.

27. Presented at the Florida Paleontological Society Meeting by Dr. Gordon Hubbell in 1999.

28. In fact, it is not only amateurs who have been taken in by "faked" or "reworked" specimens. The story of Piltdown Man is a quite famous historic example of a faked specimen with which most fossil enthusiasts are familiar. *Unraveling Piltdown*, by

John Evangelist Walsh (1996), gives a complete account of this fraud. Perpetrators of fraud are still around, however, and have gotten better at their craft. As late as 2000, Stephen Czerkas, a well known avocational dinosaur paleontologist, Phillip Currie of the Royal Tyrrell Museum in Canada, and *National Geographic Magazine* were all duped by a forged Chinese fossil purported to be the earliest bird. This episode was well documented by Paul Chambers (2002) in *Bones of Contention*.

29. The fact that reptiles have homodont dentition was one of the first clues that led early naturalists like Gideon Mantell and Richard Owen to identify early dinosaur finds as giant reptiles. *The Dinosaur Hunters: A True Story of Scientific Rivalry and the Discovery of the Prehistoric World* by Deborah Cadbury (2001) is a comprehensive account of this saga in the history of dinosaur science.

30. Only mammals alone of living vertebrates have permanent teeth.

Chapter 4. Natural Alterations to Fossils

1. *Pleistocene Bone Technology in the Beringian Refugium*, by Robson Bonnichsen (1979), presents an analysis of geological alterations that can occur to bones and fossils.

2. According to Greg Ericson, "Paleobiologists therefore view the majority of the world's natural history museums as deserts of behavioral evidence" as a result of their desire to present complete skeletons that died from causes other than predation or scavenging. Complete skeletons were usually buried quickly after death and not transported by water currents, as opposed to partial skeletons or bones that may show evidence of various taphonomic factors having worked on them.

3. In *Animal Bone Archaeology*, Brian Hesse and Paula Wapnish (1985) describe seven processes affecting bone samples. In addition to the processes described in chapter 4 of this text, anataxic processes, sullegic processes, and trephic processes also exist. Anataxic processes describe anything that moves a bone from a buried state to one where it is exposed to agents of attrition, for example, erosion, construction, mining. Sullegic processes are procedures by scientists that may bias a bone sample, such as collecting/digging procedures, deciding which specimens to keep, recognizing specimens, and deciding from which areas to collect at a large site. Trephic processes are the curatorial processes of sorting, recording, and reporting, all areas where mistakes can be made.

4. *Bones: Ancient Men and Modern Myths*, by Lewis R. Binford (1981), presents an in-depth discussion of all possible mimics that naturally occur in the archaeological record. These mimics are no different in the paleontological record.

5. Lewis R. Binford (1981) presents many examples of scientists who have gone astray by not looking first at the possibility of natural mimics before attributing anomalies in bones to cultural modifications.

6. The most complete treatment of the subject of taphonomy appears to be *Bonebeds: Genesis, Analysis, and Paleobiological Significance*, edited by Rogers, Eberth, and Fiorillo (2007).

7. Dale Guthrie (2005), in *The Nature of Paleolithic Art*, describes several other instances of biased taphonomic preservation in the fossil record. If these biases are not carefully studied and accounted for, they can lead to some diverse conclusions.

8. The acid level in soils and waters varies and can be measured on a pH scale, where pH of 6 or less indicates acid soil, and pH of 8 or more indicates alkaline soil. A pH of 7 is considered neutral. Bones and teeth generally do not survive well in acidic soils; however, in soils with little or no oxygen and minimum water movement, bones and teeth may survive in great condition even if the acid level is high, because of lack of bacteria to break down the organic matter as well as lack of water to leach the acids into the bone.

9. Michael J. Benton (2003), in *When Life Nearly Died* (pp. 176, 269) gives a good description of the various colors in fossils and the surrounding matrix and what those colors can tell scientists about the sediments where they were first laid down.

10. In addition, fossil bones suffer much breakage during the collection process as the result of poor preservation and/or sloppy collecting methods.

11. Abrasion and corrosion are covered in great detail in chapter 5 of *Bonebeds* by Eberth, Rogers, and Fiorillo (2007).

12. Fading (and two-tone) are not scientific terms that the author could find in any of the technical literature; however, many beginners are often confused by two-toned and faded specimens. Therefore, the author coined simple terms to explain these phenomena.

Chapter 5. Pathologies in Fossil Bones

1. Paleopathologies have been reported in the literature as early as 1774. Giants of nineteenth-century paleontology also recognized paleopathologies: Cuvier in 1820 and Leidy in 1886. The first compilations of various paleopathologies were not done until early in the twentieth century by Metchnikoff; however, as a whole, paleopathology is still quite overlooked in the popular literature on fossils.

2. Books such as *Paleopathology*, edited by Shelton and Rothschild, and other publications such as *Journal of Paleopathology* are evidence that the subject of paleopathology is emerging as a field unto itself.

3. The author is deeply indebted to one such team of collaborators, Bruce M. Rothschild and Larry D. Martin. Their seminal work in this area, *Paleopathology: Disease in the Fossil Record* (1993), is a must read for anyone delving into this area. Bruce Rothschild also took considerable time to review this chapter and give corrective feedback; however, the author still takes responsibility for any errors in this chapter.

4. The author had the most difficulty with this section on arthritis. Without the use of specialized equipment and specific training in this field, diagnosis beyond rudimentary arthritis should probably be left to those specializing in the field of paleopathology. Refer to the work of Rothschild and Martin (1992), *Paleopathology: Disease in the Fossil Record*, chapters 7–10, for in-depth reading on this subject. Also see *Skeletal Impact of Disease* by the same authors.

5. Rheumatoid arthritis is a type of polyarticular erosive arthritis so far found only in humans. The term polyarticular refers to the fact that rheumatoid arthritis affects multiple joints, often bilaterally and symmetrically (therefore, multiple bones from an individual animal make it easier to diagnose).

6. In *The Big Cats and their Fossil Relatives*, Alan Turner (1997) reports that more than 5,000 bones from saber-toothed cats found in the La Brea Tar Pits show some

type of pathology. Especially prevalent is osteoarthritis from overexertion, presumably caused by taking down large prey animals.

7. Bonnichsen (1979) reports extensive finds of artiodactyls gnawing on bones in the Baringian Refugium.

8. With the combined use of modern analogues and well-preserved fossil sites such as dire wolf dens, various bear dens and caves, and large cat lairs, scientists have made much headway in determining the specific animals that leave particular marks on bones. Dire wolves left the majority of gnaw marks on Pleistocene bones, large cats tended to leave light scratch marks on bones as they used their incisors to strip away skin and flesh, and smaller bears did not break bones the way larger bears did, such as *Arctodus*, which tended to break and crush even fairly large bones.

9. In the La Belle site, a Pleistocene deposit in south Florida excavated by author Mark Renz and studied by the University of Florida, many long bones of camels and horses were missing their proximal ends. In *Giants in the Storm*, Renz (2005) gives a complete account of the amateur paleontological community, led by Renz, working with professionals excavating and donating the finds from this location to science.

10. Spina bifida occulta generally has no outward effects on the animal (asymptomatic), as opposed to spina bifida cystica, which involves neural tube defects and neurological complications. It is unlikely that any animal could survive in the wild with spina bifida cystica.

Chapter 6. Pathologies in Fossil Teeth

1. The pH scale is a logarithmic scale of the activity of dissolved hydrogen ions and expresses the alkalinity or acidity of a substance. A pH of less than 7 is considered acidic; greater than 7 is considered alkaline. Thus, if the pH level in saliva is reduced to less than 7, acids are formed in the mouth. An acidic saliva is detrimental to tooth enamel and can cause dental caries. pH stands for the potential or power of hydrogen ions in solution.

2. Although rare, dental caries have been reported from the Devonian, Permian, and Triassic time periods.

3. Dinosaurs had reptile-like teeth, which gave early paleontologists a clue to their classification. *The Dinosaur Hunters* by Deborah Cadbury (2001) gives a detailed account of the problems that dinosaur teeth presented to early paleontologists: Cuvier, Mantell, and Owen.

4. For in-depth discussion of the giant squid, *Architeuthis*, read Richard Ellis's (1998) book *The Search for the Giant Squid*. Ellis separates myth from reality; however, even the real giant squid is something to marvel at.

5. The private shark tooth collection of Dr. Gordon Hubbell is an excellent example of the use and display of both comparative anatomy and modern phylogenetic analogues.

6. Again, the private collection of Dr. Hubbell includes a complete set of modern great white jaws exhibiting side spurs on every tooth.

7. Teri Lear (2002) describes many atavistic traits expressed in modern horses in "Atavisms or What Goes Around Comes Around." For an even more in-depth discussion of atavisms, read *Hen's Teeth and Horse's Toes* by Stephen Jay Gould (1984), also

included in *Further Reflections in Natural History* by W. W. Norton and Company and excellent reading for anyone interested in paleontology or natural history.

8. While taking photographs for this book, the author saw literally hundreds, perhaps more than a thousand, pathological shark teeth. Pathological mammal teeth were very rare in comparison, and the author spent much time finding specimens to photograph to illustrate the text.

9. An article titled "A Study of a Molar Tooth Found in the Coronoid Process" (J. L. Gomez, 1996, *Journal of Paleopathology* 8[1]) discusses how embryonic buds can travel to different areas of the jaw during very early stages of development, in this case carrying all the encoded sequences of a fully developing tooth to an anomalous area of the jawbone. In this situation, the scientists researched the entire embryonic dental development in order to determine how one tooth could erupt in an anomalous position.

Chapter 7. Cultural Modification of Bones, Antlers, and Teeth

1. Lewis Binford's (1981) *Bones: Ancient Men and Modern Myths* presents a very in-depth conservative view of what can be confidently attributed to cultural modification. What many professional archaeologists and paleontologists refer to as culturally modified bone Binford believes is actually the work of natural elements and animal actions, such as gnawing or trampling. Binford backs his position with detailed research on the results of animal actions and natural phenomena (weather, ground acids, etc.)

2. In 1895 and 1896, Frank Hamilton Cushing led an exploration of the Key Marco site in Florida that unearthed a vast quantity of finely carved and painted wooden artifacts. These items included ceremonial masks, tablets, utensils, tools, weapons, boat paddles, and what are believed to be toys. Cushing's (2000) accounts of these explorations and discoveries are well documented in his *Exploration of the Ancient Key Dweller Remains on the Gulf Coast of Florida*, recently republished by University Press of Florida. Note: Wooden artifacts disintegrate almost immediately after being unearthed, and sites containing such items should be handled only by professionals.

3. *Archaeology of Precolumbian Florida* by Jerald T. Milanich (1994), *Indian Mounds You Can Visit* by I. Mac Perry (1993), and *Florida's First People* by Robin C. Brown (1994) all give excellent detailed breakdowns of the chronological cultural period stages of Native American occupation of North America.

4. In *The First Americans: In Pursuit of Archaeology's Greatest Mystery*, J. M. Adovasio and Jake Page (2002) review the evidence for sites considered pre-Clovis (earlier than 12,000 to possibly 40,000 years ago) and make a strong case for very early occupation of the Americas.

5. Some archaeologists also include a brief protohistoric period. This very brief period of time would have occurred shortly after Columbus first landed in the Caribbean and South America, when natives fled to other areas of the New World to escape Spanish atrocities. They may have brought cultural items, ideas, or techniques to other Native Americans they encountered, ahead of actual first contact for those groups with European settlers and explorers.

6. Many stages and periods may have different names and slightly varying chronologies depending on the researcher, location, and constant arrival of new discoveries and research concerning dating techniques.

7. The discovery of Kennewick Man, a 9,000-year-old skeleton with purported Caucasoid features, has caused a major controversy in the chronology of who arrived first (and from where) in North America. *Skull Wars* by David Hurst Thomas (2000) is the best attempt to present Kennewick Man, the arrival of Paleo-Indians, and the feelings of current Native Americans toward archaeology.

8. *The Overstreet Indian Arrowheads Identification and Price Guide* is a readily available, regularly updated, and well-organized pictorial guide that can assist amateur and vocational collectors alike in identifying more than 1,000 stone implements from all over the United States.

9. Barbara A. Purdy (1996), in her book *Indian Art of Ancient Florida*, devotes a short chapter to bone and antler items that have been worked into objects of art. Her book also describes wood, shell, stone, ceramic, and metal items crafted by ancient Native Americans.

10. *The Art and Archaeology of Florida's Wetlands* by Barbara A. Purdy (1991) is an entire book focusing on the more perishable items that can be preserved in wet environments, including artifacts of bone, antler teeth, wood, and even textile and cordage made from plants. Included in these sites are raw plant materials, including seeds, leaves, and unprocessed wood. Note that only expert archaeologists with technical skills relating to these environments can salvage anything from these sites. Items discovered in such settings can often perish within hours, sometimes minutes, of being exposed to the atmosphere for the first time in thousands of years. If a site like this is discovered, accidentally or while fossil or artifact hunting, state or federal authorities should be notified immediately or all will be lost.

11. Florida's unique geological structure offers more opportunities for the preservation, and ultimate discovery, of bone artifacts than most other locations in the United States.

12. Trampling may result in shallow parallel scratches left on bones. Carnivores generally leave deep U-shaped grooves on bones, and rodent gnawing generally leaves closely spaced repetitive parallel markings.

13. In an extensive study of Nunamiut Eskimos, Lewis Binford (1981) identified many traits and locations of butchering marks left by native cultures as they dismembered and procured meat from a carcass. Using these observations to determine how early Native Americans would have butchered animals, Binford has come to the conclusion that much of what we consider butchering marks are in actuality the markings left by carnivores and scavengers.

14. For an in-depth discussion of Binford's research in the area of splitting bones for marrow extraction, see his *Bones: Ancient Men and Modern Myths* (1981).

15. Larry G. Marshall's chapter titled "Bone Modification and The Laws of Burial" in *Bone Modification* (edited by Bonnichsen and Sorg, 1989), cautions readers not to conclude that association of stone tools with broken bones is concrete evidence of human modification, and then gives an in-depth description of what to look for in bones modified by humans.

16. Those interested in discussion of prehistoric fishhooks, their construction, terminology, and typology, should review "A New Type of Prehistoric Fishhook from North Florida" by Ryan and Harley Means (2004).

17. The book *Indian Fishing: Early Methods on the Northwest Coast*, by Hillary Stewart (1977), is an excellent source of information on development of various fishing methods, including hooks utilizing bone pin barbs, by Native American cultures on the Pacific Coast.

18. The author has found numerous bone pins himself and been present during the discovery of many more. The vast majority of bone pins found are usually broken at one end or the other. When only the pointed end is found, it is virtually impossible to tell whether the whole pin would have been a single-pointed or bi-pointed bone pin. This makes it even more problematic to determine the intended function of broken bone. Furthermore, it is also virtually impossible to tell the length of an incomplete pin, no matter which end one finds of a broken bone pin.

19. Karen Jo Walker (1992), in a monograph titled "Bone Artifacts from Josslyn Island, Buck Key Shell Midden, and Cash Mound: *A Preliminary Assessment*," provides a detailed account of bone pin technology, including the differences between bone pins and bone points and other facts concerning bone pin technology.

20. In *The Nature of Paleolithic Art*, R. Dale Guthrie (2005) goes to great lengths to make a compelling case for not attributing the majority of Paleolithic art to the magico-religious paradigm, but rather to a naturalistic observer paradigm. His overall work also addresses the nature of art made by children and teens, practice art, and the accuracy of representations in very early art. Although he is generally discussing art earlier than that from North America (mostly cave art from Europe), he gives many examples of New World art. His work is worth reading by anyone interested in prehistoric art of any type.

21. For further discussion of the theory of use of altered states in prehistoric or primitive art, read *The Mind in the Cave* by David Lewis-Williams (2002). Although the book focuses mainly on cave art in Europe, Lewis-Williams briefly discusses modern-day primitive art, including some examples from North America. The author feels a strong connection might exist between this theory and many of the examples shown in the book. This theory may provide a good explanation for the first appearance of these patterns on objects; after that, they might have become culturally engrained and produced as part of everyday life, without an altered state being reached every time a bone was incised or a pot decorated.

22. According to Dale Guthrie, several items can be termed spears from prehistoric times: (1) a long, handheld thrusting spear is called a "pike"; (2) If that thrusting spear is held by a horseman or charioteer it is called a "lance"; (3) a spear held in the middle for throwing is called a "javelin"; (4) A spear thrown with the use of an atlatl is called a "dart"; (5) smaller fletched darts shot from a bow are called "arrows"; and (6) any of the above forms tethered to a cord of some sort are termed "harpoons" and generally barbed at the point.

23. At this time there is no direct evidence that Paleo-Indians had use of the atlatl in North America; however, European discoveries predate the arrival of the first humans in North America.

24. In *Clovis Revisited*, Boldurian and Cotter (1999) deliver a comprehensive dis-

cussion of the possible uses of foreshafts in Paleo-Indian hunting technologies, specifically those related to the Clovis culture.

25. The term bannerstone reflects the predominance of magico-religious interpretations of early archaeology. Without knowing the use of these carved stones or bones, early archaeologists termed them bannerstones, meaning charmed stones, and believed they were used in some sort of religious ceremony. For further information on the exact mechanics of bannerstones in use of the atlatl, refer to R. Dale Guthrie (2005), *The Nature of Paleolithic Art*, pages 283–292.

26. The author has recovered more than 100 fossilized antler bases from various sites and has never once found one with a base naturally hollowed out. Fossilized antler has little or no marrow cavity and often appears to be almost solid all the way to the core.

27. Although some believe antler bases were used in the initial manufacture of stone implements, Purdy (1986) points out that antler material is probably too light for the early manufacture stages of stone working. She mentions use of deer tibiae and metapodials discovered at a few sites potentially as flakers for initially removing larger flakes from the core material. A more dense bone, such as manatee or whale rib, possibly already in a fossilized state, would be far more suitable for the beginning stage of core reduction. These denser bones were also readily available to many Native Americans, especially in Florida and the southeastern United States.

28. An index often used to demonstrate the fine craftsmanship of stone implements is the ratio of width to thickness ratio. In the case of the Newnan Point pictured in figure 7.70, its width is 5.5 cm and thickness is 0.8 cm, for a width/thickness ratio of nearly 7:1.

29. For a complete description of the way arrow shaft wrenches work, refer to R. Dale Guthrie's (2005) *The Nature of Paleolithic Art*, pages 294–296.

30. It is quite possible that bison were far rarer in the prehistoric past for any number of reasons. There is growing evidence that the Native American population in North America may have been far more abundant before first contact with Europeans. Hunting of bison may have kept the bison populations in check; after Native American populations were decimated by disease and other hardships caused by European contact, bison populations may have exploded.

31. The author is deeply indebted to Hermann Trappmann for this insight and many others pertaining to Native American cultures; especially freeing the author from purely Euro-centric or ethnocentric thinking when it came to determining the meaning and uses of many Native American artifacts. Understanding these cultures often takes a lifetime of work and open-mindedness. These indigenous peoples were neither worse nor better than ourselves; just extremely culturally different. Many of these cultural differences are so great that it becomes hard for many of us (amateurs or professionals) to figure out what many items were used for, or their spiritual or cultural meaning. The cultural difference is often so great that we are either unable to give meaning to an item or unwilling to accept a meaning once one is put forth. The author does not purport to have become an expert in any spiritual or cultural ways of current or past Native Americans, only to have become more open minded as a result of the enlightenment of Hermann Trappmann.

32. *Decorative and Symbolic uses of Vertebrate Fossils* by Kenneth Oakley (1975)

provides some great examples of the use of fossilized materials by prehistoric and ancient cultures.

33. Personal communication from Robert Austin.

34. For further examples and discussion of geofacts and manuports, refer to *The Lost Civilizations of the Stone Age*, by Richard Rudgley (1999).

35. Do not mistake Purdy's use of the phrase "not significant" for lack of scientific importance. The first of a new genre of artifacts may often appear idiosyncratic, but upon further investigation, additional items and information may lead to a fuller understanding of the item in hand.

36. The author found two different viewpoints in the professional literature regarding use of toe bones as whistles. Lewis Binford (1981), in *Bones: Ancient Men and Modern Myths*, vehemently opposes attributing marks on bones to humans when they can easily be attributed to the action of animals. In his discussion of tooth marks, he specifically mentions that toe bones with holes have been erroneously categorized as primitive musical whistles; however, in *Bone Modification*, edited by Bonnichsen and Sorg (1989) and published by and for professionals, a chapter by Sollorzano pictures several deer toes as possible whistles.

37. Once again the author is indebted to Hermann Trappmann for opening his eyes to alternative possibilities when investigating culturally different items, as explained in note 31 in this chapter.

38. The use of a deer toe bow bearing and drill are illustrated in *The First Civilizations* by Giovanni Caselli (1983), page 11.

Selected References

Adovasio, J. M., and Jake Page. 2002. *The First Americans: In Pursuit of Archaeology's Greatest Mystery*. New York: Random House.

Alexander, R. McNeill. 1989. *Dynamics of Dinosaurs and Other Extinct Giants*. New York: Columbia University Press.

———. 1992. *Exploring Biomechanics*. New York: Scientific American Library.

———. 1994. *Bones: The Utility of Form and Function*. London: Weidenfeld and Nicolson.

Bahn, Paul (Ed.). 2002. *Written in Bones: How Human Remains Unlock the Secrets of the Dead*. Toronto: Firefly Books.

Benedict, Jeff. 2003. *No Bone Unturned*. New York: Harper Collins.

Benton, Michael. 1998. *The Rise of the Mammals*. London: Eagle Editions, Quantum Books.

———. 2003. *When Life Nearly Died*. New York: Thames and Hudson.

Binford, Lewis R. 1981. *Bones: Ancient Men and Modern Myths*. New York: Academic.

Boaz, Noel T., and Russell L. Ciochon. 2004. *Dragon Bone Hill: An Ice Age Saga of Homo Erectus*. Oxford: Oxford University Press.

Boldurian, Anthony T., and John L. Cotter. 1999. *Clovis Revisited: New Perspectives on Paleoindian Adaptations from Blackwater Draw, New Mexico*. Philadelphia: The University Museum, University of Pennsylvania.

Bonnichsen, Robson. 1979. *Pleistocene Bone Technology in the Beringian Refugium*. Ottawa: National Museums of Canada.

Bonnichsen, Robson, and Marcella H. Sorg. (Eds.) 1989. *Bone Modification*. Orono: Center for the Study of the First Americans, University of Maine.

Brothwell, D. R. 1981. *Digging Up Bones*. Oxford: Oxford University Press.

Brown, Robin C. 1994. *Florida's First People*. Sarasota, Fla.: Pineapple Press.

Cadburry, Deborah. 2001. *The Dinosaur Hunters*. London: Harper Collins.

Caselli, Giovanni. 1983. *The First Civilizations*. New York: Peter Bedrick Books.

Chambers, Paul. 2002. *Bones of Contention: The Archaeopteryx Scandals*. London: John Murray Publishers.

Chandler, Richard, and John Timmerman. 1994. *Neogene Fossils of North Carolina: A Field Guide*. Durham: North Carolina Fossil Club.

Chaplin, R. E. 1971. *The Study of Animal Bones from Archaeological Sites*. New York: Seminar Press.

Chatters, James C. 2001. *Ancient Encounters*. New York: Simon and Schuster.

Cohen, Claudine. 2002. *The Fate of the Mammoth: Fossils, Myth, and History*. 2nd ed. Trans. William Rodamor. Chicago: University of Chicago Press.

Corfield, Richard. 2001. *Architects of Eternity: The New Science of Fossils*. London: Headline Book Publishing.

Cushing, Frank Hamilton. 1896 (2000 reprint). *Exploration of Ancient Key-Dweller Remains on the Gulf Coast of Florida*. Gainesville: University Press of Florida.

Cutler, Alan. 2003. *The Seashell on the Mountaintop*. New York: Dutton.

Dingus, Lowell, and Timothy Rowe. 1998. *The Mistaken Extinction*. New York: W. H. Freeman.

Ellis, Richard. 1998. *The Search for the Giant Squid: The Biology and Mythology of the World's Most Elusive Sea Creature*. New York: Penguin Books.

Ferllini, Roxana. 2002. *Silent Witness: How Forensic Anthropology Is Used to Solve the World's Toughest Crimes*. Ontario: Firefly Books.

Garcia, Frank A., and Donald S. Miller. 1998. *Discovering Fossils: How to Find and Identify Remains of the Prehistoric Past*. Mechanicsburg, Pa.: Stackpole Books.

Gilbert, B. Miles. 1990. *Mammalian Osteology*. Columbia: Missouri Archaeological Society.

Gilbert, B. Miles, Larry D. Martin, and Howard G. Savage. 1985. *Avian Osteology*. Flagstaff, Ariz.: B. Miles Gilbert.

Gill, Anton, and Alex West. 2001. *Extinct*. London: Pan Macmillan.

Gould, Stephen Jay. 1981. *The Mismeasure of Man*. New York: W.W. Norton.

———. 1984. *Hen's Teeth and Horse's Toes*. New York: W.W. Norton.

Gray, Henry F. R. S. 1901. *Gray's Anatomy*. New York: Barnes and Noble Books.

Guthrie, R. Dale. 2005. *The Nature of Paleolithic Art*. Chicago: University of Chicago Press.

Haynes, Gary. 1991. *Mammoths, Mastodonts, and Elephants*. New York: Cambridge University Press.

Herrera, Joan. 1999. Determining the Species Source of Prehistoric Ivory. *Aucilla River Times* 12(1).

Hesse, Brian, and Paula Wapnish. 1985. *Animal Bone Archaeology: From Objectives to Analysis*. Washington, D.C.: Taraxacum.

Horner, John R., and Edwin Dobb. 1997. *Dinosaur Lives*. New York: Harcourt Brace.

Hulbert, Richard C., ed. 2001. *The Fossil Vertebrates of Florida*. Gainesville: University Press of Florida.

———. 2004. The Last Decade (More or Less) of Equid Paleobiology. *Pony Express* 13(2): 5.

Jacobs, Louis. 2000. *Quest for the African Dinosaurs: Ancient Roots of the Modern World*. Baltimore: The John Hopkins University Press.

Jones, Douglas S., and Stephen J. Gould. 1999. Direct Measurement of Age in Fossil *Gryphaea*: The Solution to a Classic Problem in Heterochrony. *Paleobiology* 25(2): 169–70.

Kent, Bretton W. 1994. *Fossil Sharks of the Chesapeake Bay Region*. Columbia, Md.: Egan Rees and Boyer.

Keynes, Randal. 2002. *Darwin, His Daughter, and Human Evolution*. New York: Riverhead Books.

Keynes, Richard Darwin. 2003. *Fossils, Finches, and Fuegians: Darwin's Discoveries and Adventures on the* Beagle. Oxford: Oxford University Press.

Kocsis, Frank. 1997. *Vertebrate Fossils: A Neophyte's Guide*. Palm Harbor, Fla.: Ibis Graphics.

Kreling, Kai. 2004. *Horse's Teeth and Their Problems*. Guilford, Conn.: The Lyons Press.

Kuhn-Snyder, Emil, and Hans Rieber. 1986. *The Handbook of Paleozoology*. Trans. Emil Kucera. Baltimore: John Hopkins University Press.

Kurten, Bjorn. 1982. *Teeth: Form, Function, and Evolution*. New York: Columbia University Press.

Lange, Ian M. 2002. *Ice Age Mammals of North America: A Guide to the Big, the Hairy, and the Bizarre*. Missoula, Mont.: Mountain Press Publishing.

Larson, Clark Spencer. 2000. *Skeletons in Our Closet: Revealing Our Past through Bioarchaeology*. Princeton, N.J.: Princeton University Press.

Lear, Teri L. 2002. Atavisms or What Goes Around Comes Around. *Pony Express: Florida Fossil Horse Newsletter* 11(1).

Lewis-Williams, David. 2002. *The Mind in the Cave: Consciousness and the Origins of Art*. London: Thames and Hudson.

Lister, Adrian, and Paul Bahn. 1994. *Mammoths*. New York: Macmillan.

MacDonald, David. 1992. *The Velvet Claw: A Natural History of Carnivores*. London: BBC Books.

MacFadden, Bruce. 1993. Mammal Tooth Structure. *Pony Express* 2(3).

———. 1992. *Fossil Horses: Systematics, Paleobiology, and Evolution of the Family Equidae*. New York: Cambridge University Press.

Martin, Paul S. 2005. *Twilight of the Mammoths: Ice Age Extinctions and the Rewilding of America*. Berkeley: University of California Press.

Mayor, Adrienne. 2005. *Fossil Legends of the First Americans*. Princeton, N.J.: Princeton University Press.

Means, Ryan C., and Harley Means. 2004. A New Type of Prehistoric Bone Fishhook from North America. *The Amateur Archaeologist* 10(2).

McCarthy, Susan. 2004. *Becoming a Tiger: How Baby Animals Learn to Live in the Wild*. New York: Harper Collins.

McGowan, Christopher. 1983. *Dinosaurs, Spitfires, and Sea Dragons*. Cambridge, Mass.: Harvard University Press.

Milanich, Jerald T. 1994. *Archaeology of Precolumbian Florida*. Gainesville: University Press of Florida.

Oakley, Kenneth P. 1975. Decorative and Symbolic Uses of Vertebrate Fossils. *Occasional Papers on Technology*, 12, Pitts River Museum, Oxford, England.

Overstreet, Robert. M. 1999. *The Overstreet Indian Arrowheads Identification and Price Guide*. 6th ed. New York: Avon Books.

Owen, David. 2003. *Tasmanian Tiger: The Tragic Tale of How the World Lost its Most Mysterious Predator*. Baltimore: John Hopkins University Press.

Oxnard, Charles. 1987. *Fossils, Teeth, and Sex: New Perspectives on Human Evolution*. Hong Kong: Hong Kong University Press.

Parker, Andrew. 2003. *In the Blink of an Eye*. Cambridge, Mass.: Perseus.

Patton, Kevin T., and Gary A. Thibodeau. 2000. *Mosby's Handbook of Anatomy & Physiology*. St. Louis, Mo.: Mosby.

Perry, I. Mac. 1993. *Indian Mounds You Can Visit*. Saint Petersburg, FL: Great Outdoor Publishing.

Poinar, George, and Roberta Poinar. 1999. *The Amber Forest: A Reconstruction of a Vanished World*. Princeton, N.J.: Princeton University Press.

Presnall, Judith Janda. 1995. *Animal Skeletons*. New York: Grolier Publishing.

Purdy, Barbara A. 1996. *How to Do Archaeology the Right Way*. Gainesville: University Press of Florida.

———. 1996. *Indian Art of Ancient Florida*. Gainesville: University Press of Florida.

———. 1991. *The Art and Archaeology of Florida's Wetlands*. Boca Raton, Fla.: CRC Press.

———. 1981. *Florida's Prehistoric Stone Technology*. Gainesville: University Presses of Florida.

Quammen, David, 2003. *Monster of God: The Man-Eating Predator in the Jungles of History and the Mind*. New York: W. W. Norton.

Raup, David M. 1991. *Extinction: Bad Genes or Bad Luck?* New York: W. W. Norton.

Renz, Mark. 1999. *Fossiling in Florida: A Guide for Diggers and Divers*. Gainesville: University Press of Florida.

———. 2002. *Megalodon: Hunting the Hunter*. Lehigh Acres, Fla.: PaleoPress.

———. 2005. *Giants in the Storm*. Lehigh Acres, Fla.: PaleoPress.

Rogers, Hugh C. 1954. *Indian Relics and Their Story*. Ft. Smith, Ark.: Yoes Printing and Lithographing.

Rogers, Raymond R., David A. Eberth, and Anthony R. Fiorillo. 2007. *Bonebeds: Genesis, Analysis, and Paleobiological Significance*. Chicago: University of Chicago Press.

Rothschild, Bruce M., and Larry D. Martin. 1992. *Paleopathology: Disease in the Fossil Record*. Ann Arbor: CRC Press.

———. 2006. *Skeletal Impact of Disease*. Albuquerque: New Mexico Museum of Natural History and Science Press.

Rudgley, Richard. 1999. *The Lost Civilizations of the Stone Age*. New York: Touchstone Books.

Schwartz, Jeffrey H. 1993. *What the Bones Tell Us*. New York: Henry Holt.

———. 1995. *Skeleton Keys: An Introduction to Human Skeleton Morphology, Development, and Analysis*. New York: Oxford University Press.

———. 1999. *Sudden Origins: Fossils, Genes, and the Emergence of Species*. New York: John Wiley and Sons.

Searfoss, Glenn. 1995. *Skulls and Bones*. Mechanicsburg, Pa.: Stackpole Books.

Shermer, Michael. 2002. *In Darwin's Shadow: The Life and Science of Alfred Russell Wallace*. Oxford: Oxford University Press.

Simpson, George G. 1980. *Splendid Isolation: The Curious History of South American Mammals*. New Haven, Conn.: Yale University Press.

Stewart, Hilary. 1977. *Indian Fishing: Early Methods on the Northwest Coast*. Seattle: University of Washington Press.

Stott, Rebecca. 2003. *Darwin and the Barnacle*. New York: W. W. Norton.

Tankersley, Kenneth. 2002. *In Search of Ice Age Americans*. Salt Lake City, Utah: Gibbs Smith.

Thomas, David Hurst. 2000. *Skull Wars: Kennewick Man, Archaeology, and the Battle for Native American Identity*. New York: Basic Books.

Thompson, Gregg. 2002. *Talking Heads: Notes on the Interpretation of the Skulls of Terrestrial Animals*. Crosbyton, Tex.: Mount Blanco Publishing.

Thulman, David. 1995. Whose Tooth Is This? *The Florida Paleontological Society Newsletter* 12.

———. 1996. Whose Tooth Is This? *The Florida Paleontological Society Newsletter* 13.

———. 1997. Whose Tooth Is This? *The Florida Paleontological Society Newsletter* 14.

Tortora, Gerald J., and Sandra R. Grabowski. 1993. *Principles of Anatomy and Physiology*. 7th ed. New York: Harper Collins College Publishers.

Turner, Alan. 1997. *The Big Cats and their Fossil Relatives*. New York: Columbia University Press.

Vrba, Elizabeth S., and Niles Eldridge, eds. 2005. *Macroevolution: Diversity, Disparity, Contingency*. Lawrence, Kans.: The Paleontology Society.

Wade, Nicholas. 2006. *Before the Dawn: Recovering the Lost History of Our Ancestors*. New York: Penguin Press.

Walker, Alan, and Pat Shipman. 1996. *The Wisdom of the Bones: In Search of Human Origins*. New York: Alfred A. Knopf.

Walker, Karen J. 1992. Bone Artifacts from Josslyn Island, Buck Key Shell Midden, and Cash Mound: A Preliminary Assessment for the Caloosahatchee Area. *Culture and Environment in the Domain of the Calusa*, Monograph 1. Gainesville, Fla.: Institute of Archaeology and Paleoenvironmental Studies.

Wallace, David Rains. 2004. *Beasts of Eden: Walking Whales, Dawn Horses, and Other Enigmas of Mammal Evolution*. Los Angeles: University of California Press.

Ward, Peter. 1994. *The End of Evolution*. New York: Bantam Books.

———. 2001. *Future Evolution: An Illuminated History of Life to Come*. New York: Times Books.

Webb, S. David, ed. 1974. *Pleistocene Mammals of Florida*. Gainesville: University Presses of Florida.

Wills, Christopher. 1993. *The Runaway Brain: The Evolution of Human Uniqueness*. London: Harper Collins.

Yochelson, Ellis L. 1998. *Charles Doolittle Walcott: Paleontologist*. Kent, Ohio: The Kent State University Press.

Zaller, John. 2003. *Bodies: The Exhibition*. Atlanta: Premier Exhibitions.

Acknowledgments

Because of the scope of the material presented here, the list of collaborators is extensive. The reader is urged to note these individuals, without whom this project could never have come to fruition. Furthermore, the specialized expertise of each represents a part of him or herself in this project. I cannot thank them all enough.

Paul Lien and Jim Tatum have extensive collections of both fossils and artifacts, many of which appear in the following pages. Their knowledge and patience in explaining worked materials from Florida and other parts of the country were invaluable in supporting the information in chapter 7. Furthermore, Jim read and edited one of the early versions of the manuscript before I sent it to a publisher for consideration. Even with the help of Jim and Paul, I did not feel comfortable without having a professional archaeologist read chapter 7. Dr. Robert Austin was an invaluable asset in proofreading chapter 7 and in offering corrective feedback that enhanced not only the information, but also the readability of the chapter.

For allowing me the privilege of handling and photographing the precious specimens in their private collections, I'd like to thank Mike and Seina Searle, Patrick McGirk, the late Marvin Preston, Barbara Fite, Brian Evensen, Mark Renz, Willy Keenan, Frank Kocsis, Tony Perez, the late Mark Condron, the late Robert "Sharky" Loster, the late Vito Bertucci, Henry Crowley, Ted Akin, the late Nita Akin, and Dominic Sinibaldi.

Every team needs a "go-to guy." Andreas Kerner was my go-to guy, often finding difficult specimens for me to photograph, and then having the knowledge to recognize their significance for this project. On many occasions when the photographic section of this project was bogged down, Andreas came through and gave it new life. Furthermore, his ability to recognize and identify obscure specimens may be unparalleled in the avocational community. He also proofread many versions of the manuscript.

Some people can always be counted on without reminders. Marge Fantosi is one of those people. She and her husband breed quarter horses, and I consulted her about horse dentition. Each time, the next time I saw her, she'd have the information I needed from a veterinary journal. This happened on several occasions. If everyone had been as efficient as Marge (including myself), this project might not have taken so long.

I met Dr. Chris Duffin almost by accident on the Internet. We have a mutual interest in fossils, and Chris has published professionally in the field. He graciously offered to review one of the early editions of the manuscript. His insights, editorial corrections, and suggestions made me look far less inept to those who later read revised versions of the manuscript.

The late Dr. Al Welberry was one of the original fossil divers in Florida's waters. His collection was extensive, and I only wish I had had the time to better document the many items he collected in the early years of Florida river diving. Many of his specimens appear in the following pages.

Dave Letasi, formerly of the Museum of Science and Industry in Tampa, Florida, provided much of the carnivore material photographed for this book. In addition, his explanations of how things worked and scrupulous record keeping and labeling of specimens made working with Dave a pleasure.

Terry Sellari has an extensive collection of precious pathological fossil specimens and worked bone materials. His collection filled in many of the gaps in chapters 5, 6, and 7. Terry was a mentor to me when I took over as president of the Tampa Bay Fossil Club, and he has been gracious enough to take me on several fossil diving expeditions, all of which were fruitful.

Dr. Richard C. Hulbert Jr., collections manager for the Division of Vertebrate Paleontology at the Florida Museum of Natural History in Gainesville, took time out of his busy schedule to pull items from storage to be photographed. I used the collection at the museum extensively to fill difficult gaps in this pictorial guide.

Frank Garcia, discoverer of the fossil laggerstatten at the Leisey Shell Pit, has been an inspiration to many amateur and avocational paleontologists in Florida and around the world (including me). Frank was always available for consultation and provided many of the splendid specimens of skulls and jaws photographed for chapters 2 and 3.

Dr. S. David Webb had retired by the time this manuscript was ready for review. He was instrumental in providing feedback for my first two books. Dr. Webb did find time in his final hours at FLMNH to pull an ivory foreshaft found in the Aucilla River project (chapter 7) and allow me to be the first non-professional to handle and photograph it for this book. This item is truly one of the treasures of Florida paleontology and archaeology.

Reid Jenkins drew the incredible illustrations at the beginning of each chapters+. When I needed more pictures, he came through with excellent work in a timely fashion.

Dr. Pennilyn Higgins took a manuscript I had circulated among amateur reviewers and put professional eyes to it. Her suggestions and editorial comments cleared up many of my misconceptions about the material with which I was working. This was the point of the entire project: to get correct information out to the interested amateur fossil community and provide a sound foundation for those going into the field professionally. Her input, especially in chapters 1–4, has given the author confidence that this pictorial guide will be of service to the paleontological community with correct explanations for the phenomena presented.

Hermann Trappmann provided alternative views on Native American ways. He attempted to free the author of his Eurocentric thinking and to consider alternative views of cultures other than his own.

Dr. Gordon Hubbell was instrumental in providing most of the fossil shark teeth specimens photographed for this project. In addition, Dr. Hubbell spent much time and effort explaining fossil shark teeth to me and reading and re-reading the rough drafts of those sections concerning fossil shark teeth.

I am also indebted to Tom and Jill Lofland for the time and energy they spent editing and enhancing the simple photos I took of specimens, then formatting them in a way acceptable to the publisher. This was a formidable and time-consuming process for the more than 500 images included in this book.

Somewhere near the eleventh hour of this project, I became painfully uneasy about the pathological sections of the book. I was expecting feedback from the paleontological professionals reviewing the manuscript, but had not received many corrections for the two chapters concerning paleopathologies. At the last minute I contacted Dr. Bruce Rothschild, a professor of medicine at Northeastern Ohio Universities College of Medicine and considered one of the foremost authorities on paleopathology. He graciously reviewed the two chapters on pathologies and provided much corrective feedback. I even imposed on him by asking him to look again at the corrected manuscript to make sure my corrections were reasonably close to accurate. The invaluable feedback I received from him added immensely to the value of this book.

Eric Vehmeier came through on every occasion I needed technical assistance with my computer. His efforts often saved me hours of work.

My brother, John Sinibaldi, assisted as a final proofreader.

John W. Byram, editor in chief, University Press of Florida, received a very rough manuscript and gave me the motivation and direction to move it forward to the work you see before you. I am also indebted to him for his patience during the more than eight years that passed between then and now. Lucinda Treadwell spent many hours editing the final manuscript for publication. The final edited edition is far more comprehensible and reader friendly after her efforts. I also thank my project editor, Michele Fiyak-Burkley.

Finally, even with all the professional and avocational help on this project, errors are still bound to exist. I take full responsibility for any misunderstandings and mistakes in the final product. In the future, as science moves forward, some of the material presented here may become outdated. This pictorial guide represents many hours of effort on my part and that of many others involved in this project, and it is hoped that the book will bring the reader to a fuller understanding of vertebrate fossils.

Index

Page numbers for a term's introduction are in boldface and for illustrations are followed by f.

Robert W. Sinibaldi is a former president of the Tampa Bay Fossil Club (TBFC) and currently a member of its board of directors. TBFC is the largest amateur paleontological organization in the state of Florida and one of the largest in the nation. He is the author of *Fossil Diving: In Florida's Waters or Any Other Waters Containing Prehistoric Treasures* and *The Handbook of Paleontological Terms*. He works for the Pinellas County School District and with the University of South Florida in the field of exceptional student education. Fossils are just a hobby, or as his wife Mary says, "By the time you get to the third book, it's an obsession."